HEROES

—— AND ——

HARD MEN

By the same author:
The Illustrated History of Boxing (Hamlyn, 1987)
The Book of Boxing Quotations (Stanley Paul, 1988)

HEROES

—— AND ——

HARD MEN

Harry Mullan

Stanley Paul

London   Sydney   Auckland   Johannesburg

Stanley Paul and Co. Ltd

An imprint of Century Hutchinson
Brookmount House, 62–65 Chandos Place,
Covent Garden, London WC2N 4NW

Century Hutchinson Australia (Pty) Ltd
20 Alfred Street, Milsons Point, Sydney 2061, Australia

Century Hutchinson New Zealand Limited
191 Archers Road, PO Box 40–086, Glenfield, Auckland 10

Century Hutchinson South Africa (Pty) Ltd
PO Box 337, Bergvlei 2012, South Africa

First published 1989
Copyright © Harry Mullan

Set by 🝖\ Tek Art Ltd, Croydon, Surrey
in 10½/12½ Rockwell Light

Printed and bound in Great Britain by
Mackays of Chatham PLC

Photographic acknowledgment
The author and publishers would like to thank the following for permission
to reproduce photographs in this book: Hulton-Deutsch Collection, Mirror
Newspapers, Sport & General, Press Association and *Glasgow Herald*.

Contents

To Frank Fee and Roger Stratford, who have shared
my lifetime's passion for the game

Preface

LISTING Britain's world boxing champions is not such a straight-forward exercise as it sounds. What about Bob Fitzsimmons, for a start? He was born in Cornwall, certainly, but was taken to New Zealand as a toddler and won all three of his world championships as an American citizen.

Can he therefore be properly regarded as a British world champion? I thought not – and, on the same grounds, disqualified the brilliant Jimmy McLarnin. Jimmy was born in Belfast, but the family emigrated to Canada when he was an infant and, like Fitzsimmons, he never boxed here.

Johnny Hill and Len Harvey were outstanding fighters, but their claims to world championship status did not bear close scrutiny. In Harvey's case, particularly, I regretted the demotion. He was a much better fighter than many who qualify for inclusion, and I was always immensely impressed by his dignified bearing when I met him in his later life.

But the 43 who survived the qualification tests include some of the finest and most colourful characters which this most exotic sport has ever produced, and it has been my pleasure to record their achievements. A few I have known personally, but I admire them all equally . . . but then any man who dares to duck between those ropes has my unqualified respect, whether he is a champion or a six-rounds loser.

It is a hard game, practised by special men, and what follows is my own small tribute to the best and the luckiest of them . . . the world champions.

HARRY MULLAN
London, 1989

Ben Jordan (1873–1945)

BERMONDSEY, once a grubby working-class area of South London, is in the process of gentrification. The yuppies have moved in, house prices are soaring, and suddenly the SE1 postcode has a certain social cachet. The streets which spawned hard fighting men such as Sid Smith, Joe Rolfe, or more recently Lloyd Honeyghan are now more likely to house stockbrokers than title contenders. Ben Jordan would never recognize the old place – and it's a fair bet that he would not welcome the changes.

Jordan, Britain's first world champion of the gloved era, was proud of his roots in shabby old Bermondsey and stayed firmly anchored to his community. Technically, of course, he was not a native of the district, having been born in the (then) much more rural and genteel Mitcham, on the Surrey borders, on 1 April 1873. But his father, a lay preacher, was offered a chapel in Bermondsey when Ben was still a toddler, and moved his family there.

Ben grew up at a time when local heroes were either boxers or villains, and his father's influence ensured that he opted for the legitimate course. Jordan junior was always a sober and sensible type anyway, so the chances of him letting the family down were remote.

He took on an apprenticeship at a local tannery, and worked at his trade as a leather dresser even when boxing was making him, by contemporary standards, a wealthy man. Inevitably, once he turned to boxing at the age of nineteen he was billed as the 'Bermondsey Tanner', and success in two 8-stone competitions at the National Sporting Club in Covent Garden quickly earned him a reputation beyond his South London manor.

His first setback came in his fifth outing, against Dave Wallace of Holloway in 1892. Some American record books list the defeat as a knockout, but it was a points decision awarded in unusual circumstances. The pair boxed their contracted eight rounds, and the referee was unable to separate them. Instead of declaring the fight a draw, he ordered them to box a deciding ninth round, which Wallace edged.

Jordan won his next eight fights in a row, all by knockout, and then trounced Wallace in a rematch held at the Wheatsheaf Hard Court in Holborn. When Jordan outscored Dave's namesake, Arthur 'Darkey' Wallace, at the NSC in October 1894, the fight trade really began to take notice of him, and he confirmed the good impression by stopping Jimmy Gough of Birmingham in the third of a scheduled twenty-rounder which carried a £25 side stake and a purse of £200, split on a 60–40 basis between winner and loser.

In April 1896 Ben won an 8 st 10 lb competition at the Excelsior Baths in Bethnal Green, beating George Wood of Hoxton in the final. A nineteenth-round knockout of Camberwell's Joe Portley followed, which earned Jordan a crack at the British featherweight title held by the Hackney veteran Fred Johnson. They met at the NSC on 22 February 1897; in those days, the autocratic National Sporting Club claimed the exclusive right to nominate challengers and stage championships.

Johnson, eight years older at thirty-two, defended grimly for twelve rounds but referee Bernard Angle rescued him in the thirteenth as Jordan battered him around the ring.

Jordan's backers, Jimmy Laws and Gus Brewer, began man-oeuvring their man towards the world title. But first it was necessary to establish some international credentials: then, as now, being British champion did not carry a lot of weight in America.

As a first stage they imported the very capable Tommy White of Fox Lake, Illinois, who had drawn with world champion George Dixon and who was unbeaten in 52 fights since abandoning bare-knuckle battling in 1890. The match took place at the NSC on 29 November 1897, and for eighteen rounds White's skilful boxing and crisp hitting provided Jordan with a painful illustration of the difference between domestic and transatlantic competiton.

One punch, a perfect left hook in the nineteenth, changed everything. White was so badly stunned that he grabbed the Londoner and held on desperately, forcing the referee to leave his ringside seat and enter the ring to haul them apart. Jordan was relentless, and the American's chief second, Jimmy Barry, jumped between the ropes to save his man from a knockout, thus incurring automatic disqualification.

Eddie Curry from Staten Island was despatched in seventeen rounds in April 1898, and Jordan was judged ready to make his move for the top. The world championship picture was muddled (what's new?). George Dixon, champion for the last five years, had been outpointed by one of his former victims, Solly Smith of Los Angeles, in October 1897 in a contest staged under championship conditions. Smith claimed the title, but Dixon's manager simply ignored the result and continued to market his man as the world champion.

In the absence of any recognized controlling body, the views of the sporting press carried more influence than they merited, and any manager who knew how to look after an amenable hack or two could be sure of a sympathetic hearing. With the backing of the New York sports writers, a Dixon v Jordan match was arranged for the Lennox Athletic Club on 1 July, twenty-five rounds with Dixon's 'world title' at stake.

Whatever the authenticity or otherwise of the billing, Jordan fought like a champion to take a runaway verdict from referee Charlie White. Dixon was beaten far more clearly than Smith had managed, and this time no amount of cajolery could change the result. The Canadian left the ring bleeding from cuts over both eyes and from the nose and mouth, while the stylish Jordan was so unmarked that he was able to box again exactly a week later in Philadelphia in a no-decision affair.

Jordan came home to spend the next ten months on the music-hall circuit, milking his world championship status for every penny it was worth, and when he next appeared in the ring, defending his world and British titles against Harry Greenfield of Camden Town at the NSC, the manner of his ninth-round knockout success brought about a change in the rules. Ben was always a wicked body puncher, and he finished off Greenfield with a right to the kidneys which caused the challenger so much pain and distress that the NSC ruled that henceforth kidney punches would be illegal.

The Americans, meanwhile, had come up with a challenger: Eddie Santry of Chicago, a hard-punching twenty-two-year-old with 17 knockouts in 31 fights. Santry had been stopped by Tommy White and, in his previous fight, been held to a draw by George Dixon, who was defending the portion of the championship which he had reclaimed by beating Solly Smith's conqueror, Dave Sullivan.

On form, therefore, it looked a fairly safe defence for the Londoner, even though it took place at the Lennox AC in New York. Jordan was installed as a 100–30 favourite, and boxed like it for fifteen rounds despite suffering a shock first-round knockdown.

Santry was cut, confused and outboxed – but then Jordan unaccountably dropped his guard and was flattened by a single, sweeping right.

There was not much left for him after that. A couple of minor fights were followed by a two-year layoff, which he ended at the request of the NSC who wanted him to headline a special tournament in honour of King Edward VII's Coronation. The opponent was George Kid McFadden of California, and the club billed the fight as being for the 8 st 8 lb championship of the world. Nobody took the claim too seriously, but Jordan's performance in knocking out the younger man with a straight right to the chin in the fifteenth round was good enough to revive interest in his career.

He accepted a British title challenge from Jack Roberts of Drury Lane, knocked him out in five rounds, and then outscored his old rival George Dixon. By that stage, though, Dixon was a shadow of the magnificent fighter he had once been, and the former champion won only nine of his subsequent 30 fights.

Jordan finished his career on a more up-beat note, retaining the British title with a splendid points win over the former world bantamweight champion Pedlar Palmer at the NSC on 12 December 1904. He retired to Bermondsey where he opened a school of boxing and became a successful bookmaker, with a regular pitch at leading race courses. He died, aged seventy-one on 18 January 1945.

CAREER RECORD: 36 fights, 32 wins (22 by knockout or stoppage), 1 draw, 1 no-decision, 2 defeats.

Billy Plimmer (1869–1929)

ANY BRITISH boxer who wins a world title in America and successfully defends it there three times should be assured of immortality – yet Birmingham's Billy Plimmer, who did just that almost a hundred years ago, is merely a footnote in the record books. He deserves better.

Plimmer was a classical left-hand stylist in the British tradition, yet when necessary he could be rugged enough to capture the affection of the New York fight crowds, who were never best known for their appreciation of the game's finer arts and sciences.

He was born in Birmingham on 6 February 1869, and by the age of fifteen was appearing regularly on the local boxing booths. He always boasted that he had never had a single boxing lesson in his life: his text-book skills were partly instinctive and partly self-taught, and he perfected them in hundreds of bruising encounters on the booths. By the time he took up boxing as a profession in 1888, he was already an accomplished and experienced performer.

A string of wins in his home town encouraged him to try his luck in a 104 lb competition in London, staged by Frank Hindes. Plimmer won twice to reach the final, but was narrowly outpointed over four rounds by Patsy Sheehan. A pair of wins over Chappie Moran quickly re-established him on the local scene – results which looked even better when Moran went over to America later that year and claimed the world bantamweight title after beating Frank Donovan in fourteen rounds.

Quite how Moran qualified as a title contender is another matter: going into the Donovan fight his record showed two wins and three losses, two against Plimmer and the other to Patsy Sheehan.

Stoppages against Tim Buckley and the former amateur star Arthur Westley, as well as winning the £100 prize in the Kennington Social Club's 7 st 12 lb competition, earned Plimmer the chance to contest the vacant British bantamweight title with Jem Stevens of Bethnal Green at the National Sporting Club. Stevens had wealthy and influential backers in Tom Symonds, who kept the Blue Anchor public house in Shoreditch, and Teddy Mills, a former professional race walker who along with his brother Charlie had made a fortune with a chain of cut-price pubs.

These were serious betting men, but they met their match in Plimmer. The Birmingham boy was so convinced that he had the beating of Stevens that he quite literally bet everything he owned on himself. He put up most of his £100 side stake, pawned all his jewellery, and raised a mortgage on his house and furniture to finance a gigantic bet.

He collected, when the Londoner quit in the fifteenth round. It had been a fast and well-contested affair, but during the fifteenth Stevens walked back to his corner, burst into tears and said to cornerman Dan McGannon: 'Dan, I can't go on. I can't see him.' His eyesight had always been weak, but the punishment Plimmer administered had almost blinded him. He had to be helped from the ring, and it was several days before his sight was restored to normal.

Plimmer's winnings financed a working trip to the States, and he installed himself at Billy Norton's saloon in Newark, New Jersey. His American debut was arranged for nearby Paterson, a four-rounder against Jim Watson, and Plimmer won so easily that a local sports writer was moved to write, in the quaint style of the day:

The first appearance of Billy Plimmer was what the theatrical critics might term a howling success. The Briton proved himself a great little fighter: clever, strong, game and a grand technician.

There is no man at his weight in America who would have more than an even-money chance with him, and I do not bar my old friend Spider Kelly either. Plimmer is a downright good man, and there is no wiping it out!

Tommy 'Spider' Kelly, a New York Irish-American, had gained recognition as world bantamweight champion by beating Plimmer's old adversary Chappie Moran, with whom he had previously split a pair of points verdicts. He was Plimmer's target, and a string of successes in Philadelphia, New York and New Jersey moved the Englishman into a challenging position.

They met on 9 May 1892 at an old skating rink about 12 miles out of New York, over twenty rounds for a purse of £400. There was some speculation that the local police chief, John McKane, might stop the fight going ahead, but in fact that was hardly likely: many years later McKane was revealed as the major shareholder in the club which promoted the fight!

They weighed in at 2 p.m. on the afternoon of the fight, at the agreed weight limit of 110 lb (7 st 12 lb). The bantamweight championship limit had previously been 105 lb (7 st 7 lb), which is actually the limit of the modern straw-weight category – four full divisions below today's bantamweight limit of 8 st 6 lb (118 lb).

Ten thousand fans, paying up to $100 for a ticket, packed the hall to see how the 'Harlem Spider' would cope with his latest challenger. For a minute or two it looked as though the whirlwind, ungainly aggression which had earned him his nickname would overwhelm Plimmer – but then Billy's left jab smashed into the American's mouth, gashing his lips and splattering his white silk breeches with blood.

That set the pattern of the exchanges – Kelly chasing relentlessly, but running on to Plimmer's left hand. Thirty years later, sports writer James Butler recalled Plimmer showing him the gloves he wore that night:

The gloves, made of yellow dog-skin and lightly padded with cotton wool instead of hair, weighed only two ounces each! They were the nearest thing to bare knuckles it was possible to contrive. Holding them in my hands and examining them, I could read the whole story of that famous fight – for while the right glove was comparatively clean, the left was darkly stained with blood where it had played ceaselessly on the American champion's nose and mouth.

A right cross dropped the champion for five in the seventh, and Kelly was on the floor again as the bell ended the ninth. Plimmer thought he had won, and ran across to shake Kelly's hand. But Kelly, dazed and bewildered, lashed out at Plimmer and there was a heated exchange before the referee separated them. A round later, Plimmer was world champion: Kelly went down three times, and he didn't get up from the last knockdown.

The win made Plimmer a big attraction, and for the next couple of years he campaigned across America, retaining his title against Joe McGrath in eight rounds on Coney Island and with a twenty-five round draw against Johnny Murphy in New Orleans. He also had the best of a four-rounder in New York with George Dixon, former bantam and featherweight champion of the world.

A contender had emerged at home – George Corfield of Sheffield – and Plimmer accepted an offer of £300 plus £50 expenses from the NSC to risk his world and British titles. Corfield held out for the same expenses as the champion, ignoring the fact

7

that it was considerably less expensive to travel from Sheffield than from New York, and the Club reluctantly paid up.

But that was all Corfield won; he seemed completely overawed by the occasion, and Plimmer had one of the easiest wins of his career, knocking him out in the seventh. Watching at ringside, and distinctly unimpressed, was Alf Snelling, an East End bookie who was the backer of Thomas 'Pedlar' Palmer, the brilliant youngster from Canning Town. Snelling offered a side stake of £500 and a purse of the same amount, which Plimmer accepted, but the champion insisted that the weight limit be increased to 8 st (112 lb). This was mainly because Plimmer had contracted what might discreetly be called a 'social disease' after the Corfield fight, as a result of which his weight had ballooned to 8 st 12 lb.

The efforts of weight reduction left Plimmer drained, and he had nothing left to offer when he faced Palmer at the NSC on 25 November 1895. His brother Jack entered the ring in the fourteenth round to save Billy from an inevitable knockout, and the automatic disqualification that ensued left Plimmer an ex-champ.

Corfield's connections, unhappy with their man's showing first time around, fancied his chances in a rematch with Plimmer, especially in view of Plimmer's dismal performance against Palmer. The match went on at the Drill Hall, Sheffield for £500 a side and a purse of £400, and Plimmer's stinging left jabs earned him an easy twenty-round points verdict from referee Bob Watson.

The victory should have put Plimmer back in contention, but in fact he never won another fight. Sammy Kelly of America knocked him out 15 seconds from the end of a twenty-rounder at Birmingham, when Plimmer had won all previous nineteen rounds and had gone out to try for a big finish.

Palmer stopped him in seventeen rounds in a return fight, and Harry Ware – who beat Palmer for the British bantamweight title the following year – outpointed him. There was only one more, a draw with Corfield at Stalybridge, before Plimmer retired at thirty-one. Like so many other ex-fighters, a combination of bad management and a liking for a bet had accounted for most of his ring earnings, and he lived out the remaining twenty-eight years of his life in obscurity. He died in Birmingham on 23 February 1929.

CAREER RECORD: 46 fights, 33 wins (14 by knockout or stoppage), 5 draws, 3 no-decisions, 5 defeats.

Pedlar Palmer (1876–1949)

PEDLAR PALMER'S curriculum vitae included winning the world bantamweight championship, getting arrested for murder, and squandering a fortune of, in modern terms, around a quarter of a million pounds. Nobody could ever have accused the Cockney from Canning Town of leading a dull life.

Palmer was nicknamed the 'Box O' Tricks', which could have owed as much to his activities outside the ring as to his uncanny defensive skills in it. The Pedlar was an enigma, a wonderful athlete with the appetites of a libertine.

He broke all the rules, and got away with it. He was an instinctive genius in the ring, and a hard-drinking, hard-living spendthrift the rest of the time. He pre-dated the heyday of the British cinema by forty years, but could have served as role model for the archetypal cheeky Cockney Sparrow who was the comic standby in so many films of the forties and fifties, right down to the regulation dress of bowler hat and 'choker'. But at least with Palmer it wasn't acting: he was Cockney to the bone, even if he spent the last twenty years of his life in 'exile' in Brighton.

Fighting was in Palmer's blood. His father Jack, a 14-stone six-footer who boxed as 'Palmer the Peddler', had claimed the bare-knuckle championship of Essex, while his mother (as a contemporary sports writer wryly noted) could, and frequently did, beat any woman in the East End.

Nevertheless, for all the instinctive ability that carried Pedlar to the bantamweight championship in 1895, he could not even claim to be the best boxer in his own family. His brother Matt could outbox him over three rounds at any stage in Pedlar's career, but the heart condition which eventually killed him at the age of thirty prevented Matt from taking up the game professionally.

The pair developed their skills so rapidly that long before they reached their teens they were regular performers on the music-hall circuit, giving boxing exhibitions as 'The Palmer Brothers – Midget Boxing Act'. Pedlar played the clown, missing punches by rolling, swaying, or even somersaulting, while Matt was the straight man.

This apprenticeship on the boards was responsible for the 'showbiz' elements of Palmer's later ring performances. In many ways he anticipated Muhammad Ali: he specialized in frustrating, taunting and infuriating opponents – what Ali would later term 'messing up their minds' – before turning his attention to the physical side of the contest.

He boxed like a nineteenth-century Herol Graham, almost impossible to hit and throwing his counters from bewildering and unpredictable angles. Palmer was as unorthodox in his training methods as he was in the ring. His long-time friend James Butler recounts how his trainer Joe Palmer, a leading professional runner, was baffled by the way that Pedlar kept putting on weight despite his apparently rigorous roadwork every morning.

There was a steep hill on the route that Pedlar ran regularly, and as they approached it Pedlar would invariably tell Joe: 'You take it easy, and I'll wait for you over the top.' The trainer solved the mystery one morning by letting Pedlar run ahead as usual, and then sprinting after him to find him sitting outside the pub at the bottom of the hill, drinking heartily from a pewter pot which he had arranged for the landlord to leave ready for consumption each morning.

On another occasion he produced a bottle of stout after a weigh-in, drank from it, and offered the second swig to his opponent for the evening, Joe Bowker. 'No thanks, Tom,' Bowker said. 'Drink for the both of us, and good luck.' Bowker knew what he was about: he stopped Pedlar in twelve rounds that night, to win the vacant British featherweight title and end Pedlar's career at championship level.

Like most youngsters of his background and time, Palmer had only the shakiest grasp of the principles of banking and finance. His backer, bookmaker Alf Snelling, persuaded him to open a bank account when Pedlar started earning worthwhile amounts. Palmer duly sprayed cheques like left jabs around the shops and restaurants of London, as well as amongst the host of hangers-on who were constantly borrowing a fiver here and a tenner there.

Within a couple of weeks, the inevitable summons arrived from the bank manager. 'I'm sorry to tell you that your account is overdrawn,' he said. 'Don't be daft,' said Palmer, producing a half-full chequebook and waving it under the manager's nose. 'How can I be overdrawn when I've still got all these cheques left?'

Palmer earned a fortune during his long career. He claimed to have had more than 400 fights, although he was probably counting bare-knuckle engagements, booth fights, and sparring exhibitions. Record-keeping was sketchy at that time, and only 64 contests can be verified in a career which began, officially, in 1891. But he had been fighting for money for a couple of years before then, and acknowledged that he had lost a few in the process of mastering his trade, although the accepted version of his record has him unbeaten until 1899.

He was launched on a professional career when he was only thirteen. His father took him to the Blue Anchor, a famous boxing pub in Shoreditch, and put him in to spar with a seasoned pro called Fred Johnson. The landlord, Tom Symonds, watched in amazement as the youngster toyed with the professional, and promptly dubbed him 'Box O' Tricks'. Alf Snelling, one of the East End's leading bookies, got to hear of the prodigy and took him under his wing.

A long run of wins in London's minor arenas during 1891 and 1892 eventually brought him to the attention of the National Sporting Club, who matched him with the ill-fated Walter Croot (who died after a fight with the American Jimmy Barry at the NSC four years later). Palmer was only eighteen, but boxed with the maturity of a veteran to outclass and stop Croot in seventeen rounds.

A.F. 'Peggy' Bettinson, matchmaker at the Club, was sufficiently impressed to take an active interest in Palmer's career, and Pedlar was quickly moved up the ladder. He took the world title from Billy Plimmer at the Club on 25 November 1895, and defended it successfully five times, including a smashing points win over Cork-born Dave Sullivan, who went on to win a version of the world featherweight title.

Palmer's backers were so delighted with his display against Sullivan that they held a collection to fund the purchase of a £1000 diamond-studded belt, which was duly presented to him. The ever-obliging Pedlar often loaned the belt to a few of his less reputable friends, who would invariably return it promptly. Some years later, Palmer took the belt to be valued. It was worthless: the diamonds had been replaced by coloured glass.

The Americans disputed Palmer's right to call himself world champion, and instead recognized 'Terrible' Terry McGovern. Bettinson negotiated for a deciding match between the two. It took place at Tuckahoe, New York, on 12 September 1899, and resulted in one of the oddest excuses for defeat ever offered by a world champion. Palmer entered the ring first, and as he sat down to await McGovern's entrance he was dazzled by the glare of fierce arc lights blazing down and directed on the English corner. McGovern did not appear for almost ten minutes, and by the time Palmer was led to the centre of the ring for the referee's instructions he was, effectively, blind. Two minutes and 32 seconds later, he was an ex-champion. As *Boxing News* noted in Palmer's obituary, it was 'surely the first time a champion has lost his crown without ever seeing his challenger'.

The sparkle left Pedlar that autumn evening, and he was never the same again. He came home to retain his British title against Harry Ware, but lost it in a rematch in September 1900. He was still capable of good performances, including two wins each over Digger Stanley and George Dixon and a classy points win over the tough American featherweight Spike Robson, but the losses began to mount up.

Ben Jordan and Joe Bowker beat him in successive fights for the British featherweight title, and by the end of 1905 he was losing to obscure individuals such as Cockney Cohen and Charley Lampey. He drifted away from the game after outpointing Cockney Cohen in a four-rounder at Plymouth in May 1906, but reclaimed the headlines in tragic circumstances a year later.

Palmer got involved in a brawl with another race-goer on the Epsom train, and the man died of his injuries. The charge was originally murder – then, of course, a capital crime in Britain – but at the trial in Guildford it was reduced to manslaughter.

He served nearly four years of his five-year term, and launched the inevitable comeback on his release. He was thirty-five, and while enough of the skills remained to keep him out of trouble for seven or eight rounds on his return to the ring against Darkey Haley, the ageing legs let him down and he was knocked out in the tenth. He scuffled through half a dozen minor engagements in 1912, losing one on a disqualification, and retired after outpointing Jim Lloyd at Liverpool on 12 August that year.

That should have been the end, but the old boy surfaced again six and a half years later, taking on former world featherweight champion Jim Driscoll at the NSC. It was a curious pairing: Palmer was forty-two and had not boxed since August 1912, while Driscoll, thirty-nine, had been out of the ring since drawing with Owen

Moran in January 1913. In their respective primes the match would have been a classic, but instead it was a farce, with Palmer being stopped in four rounds.

He was seen in a ring only once more, when he boxed an exhibition with world flyweight champion Jimmy Wilde in 1922.

Pedlar retired to Brighton, where he made an adequate living first as a bookmaker and then as a backer until his sudden death from pneumonia on 13 February 1949.

CAREER RECORD: 64 fights, 47 wins (18 by knockout or stoppage), 4 draws , 13 defeats.

Joe Bowker (1883–1955)

NOBODY remembers him now, but Bill Johnson of Ardwick was, in a roundabout way, responsible for two significant developments in the history of boxing in Britain. Johnson was a booth fighter in the late 1890s, a black journeyman of no great distinction. But his son Len became one of the finest boxers of his day, and only the existence of the odious 'colour bar' prevented him from contesting a British title. The rank injustice of the Johnson case sparked a campaign for the abolition of this racial discrimination, which finally came about in the late 1940s.

Bill's other contribution to posterity was even more unwitting: when he quit his job with Harry Hughes' booth, which was pitched on an open site known as the Flat Iron Market in the Lancashire town of Salford, the vacancy was filled by an eager youngster called Tommy Mahon. For Mahon it was the first step on the road to the bantamweight championship of the world, which he won under his ring name of Joe Bowker. (Bowker was his mother's maiden name.)

Bowker, only 5 feet 3 inches, had a passion for the game and the busy booth was the ideal place to nurture his skills. For anything up to half a sovereign a night, Bowker lined up on the platform outside the booth with the other 'house fighters', accepting challenges from anyone, regardless of size. He proved a quick learner – he had to be, for in that kind of environment you either mastered your trade or sank without trace.

By the time he was sixteen Bowker was supplementing his booth earnings with regular appearances in formal matches around the Salford and Manchester areas, and his reputation soon spread outside Lancashire. Peggy Bettinson, drawing up the lists for a novice competition he was staging at the NSC, decided to give him a chance. He wrote to Bowker inviting him to take part, but there was a slight problem: Bowker was broke, and the rail fare to London was beyond his reach. Instead, he walked there – ten days on the road, sleeping rough and eating whatever, whenever and wherever he could.

Bettinson was irate when the weary Bowker arrived at his office. 'I thought I told you to come at once.' Joe, looking sheepish, replied:

14

'But I did – I walked as quick as I could.'

Bowker rounded the story off in style by winning the competition, and he never looked back. The Club members enjoyed his style, and the bookings were regular and increasingly lucrative – in fact, his next 15 fights were all at the club. Within two years Joe had won recognition as British bantamweight champion by beating Harry Ware of Northampton, and he retained the title impressively in 1903 against Andrew Tokell and Bill King.

Bettinson decided it was time to test him against American opposition, and the ideal opponent was already to hand. Al Fellows had paid his own way from Chicago to London earlier in 1903 and, armed with letters of recommendation from various American sportsmen, presented himself at Bettinson's office and asked for work. Bettinson, never a man to take anyone on trust, asked him to box a three-round trial with Bowker, and the shrewd little Lancastrian saw a chance of making some easy money.

Bowker had the knack of making himself appear very much more gullible and innocent than he actually was, a ploy he later used to profitable effect against Frankie Neil when they met for the world title. He deliberately boxed badly in the trial, so the American did not need much persuasion to agree to Bowker being his opponent on his formal debut at the Club on 9 November 1903. Bowker innocently suggested a bet, and Fellows confidently offered him odds of 100–30. Bowker backed himself with his entire purse for the fight, £300, and gave the American the worst beating of his career.

Fellows could not lay a glove on him, while Bowker's precise and scientific hitting chipped away at the visitor's morale until, when the bell rang to start the ninth round, the towel fluttered in from the American corner.

With his £300 purse and £1000 winnings, Joe bought himself a tobacconist's shop in Deptford, South-East London, ready for his eventual retirement. It was a typically pragmatic move by Bowker: while his contemporaries such as Digger Stanley and Pedlar Palmer spent their ring earnings in the pubs and at the race tracks, Bowker believed in providing for his future. He was an unassuming, philosophical man, content to enjoy the quiet life. He was never interested in travelling abroad, and was not above making the occasional return to his roots on the booths to sharpen his skills – or perhaps to save on sparring bills.

Bowker's stylish defeat of Owen Moran in defence of the British championship convinced the NSC that he was ready for the best, and world champ Frankie Neil of San Francisco accepted a hefty offer to risk his title at the club on 17 October 1904. Once more Joe acted the gormless, gullible yokel when the American's manager George Constandine suggested a side stake, and did it so convincingly that Constandine upped the bet to winner-take-all.

Neil was so sure of the outcome that he booked a victory banquet, and arranged to go on from London to Paris with his father and Constandine, to do some serious celebrating. They never got that far: Bowker handled Neil as easily as he had beaten Fellows, even though he had to go the full twenty rounds to do so. Peggy Bettinson organized an informal collection to pay the Americans' fare home.

Bowker became a double champion in his next outing, flooring Pedlar Palmer three times to force a twelfth-round stoppage for the British featherweight title. Two months later he struggled down to the bantamweight limit to retain the world title against New York challenger Pinky Evans. Weight-making was becoming increasingly difficult, however, and Bowker decided to concentrate on the featherweight championship.

He managed one successful defence, outpointing Spike Robson of South Shields, before the immaculate Jim Driscoll – who had outpointed him in a non-title fifteen-rounder in 1906 – battered him to a painful seventeenth-round stoppage to end his reign. In his only outing in 1908, the New Zealander Charlie Griffin stopped him in eight.

Joe tried to rebuild his career the following year with a trip to America, but it was a disaster. Al Delmont outpointed him in Boston, and Tommy O'Toole knocked him out inside two rounds in Philadelphia. His career seemed to be over, but Bowker had one last card to play. The European bantamweight title was vacant, and he got himself matched for it with Jean Audony of France, whom he flattened in eight rounds.

Bettinson offered him £200 and a £100 side stake to put up both titles (British and European) against Digger Stanley at the NSC on 17 October 1910. Theoretically the world title was also at stake, but in reality Bowker's claim to the championship had been allowed to lapse. He had never defended it since beating Frankie Neil six years earlier (to the very night), and title recognition had passed to other, more active performers with the American Jimmy Walsh having the strongest case.

The first Lonsdale Belt in the bantamweight division was on offer to the winner, and for seven rounds that looked like being Bowker. But in the eighth, Stanley – whose reputation for dirty fighting was notorious – swung a low left and Bowker collapsed on to his hands and knees, his head bowed to the canvas. He stayed in that position while he was counted out, but the referee then asked a doctor to inspect him for evidence of a foul blow before formally declaring Stanley the new champion.

That was the end of Bowker's championship career, although he boxed sporadically until 1919 and lost only one of his subsequent 11 fights. Charles Ledoux, the hard-hitting Frenchman, was near his peak when he faced Bowker at the Club in January 1912, but found himself being outboxed for round after round. Bowker himself could not believe how easy it was, and in the eighth round turned to give a cheeky wink to his cornermen. That piece of bravado cost him the fight, and his last chance to stay in boxing's big-time.

Ledoux smashed a right to the unguarded jaw, and Bowker wobbled his way through the remainder of the round. The ninth was one-way traffic, and Bowker was finally rescued by the referee in the tenth after being put down twice. Ledoux, according to one flowery translator, said afterwards:

Your Joe Bowker – I did not beat him. Oh, no. He fooled me, but a bigger fool, which was himself, took him off his guard and I helped myself to his jaw. It was so simple when it should have been so difficult. I go back to France the conquerer instead of the vanquished, all because your Joe Bowker is a very funny man.

As reported post-fight quotes go, it's as improbable as any.

Joe's last appearance in the ring was in New Cross, a couple of miles from his adopted home of Deptford, and he went out a winner when he kayoed Charlie Ward of Deal in the fifteenth round. He quit to run his tobacconist's, but never lost his love for the ring and, in 1924, served as trainer to the British Olympic team which won two gold medals at the Paris Olympics. He died in Deptford on 22 October 1955.

CAREER RECORD: 51 fights, 40 wins (14 by knockout or stoppage), 1 draw, 2 no-decisions, 8 defeats.

Ted 'Kid' Lewis (1894 – 1970)

WHEN former world welterweight king Ted 'Kid' Lewis serialized his astonishing life story in *Boxing News* in the summer of 1948, he claimed to have had 800 fights and to have earned over half a million pounds. The truth was so remarkable anyway that one wonders why the old champion felt it necessary to exaggerate at all.

His verifiable career record showed 282 fights over a twenty-year span during which he won nine major championships and fought for a tenth. He contested titles at every weight from feather to light-heavy, and until Lloyd Honeyghan won the same title sixty years later Lewis was the only British fighter to win and successfully defend a world title in America.

He and Jack Britton shared one of the ring's great rivalries. They met at least 20 times (Lewis claimed 24) and the world title was on the line in five of them. He earned certainly a quarter of a million pounds, and probably more, and he spent, squandered, or gave away every penny of it. In his heyday Lewis estimated his living expenses at £1000 a week – at a period when men of his background regarded £2 as a decent weekly wage.

There are people still living who can recall him making a regular royal progress through Whitechapel and environs in an open-top tourer, scattering notes and coins like confetti. Such behaviour guarantees immediate popularity, although this is usually as transient as the cash that buys it. But it was different with Lewis, who retained the affection of his own community to the very end – and that despite an extraordinary aberration in the 1930s when he served as minder and fund-raiser for the British fascist leader Oswald Mosley. Lewis was probably the only Jew in Britain who could have filled that role and still be treated with respect by his own people.

He was, by any standards, a larger-than-life character, and the published versions of his story are so full of incredible tales that it is difficult to know where truth ends and fiction takes over. Was he really persuaded to go to South America along with a troupe of leading European professionals to stage a private show for a boxing-mad millionaire, and did he really leave his Lonsdale Belt behind when the deal went sour and the Kid had to leave in a hurry? We'll never know, but like so many other Lewis legends it just *might* be true.

Even his date of birth is in dispute. The record books list it as 24 October 1894, but Reg Gutteridge, in *The Big Punchers* (Stanley Paul, 1983), insists that Lewis was a year older than his 'official' age. Lewis himself claimed to have been born in 1896, which would have made him only sixteen when he beat Alec Lambert for the British featherweight title.

He was born at 56 Umberston Street, Aldgate, into a Russian immigrant family. His real name was Gershon Mendeloff; Lewis was the 'nom de ring' he adopted (from a *Sporting Life* headline about Harry Lewis) to hide from his disapproving father the fact that he had taken up boxing. The elder Mendeloff, a carpenter, would have preferred his son to spend more time at the Jews' Free School, but once the fourteen-year-old Gershon had won an impromptu tournament organized by a boxer friend of his, Darkie Daniels, he was hooked on the sport.

But it was an old-fashioned beat bobby who pointed him in the direction of a professional career. He caught Mendeloff and another boy squaring off for a street fight, and instead of dissuading them he suggested that they go along to the Judean Athletic Club in Princes Square, Cable Street, where they could settle their differences and be paid for doing so. The club, founded in 1902 by the brothers Dave and Barney Stitcher to encourage Jewish participation in all sports, had evolved into a semi-professional fight arena in a converted stable loft.

Amenities were basic and the pay was poor, but with a membership of over 1000 the club's shows were always packed. Lewis showed up there the following day, as agreed, but his street-fighting opponent had second thoughts and stayed away. Instead, club secretary Sam Kite paired Lewis (as he had suddenly become) with a boy called Young Cohen, for a purse of a shilling (5p) to the winner and sixpence (2½p) to the loser. Cohen had some experience of 'formal' boxing, and comfortably outpointed Lewis over six rounds.

The sporting winner recognized potential, however, and suggested to Lewis that he join the club and get regular training. Cohen's own career as a boxer did not progress further, but he later became well known in the sport as Johnny Sharpe, a leading manager and agent who also served for many years as British correspondent of *Ring* magazine.

Lewis was a quick learner, and his tearaway style ensured that the club gave him as much work as he could handle. But his father was bitterly opposed to his son boxing, and gave him an ultimatum: he could settle down to becoming a cabinetmaker or, if he persisted in boxing, he could leave home. Reluctantly, he left.

By modern standards, where 50 fights entitle a man to regard himself as a seasoned veteran, Lewis' apprenticeship in the game was ferocious. He crammed 56 engagements into his first 24 months in the game, losing here and there but learning all the time. He would often fight three times a week; in April 1911 he lost over six rounds to Jack Fisher on the 22nd, stopped Joe Marks in seven on the 23rd, and outpointed Young Hyams over six on the 24th.

By the end of 1912 Lewis had managed an astonishing 104 fights, and despite the occasional points loss to men such as Nat Brooks, Jack Fisher and Fred Halsband there was only one bad setback, against Duke Lynch. Lewis had outpointed Lynch, from Camberwell in south-east London, at Premierland in February 1912, but it had been a controversial verdict which outraged a member of the NSC who was 'slumming' at the East End arena. He told the twenty-year-old Lynch to go along to the NSC matchmaker Peggy Bettinson next morning and tell him that he would back Lynch for £25 in a rematch with Lewis.

Bettinson made the match for 1 April, for purses and side stakes of £80. It was an important break for Lewis, whose previous outings had mostly been staged in the minor halls of east London. He was unbeaten in his last 34 fights, and was overdue for some big-time exposure.

Lewis started as 2–1 favourite, but took a solid right to the chin in the opening 15 seconds and went down for eight. He got up shakily, and Lynch immediately floored him again, this time for seven, before a final right dispatched him for the full count. It was all over in 55 seconds – but nobody did that to Lewis again for another ten years and 165 fights.

The indefatigable Lewis turned up in Paris only two nights later, where he showed that no lasting damage had been done by outpointing Leon Truffler in a ten-rounder, and then rounded off a hectic week by knocking out Gus Venn in seven rounds back in

London on 6 April!

By late 1913 Lewis had worked his way up to leading contender for the British featherweight title, and the NSC matched him against Alec Lambert, the twenty-two-year-old son of the Club's chief whip. A new Lonsdale Belt was also at stake, Jim Driscoll having won the previous Belt outright. Lambert, a stylish ex-amateur, outboxed the Kid for sixteen rounds but could not match his pace and slumped to a stoppage defeat in the seventeenth.

A few months later Lewis was a double champion, beating Paul Til of France on a twelfth-round disqualification to take the European title, but he was still a teenager and was fast outgrowing the division. By the time he left for Australia, later that year, he was already almost a welterweight.

Lewis, busy as ever, packed five twenty-rounders into a hectic 63-day tour of Australia, losing only one, and then moved on to America. He based himself in New York under the guidance of Charlie Harvey, who specialized in handling English boxers, and made his debut there in November 1914 with a 'newspaper decision' over Phil Bloom in New York. The Americans loved Lewis, and he was just as keen on them. In fact, he did not box in Britain again until December 1919, 101 fights later.

The welterweight championship was in one of its periodic spells of confusion at the time, but the claim most widely accepted was Jack Britton's. Lewis had the better of a no-decision ten-rounder with Britton in March 1915, and a string of good performances subsequently – including a decision over Britton's predecessor as champion, Mike Glover – earned Ted a rematch for the title in Britton's home town of Boston on 31 August 1915.

Unlike in New York, points verdicts were permissible in Boston, and Lewis's twelve-round victory completed the long road from Judean Club novice to world champion. When Lewis got the better of Willie Ritchie in a New York meeting in December that year, he was universally accepted as champion.

Over the next four years Lewis met the cream of the welter-weight and middleweight divisions, earned a fortune, and established himself as probably the best and most consistent European ever to box in America. He lost the title back to Britton in New Orleans in April 1916 but regained it from him in Dayton, Ohio 14 months later, before Britton ended his reign with a ninth-round knockout in Canton on St Patrick's Day 1919.

By rights Lewis should have been nearing the end of his career; although he was still only in his mid-twenties, he had been fighting professionally for a decade and had already had more than 220 recorded contests. But instead he returned to Britain late in 1919 and embarked on the second phase of his career which saw him win British, Empire and European titles at welterweight and middleweight, as well as making an audacious challenge for the world light-heavyweight crown.

Jack Britton foiled his final bid for his old welterweight title in 1921, but wins over Johnny Basham and Jack Bloomfield confirmed that the Kid was still unbeatable in two divisions at domestic and European level. He beat Bloomfield for the British middleweight title when he weighed 1½ lb inside the welterweight limit, and then five months later ate himself up to 11 st 9 lb to tackle the British light-heavyweight champion, Irishman Noel 'Boy' McCormick, whom he stopped in fourteen rounds.

His next performance was even more remarkable: weighing only 11 st 6 lb, he took on Tom Gummer, a decent heavyweight who scaled 13 st 10 lb, and knocked him out in the first round. On the strength of those two results, he was paired with the charismatic Frenchman Georges Carpentier for the world light-heavyweight title. It was a crazy match – Lewis weighed 10 st 12 lb, less than the modern light-middleweight limit and 23 lb lighter than the champion – yet such was Lewis's reputation that the show was a huge success.

It was staged at the London Olympia on 1 May 1922, and the receipts of £43,000 broke the record for an indoor promotion. There was so much interest in the match that it was arranged to fire off Very lights to signal the result to the crowds outside – green for a Lewis victory, red for defeat. Within two minutes, the red lights were in the sky.

Lewis went at Carpentier in his usual brawling style, and the Frenchman complained to referee Joe Palmer that he was being fouled. As Palmer cautioned Lewis, his hand on the Englishman's wrist, Carpentier fired a straight right to the jaw which knocked Lewis cold. He should have been disqualified, but was not, and that was the end of Lewis as a world contender. Carpentier's recollection of the event must have been hazy, as he recorded in his autobiography (*Carpentier*, Hutchinson & Co., 1955) that, 'I hit him a real welt on the point of the jaw and down he went on his back with his arms outspread to take the count. The fight had hardly lasted ten minutes.'

There were a few good results at British level to come, but by November 1924 the last of the Kid's titles was gone. He fought on until the late 1920s, turning up in rings from Paris to Toronto, Hamburg, Milan, Hollywood and Johannesburg, and made his farewell appearance at Hoxton Baths – only a couple of miles from where it had all begun – in December 1929, when he came out of a year's retirement to beat an old rival, Johnny Basham, in three rounds.

He went on to serve the sport in any number of capacities from referee to promoter, manager and trainer, and was a familiar and respected figure at boxing shows and functions until his death, four days before his birthday, in 1970.

CAREER RECORD: 282 fights, 173 wins (71 inside schedule), 14 draws, 30 defeats, 65 no-decisions. Research by Herb Goldman for the 1986 *Ring Record Book* indicates that Lewis won the 'newspaper verdict' in 40 of these no-decision affairs, lost it in 14 of them, and was awarded a draw in 10 others. No newspaper verdict could be traced in the remaining instance.

Digger Stanley (c. 1878–1919)

THE scenery props outside Billy le Neve's travelling boxing booth included one which depicted Billy's wife Norah apparently lifting a horse by means of a leather harness over her shoulder, and it may well have been the (unfulfilled) expectation of actually witnessing this extraordinary feat which tempted young George 'Digger' Stanley, one afternoon in 1887, to crawl under the back of the tent for a free show.

But instead of the formidable Norah, there was only boxing going on – and after watching for a while the youngster decided he could do just as well as the men in the ring. He somehow persuaded the ringmaster to let him try, and gave an exhibition of the game's arts and skills which was so remarkable that le Neve himself was summoned to watch.

The showman was spellbound by the child's talent, and immediately opened negotiations with the boy's father about taking him on as part of the touring team. Stanley senior, a gypsy from Norwich, was hazy about his son's age, but reckoned that as he was only about nine, negotiations would have to be suspended until he reached fourteen.

He kept his word, and when George attained that age (at least by his father's reckoning) he was brought back to le Neve's booth and the deal was concluded: for ten shillings and a pot of beer, Stanley renounced all future interest in the boy and handed him into the le Neves' charge. It was a decidedly unorthodox beginning to a career which would eventually take him all the way to the bantamweight championship of the world – but then, there was very little orthodox about anything connected with Stanley.

His age remained a mystery: from 1908 until his retirement ten years later, Stanley always gave his age as 'twenty-seven'. Some record books list his date of birth as 28 February 1883, but if his father had calculated in 1887 that Digger would be fourteen in five years' time, he must have been born around 1878. But age never troubled Stanley much anyway – he regarded the question as irrelevant, and dismissed the years so lightly that he continued boxing untl 1918 when he was, by the most generous estimate, at least thirty-five years old.

Life on the booth suited the youngster, who relished the opportunity to master his chosen trade by taking on all comers, regularly conceding three or four stone, for six or more hours every day during the season. I have a vivid memoir from John Spooner, writing in 1965 when he was almost seventy-nine, recalling Stanley in those days:

Le Neve's greatest star was Digger Stanley, standing on the rostrum bright and unexhausted after boxing all the morning and sometimes drinking from a penny bottle of mineral water. As Stanley's given weight was only 7 st 12 lb, he was a marvel, for most of his partners were three to five stones heavier.

On one afternoon he had a real fight with a rival from Notting Hill, about his own weight and build. His ability was quite good, but Stanley floored him once and mastered him, and considering at that time in the afternoon Stanley had been boxing for five hours already there is no doubt a Stanley as fresh as his opponent would have had a clear victory.

The long apprenticeship on the booth gave Stanley a mastery of the tricks of the trade that was unmatched by anyone of his generation, and which enabled him to last as long as he did in top-level competition. He also became the acknowledged master of the game's darker arts: Digger knew every foul strike in the book, and invented most of them. But he was such a chirpy, charming, cocky character that he got away with it, and a style which in another man would have made him a ring 'villain' to match any TV wrestler instead endeared Digger to his public.

He was disqualified seven times during his formal career, although he probably deserved to be thrown out many times more. But he had the knack of making even the worst fouls appear accidental, which would infuriate referees. The official would know full well that Digger was 'at it', but the fouls were invariably so cleverly disguised that he could not spot them. Eventually he would throw Stanley out for some imagined offence, and Digger, realizing that he had already got away with enough genuine fouls to merit disqualification, rarely complained.

Stanley's formal career began on 17 June 1901, and he could hardly have picked a more formidable opponent – Owen Moran, the world-class bantamweight from Birmingham. Stanley beat him clearly on points, a result he repeated two years later, and never looked back.

In his first three years as a pro he lost only three times, twice to the great Pedlar Palmer and once to the former world champion George Dixon, whom he beat in a rematch. A win and a draw against the capable American Jimmy Walsh in 1904 moved him into international reckoning, and in October 1905 he travelled to America to face Walsh again for the world title, or a version of it, at Chelsea, Massachusetts.

But Digger was not a good traveller, and was fairly outpointed. He could have stayed on for more fights in the States, but homesickness got the better of him and he was back in Britain a few weeks later to draw with Darkey Haley. Stanley fought on, winning more than he lost but seemingly getting no nearer a title fight, although wins over the likes of Ike Bradley and Sam Kellar ensured that he stayed in the front rank.

He finally got a second chance in October 1910, and this time it was on home ground against Joe Bowker in London for Bowker's share of the world bantamweight title. Bowker had been boxing at featherweight, and drained himself to get down to the bantamweight limit. Stanley knew where he was most vulnerable, and concentrated his attack on the body – especially the kidneys – for round after round until the champion finally collapsed in agony in the eighth round, trying unsuccessfully to claim a foul as he was counted out.

Digger and his bookmaker backer Alf Mack were in the money – but like so many fighters of his time, Stanley had no idea how to handle it. He opened a bank account, even though he was illiterate; his sole accomplishment in this area was the ability to copy, laboriously, the signature 'George Stanley' on to a contract or a cheque. Fight promoters must have loved him.

A dandy dresser, Stanley proudly sported an expensive fob watch which he would produce with a flourish from his waistcoat – only to spoil the effect by having to ask someone else to tell him the time, another accomplishment which had eluded him.

Stanley kept busy with defences against Johnny Condon and Ike Bradley, and sandwiched between these was another American venture. This time he stayed for two no-decision fights, in New York and Philadelphia, before homesickness again drove him back home.

He retained his title at the NSC against the Fench pastry cook Charles Ledoux, but then gave the Frenchman a rematch in Dieppe two months later, on 23 June 1912. Accounts vary as to what really happened that night. Some reports had Stanley, who was in a comfortable lead, suddenly dropping his hands in the seventh and taking almost twenty unanswered punches before sinking, unconscious, to be counted out. But Stanley himself had a more sinister explanation: he told James Butler, then the respected boxing writer for the *Daily Herald*, that he had taken a dive. According to Butler, Stanley told him: 'I needed the money – that was the reason I let them persuade me to take the dive. I did what they told me to, but as I went down in that seventh round I said to myself: "If I ever get you in a ring again I'll knock spots off you."'

But he never got the chance either of a third meeting with Ledoux or to contest the world title again. He put a second notch on a Lonsdale Belt by beating the Scot Alec Lafferty, but then lost the British title to the Welsh miner Bill Benyon in June 1913. By then he was at least thirty, and probably considerably older, and it was generally felt that he was firmly on the downward slope.

Instead, like all genuine champions, he summoned up one last great performance to regain the championship from the young Welshman four months later. It was vintage Stanley: he broke both his hands, but used dazzling footwork and technique to outclass Benyon and win the Lonsdale Belt outright. (Typically, he did not manage to hold on to the trophy – after his death it turned up in a pawnshop.)

There was only one more championship fight, in 1914, when for the first time he met a referee (the notoriously strict 'Pickles' Douglas) who was not deceived by his protestations of innocence and disqualified him in the thirteenth round against Curley Walker. Stanley fought on as a fading ex-champion through 1915 and 1916, but although he was still meeting top-flight opposition the wins were becoming harder to find – only three in eight attempts.

His money was fast disappearing, consumed by his passion for trotting horses. He took a nasty fall in a trotting match in 1916, sustaining a broken hip which left him with one leg two inches shorter than the other, but despite this handicap he returned to the ring in January 1918 after a 15-month layoff and had a further seven fights, winning two and losing the last three of his career on disqualification.

He was always supremely fit, and had never experienced the slightest difficulty in making weight, and so he was entitled to expect a long and healthy retirement when he finally quit the ring in July 1918. But instead he was injured again in a trotting match, when the mare he was driving fell back on him.

While he was still convalescing he went to a gypsy gathering and contracted pneumonia, dying on 7 March 1919. He was a member of the gypsy royal family, and as such was given the full ceremonial funeral.

CAREER RECORD: 81 fights, 51 wins (13 inside schedule), 7 draws, 21 defeats, 2 no-decisions.

Sid Smith (1889–1948)

THE AMERICANS, who don't like to lose at anything, claim that Jimmy Barry of Chicago became the first flyweight champion of the world by beating Walter Croot on a twentieth-round knockout – which cost Croot his life – at the National Sporting Club in 1897. In fact, as any South London boxing fan will tell you, that distinction belongs to a Bermondsey boy, Sid Smith, who won the first generally recognized world flyweight title fight in Paris sixteen years after Barry's fateful clash with Croot.

Indeed, Smith was the first man to style himself flyweight champion of anywhere, so Barry's claim deserves to disappear. Smith was describing himself as the British flyweight champion in 1909, two years before the NSC deigned to recognize the new category by awarding a Lonsdale Belt for the eight-stoners.

Smith, like so many Bermondsey youngsters, was always keen on the sport. His first job was as a van boy for a firm of carriers who worked the London docks, and his driver was a well-known local scrapper called 'Young Nipper', whose real name was Charlie Wood. The pair used to tie up their horse and cart in Tooley Street, just on the south side of London Bridge, and there entertain passers-by with vigorous sparring sessions using hay stuffed into their caps as gloves.

In early 1907, just after his eighteenth birthday, Smith earned his first purse with a points win over Jack Brooks at Wonderland, the East End arena which was to become his principal fighting base until it was burned down in 1911. He was strictly a boxer rather than a puncher (only ten of his 105 fights ended inside schedule, and of those only four were won by count-out). But the Wonderland clientele were knowledgeable boxing people who could appreciate skill as much as hitting power.

The youngster got regular work there, but his appearances at 'headquarters', the NSC, were restricted. Charlie Dew, whom Smith had beaten at Wonderland in his seventh fight, outpointed him three times at the NSC, and apart from that Smith had only two other minor engagements there during his first five years in the game, both of which he won.

But he was never short of work: apart from Wonderland, he was also a regular performer at the King's Hall near the Elephant and Castle in south-east London, and also at the Blackfriars Ring when that opened in 1910. He was not afraid to travel outside London either, and wins in Leicester, Birmingham, Liverpool, Glasgow and Portsmouth helped to build a national reputation.

There was a handful of losses in the early stages, but by 1911 he had proved his right to regard himself as the best eight-stoner in Britain with wins over the likes of Alex Lafferty, Louis Ruddick and Georges Galliard, who boxed a draw with future world champion Bill Ladbury a few weeks later. He billed himself as the British champion in *Boxing* (as *Boxing News* was then known) and in *Mirror of Life*, so when the NSC finally recognized the new division in 1911 and cast around for contenders for the first Lonsdale Belt match at the weight, Smith was the first choice.

He was paired with Bill Kyne, a curious selection since Smith had beaten him four times in a row after Kyne won their first fight at Wonderland in 1909. Kyne could not make the weight, so Sam Kellar was called in. When he went down with appendicitis, Joe Wilson from Hoxton got the job and the match was made for 4 December 1911, for a purse of £65 to the winner and £35 to the loser, with each man getting £5 training expenses.

It was a big night for the Club, which had just redecorated and enlarged its venue at Covent Garden to accommodate 4000 members and guests. Smith and Wilson gave them a fight to match the occasion: Smith boxed brilliantly on the retreat as Wilson chased him grimly, until a right in the fifth sent Smith sprawling. He was up at nine, but Wilson floored him again immediately, this time for eight, and Smith had a desperate struggle to survive the round.

He recovered well during the interval, and piled up the points with his stylish jabbing between then and the thirteenth, when the determined Wilson caught up with him again. This time Smith hauled himself up by his opponent's legs, and hung on until the referee – seated outside the ring, as was then the custom – managed to make himself heard above the din and ordered them to 'break'.

It was Wilson's last chance, and at the end of twenty rounds Smith had won the title and put his first (and only) notch on the Lonsdale Belt. He tried his luck briefly in America, boxing a no-decision six-rounder in Philadelphia with Young Louisiana, but became homesick and returned to London.

He packed in seven fights, all wins, between September 1912 and March 1913, before the NSC ordered him to defend the title against Bloomsbury's Johnny Hughes. But the purse they offered (£100) was insultingly low, and Smith said as much to the Club matchmaker Peggy Bettinson.

'You know you'll have to return the Lonsdale Belt if you don't accept the offer?' Bettinson asked.

'I thought you'd say that,' said Smith, as he handed over a brown paper bag containing the trophy. It was the sort of snub that did not go down at all well with the NSC, and Smith's remaining 30 fights included only four at Covent Garden.

But Sid had better things to be doing. An offer had come in from a Paris promoter to meet Eugène Criqui there on 11 April, with both the European and, for the first time, the world title at stake. They fought at Premierland in Paris, and Smith gave a dazzling exhibition to win with plenty in hand.

He came home to beat Joe Symonds – who would later become champion himself – in Symonds' home town of Plymouth, and then accepted Dick Burge's offer to meet fellow South Londoner Bill Ladbury in a title defence at the Blackfriars Ring. It was a decision which finished him in top class: Ladbury gave him an almighty hammering, flooring him eighteen times in eleven rounds.

Smith was never the same force again, although he fought on for another five years. The defeats piled up, including three inside-the-distance losses to Jimmy Wilde, and finally he announced his retirement after ending a 14-month layoff to beat Johnny Marshall at Surbiton on Boxing Day, 1919.

In his later years he made a living by guessing the weight of passers-by in the streets and markets of London. Sid would set up his scales, and tell the punters their precise weight. If he was right, the customer paid him a penny; if he was wrong, Sid paid up – but that rarely happened. He explained his secret to boxing historian Gilbert Odd: 'With men, I feel their thighs and I can usually calculate from that how much they weigh. With women, I tell them what they hope they weigh – and they never argue.'

He died in London on 28 April 1948.

CAREER RECORD: 105 fights, 81 wins (10 inside schedule), 5 draws, 1 no-decision, 18 defeats.

Bill Ladbury (1891–1917)

THE 72 men who have claimed the flyweight championship of the world in the seventy-five years since it belonged to Bill Ladbury have included many more accomplished performers than the squat little man from New Cross in south-east London, but none braver.

Ladbury was an out-and-out slugger, a short-armed 5 foot 2 inch brawler whose fighting philosophy was that it is best to knock out the other man before he knocks you out. Such an approach does not always make for a long career, but in Ladbury's case it was certainly an exciting one. He had the same combination of punching power and vulnerability that marked – and marred – the career of Charlie Magri, who brought the same title back to London over seventy years later.

A record that shows 10 inside-schedule losses as well as wins by the same route against class men such as Charles Ledoux, Joe Wilson, Sid Smith and Tommy Harrison tells its own story.

Ladbury was born in New Cross on 14 October 1891, and began his boxing in the colours of Greenwich Boxing Club. When he was fifteen, and weighing 7 st 10 lb, he entered and won an 8 st 4 lb competition organized by Battersea BC, but that apart he made no great impression as an amateur. He turned professional at seventeen, in 1908, and lost his unbeaten record in his sixth fight when Johnny Condon outpointed him in a fifteen-rounder at the National Sporting Club.

Ladbury conceded pounds to Condon, who was an established bantamweight and a regular performer at the NSC's Covent Garden venue. Just over four weeks later, on New Year's Day 1910, Ladbury went to Paris and scored a stunning upset win over Charles Ledoux, a great French favourite of the time, forcing his retirement in four rounds.

It was an astonishing result for a youngster of no great record or reputation, and it earned him a return engagement at the National Sporting Club on 28 February against Sam Kellar of Aldgate, a leading contender for the British championship. Kellar was vastly the more experienced, having boxed extensively in America, and it was an ambitious match for young Ladbury, not yet nineteen, to take on.

Kellar handled him easily for round after round. Ladbury fought with the dogged determination and courage which were to become his trademarks, walking through punishment as he tried to land the punch which might turn the fight his way. He almost managed it in the thirteenth, when a right hook sent Kellar half-way through the ropes, but Kellar's experience enabled him to box his way through the crisis and take a comfortable twenty-rounds decision.

It was almost a year before Ladbury was back in the ring, but four wins in 1911 soon re-established him. He made a return trip to Paris that year, drawing with Georges Gaillard on 4 November and then, only four days later, taking a bad beating in a rematch with Charles Ledoux. It was perfect revenge for the Frenchman as he forced Ladbury's retirement in the same round as that in which the Londoner had beaten him, the fourth.

Such a gruelling programme should have entitled Ladbury to put his feet up for the rest of the year, but instead he was back in the ring in London just eight days later against the highly rated Johnny Hughes of Bloomsbury. Hughes, a clever and skilful boxer, scored an easy third-round knockout over the battle-weary Ladbury.

Ladbury's record at this stage was an unimpressive 9 wins from 15 fights, and his career looked to be going nowhere in particular. But a surprising sixth-round stoppage of Nat Brooks in January 1912 put him back on the right road, and when he followed that with a pair of wins over Joe Fox (later to become bantamweight and featherweight champion of Britain) and a draw with title contender Joe Wilson, the fight trade began to take note.

In all, Ladbury won 10 of his 14 fights in 1912, losing a third meeting with Fox on a fifth-round knockout and being outpointed by Nat Brooks and Joe Wilson, although he avenged the Wilson result with a twelfth-round knockout in October that year and kayoed him again, this time in seventeen rounds, in February 1913. He rounded off 1912 with a satisfying revenge win over Sam Kellar, and also made a rare trip outside London to beat Tommy Harrison (later to become British bantamweight champion) in Liverpool.

The British flyweight champion at this time was Sid Smith, a neighbour of Bill's from Bermondsey. The NSC ordered Smith to defend against Ladbury's conqueror Johnny Hughes, but Smith showed an uncommon streak of independence by dismissing the Club's offer as inadequate and returning their Lonsdale Belt. Instead he went to Paris, to beat Eugène Criqui in what was billed as the first contest for the flyweight championship of the world.

The NSC tried to match Ladbury with Hughes for the Belt, but Scottish champion Johnny Best upset the plans by beating Hughes, who was then withdrawn. Dick Burge, the former British lightweight champion, was promoting at the Blackfriars Ring, a converted chapel in Blackfriars Road. He knew a good London derby when he saw one, and promptly matched Ladbury and Smith for the Bermondsey man's world title.

New Cross against Bermondsey with a world title at stake was a guaranteed box-office winner, and the rival fans packed the Ring on 2 June 1913. This time it was Smith who had to show the courage of a champion. Ladbury was outboxed for six rounds, but started his drive for victory from the seventh, when a right to the chin floored the champion. Ladbury went on to hand out one of the most one-sided beatings ever witnessed in a world championship fight: Smith took an astonishing *eighteen* counts before the referee deigned to stop the massacre in the eleventh.

The new champion took time off to celebrate and to get married before returning to action with a repeat win over Tommy Harrison in front of his home fans at New Cross Baths in November. Three weeks later he was back at the same venue for another non-title match against Jimmy Berry, the tough little Newcastle miner. Like most of Ladbury's contests it was a punch-for-punch affair, until in the tenth round he bounced off the ropes with his guard down and Berry banged over a right to the jaw.

Ladbury barely stirred until the count had reached nine, and then made a frantic attempt to rise, only to be ruled out of time. Despite the result, though, it was Ladbury rather than Berry whom the NSC chose to contest the vacant British title and Lonsdale Belt against Percy Jones, from Porth in the Rhondda. Ladbury's world title, of course, was automatically at stake since the match, at the NSC on 26 January 1914, was held under championship conditions.

Jones was a stylish, fast boxer, too clever to be caught by Ladbury's hard but predictable punches. But Ladbury would not be subdued, and almost pulled off a dramatic win when he floored Jones for eight in the nineteenth. The Welshman had to hold, maul and stagger his way through the final round to take a close points win and end the Londoner's championship career.

Bill was back in the ring a matter of six weeks later, drawing with Joe Symonds over twenty rounds at New Cross in a fight which was described as 'one of the greatest ever seen between flyweights'. When Ladbury stopped Tommy Harrison in fifteen rounds in their third meeting 35 days later, he had put himself right back in contention for his old title, but the Harrison fight proved to be his last worthwhile performance.

As he had done in the past, Ladbury went back in the ring again much too soon. Only four weeks after the fight with Harrison, he faced the brilliant Scottish ex-amateur Tancy Lee at New Cross. Lee was almost ten years his senior, but had far too much all-round technique for him, and the eight-round hammering that the former champion absorbed effectively ended his career as a top-flight competitor.

There was one satisfying win still to come, though: he outpointed Johnny Hughes over twenty rounds on 10 December, to take his revenge for that knockout in 1911.

By now the Great War was under way, and Ladbury joined the Royal West Kents. Training opportunities were limited, and in 1915 he boxed only three times – a pair of disastrous knockouts by Joe Symonds in one and two rounds, and a fifth-round defeat in a non-title rematch with Percy Jones. He carried on through 1916 and had his last fight in February 1917, but all the hard battles had taken their toll and he could win only four of his last eight outings.

His regiment was ordered up the line in France in early 1917, and on 27 June Lance Corporal Ladbury stopped a shell-burst. There was not even enough of him left to bury, but after the war his name was duly inscribed on the Menin Gate. The boxing fraternity did not forget him, and benefits were run to provide for his widow and two sons.

He had been such a popular figure in south-east London that when Deptford Borough Council built a recruiting campaign around his story and his sacrifice, more than 4000 joined up – and this at the tail-end of the war when the flag-waving fervour of the early recruitment drives had long since been smothered in the mud of the trenches.

CAREER RECORD: 52 fights, 31 wins (12 inside schedule), 5 draws, 16 defeats.

Percy Jones (1892–1922)

WEIGHT-MAKING has been the bane of many a flyweight's life, but Percy Jones, who held the world title for three months in 1915, suffered from it more than most.

The Welshman was born into a mining family at Porth, in the Rhondda valley, on – appropriately – Boxing Day 1892. Like so many of his compatriots he idolized the great Welsh featherweight Jim Driscoll and, in fact, came under the Master's tuition later in his career.

When he was a month short of his nineteenth birthday the youngster followed his hero-worship to its logical conclusion and took up the sport himself, winning a novice bantamweight competition at Pentre and thus launching an unbeaten run of 41 fights that was to carry him all the way to the world title in two short, action-packed and spectacular years.

Early in 1989 the Welsh flyweight title was contested for the first time in 38 years by two novices whose combined experience did not total a dozen fights. It was different in Jones' day: a combination of inadequate diet and hard, bad working conditions had produced an abundance of short and pugnacious men of 8 stone or less. Percy was able to learn his trade in 23 fights around the rings of Pentre, Tonypandy and Cardiff before, on 28 April 1913, he made his London debut by outpointing Gus Govarts at the National Sporting Club.

Jones crammed 24 fights into 1913 and won them all, 15 inside the distance. Three of those wins were over Joe Symonds of Plymouth, who would later take the Welshman's world title. Jones beat him on a disqualification in four rounds at Tonypandy, outpointed him in a ten-rounder at the NSC, and scored an even more decisive win in their third meeting, forcing the Englishman to retire in the eighth round at Hanley.

A points win over the well-respected Sam Kellar in November 1913 convinced the NSC that Jones was ready for advancement, and they matched him with Bill Ladbury for the world, European and British titles at the Club on 26 January 1914. Jones, incidentally, left the NSC after beating Kellar and caught the train to Liverpool where, three nights later, he stopped Alf Mansfield in eight rounds. He rounded off a hectic year with a one-round knockout of Driver Knox at Tonypandy the following week.

Jones was already suffering agonies in getting down to the division limit, and needed an hour to lose an excess half-pound at the weigh-in for the title fight. Ladbury was an unpredictable battler who had been beaten in 1912 by Joe Wilson, whom Jones had twice knocked out a year later. But form-lines do not always work out neatly, and Jones had the fight of his life to subdue the determined Londoner. It was a thrilling battle, full of fluctuating fortunes, with the Welshman being floored for eight in the nineteenth round.

He had to hold and maul his way through that round and the next as Ladbury, himself near exhaustion from the frantic pace the pair had maintained, gambled everything on a knockout. But at the final bell it was Jones who got the decision, and the title. As *Boxing* reported: 'The verdict was greeted with a terrific Welsh yell, as much relief as triumph. Percy had won, but it had been a desperately close fight.'

He was in action again just 17 days later, losing a disputed fifteen-round decision at Liverpool to the French star Eugène Criqui. Six weeks later he gave Criqui a rematch, with the world and European titles at stake. The purse was £400 with a £100 side stake, and this time Jones made sure of victory by flooring the Frenchman twice for nine counts with rights to the jaw. Criqui went on to win the world featherweight title in 1922, despite having a steel plate inserted into his jaw, which had been smashed by a German bullet in front-line action.

Jones' old rival Joe Symonds, meanwhile, had come back well from his eight-round defeat by the Welshman in September 1913. He had won seven and drawn one, against Bill Ladbury, who was himself seeking to regain lost status after dropping his title against Jones. Three losses had not convinced Symonds that Jones was the better man, and now that the world title would be involved he was even more eager to try again.

Jones was happy to oblige, for a purse of £250 and a £50 side stake. They met in Symonds' home town of Plymouth on 15 May 1914, and once more Jones fought a losing battle with the scales. Symonds was a comfortable pound inside the limit, but Jones could get no lower than 8 st 2½ lb. Strictly speaking, it should not have been accepted as a world title fight, but when Jones walked on to a right hand which knocked him out in the eighteenth round, Symonds claimed the championship anyway. In the absence of any recognized world governing body, his claim was tolerated.

According to the National Sporting Club, of course, the fight had not involved the Welshman's British title, since the Plymouth promotion had not been staged under their autocratic auspices. Jones won three minor contests inside six days in early June, and then bowed to an NSC edict that he should defend his British title against the Newcastle miner Jimmy Berry on 29 June.

This time, and for the last time in his life, Jones made the weight with something to spare – he scaled 7 st 12 lb – but it was all for nothing. Berry failed to show up for the weigh-in, and the fight was cancelled. Instead, Jones was matched with the ex-amateur star Tancy Lee at the club on 19 October, and yet again the scales beat him.

Despite three visits to a local Turkish baths, and an hour spent walking the London streets, he could not shift the final ounces and so had to surrender his title without striking a blow. He also lost the £100 side stake, which was conditional on him making the weight, but he and Lee consented to go ahead with the contest anyway as a 'catchweights' match, carrying an extra £25 side stake. Jones was drained by his efforts to reduce, and had little to offer. The Scot dominated the exchanges until the exhausted Welshman finally went down in the fourteenth round and Jim Driscoll, who was working in Jones' corner, threw in the towel.

His days as a flyweight were over, and it was almost a year before he was back in the ring, as a bantamweight. He drew with Young Swift at Plymouth and, ten days later, beat his old foe Bill Ladbury on a fifth-round retirement at New Cross, London. That was his farewell appearance, although no one knew it at the time.

Jones had joined the Royal Welsh Fusiliers at the outbreak of the Great War, and was quickly promoted to sergeant, but in 1916 he was severely wounded in the leg and was also badly affected by poison gas. He underwent 30 operations, including the amputation of his leg in 1918, but then contracted the illness which eventually killed him. He was a sad figure towards the end. In June 1922 he made a rare public appearance at a charity function for the Nazareth House, Cardiff. His weight was down to 4 st 2 lb – he had been 9 st 12 lb when he went to France. He was suffering from trench fever, and by that time his other leg had become infected, so that he was confined to a wheelchair. Six months later, on Christmas Day, he died – one day short of his thirtieth birthday.

CAREER RECORD: 51 fights, 45 wins (18 inside the distance), 3 draws, 3 defeats.

Matt Wells (1886–1953)

Australian recognition as world champion is not exactly a guarantee of a place in the Hall of Fame, but south Londoner Matt Wells has as much right to inclusion in this volume as any of the other British fighters who claimed the honour at a time when there were no regulating authorities, and when one man's claim to a title was as good as another's.

Wells won his version of the welterweight championship when the division was in absolute chaos, beating an Irishman in Sydney and losing it to an American in Boston, but his other achievements in the ring were sufficient to earn him recognition as one of the outstanding British performers of his time. He fought world champions at every weight from feather to middle, licked Freddie Welsh to win the British lightweight title and the Lonsdale Belt, and went out a winner at the age of thirty-six after thirteen years as a pro, almost all of them spent in the very top flight.

He was marked for stardom from the start, and as an amateur with the famous Lynn Athletic Club in Walworth he won the Amateur Boxing Association lightweight title four years in a row, from 1904 to 1907. He was unbeatable on the home front, and in those days there was very little organized international competiton. In 1909, when he was twenty-three, Wells decided that he had done all he could hope to do in the amateur game and turned professional under the management of George McDonald.

He was unbeaten in his first seven fights, and then took the bold step of making his own way to America, where he felt that he would benefit from the greater range of opposition available on the busy New York scene. This was during the period when it was actually illegal to give a points verdict in a New York fight, so instead bets were settled by the opinions of selected newspaper reporters.

Wells had eight of these no-decision affairs between May and September 1910, and only once, against Paddy Sullivan, did the 'newspaper verdict' go the other way. Matt made sure that the National Sporting Club was kept aware of his progress, since the Club was the sport's *de facto* governing body in Britain and claimed the exclusive right to stage British championships.

Before Christmas 1910, the invitation arrived from the club for Matt to challenge Freddie Welsh for the lightweight title. Welsh's reputation was so high that few gave Wells a chance of beating him when they met at the NSC on 27 February 1911. The Welshman was 3–1 favourite, but Wells was unimpressed. He had been at ringside when Freddie beat the other great Welsh idol Jim Driscoll on a tenth-round disqualification two months earlier, and what he saw convinced him that he would be the new champion.

'I was a close watcher of all that went on,' he told the *Mirror of Life* (a leading sports paper). 'I took mental note of all Fred's weak points. Driscoll got him so very often with a straight left; I was quite surprised and I determined there and then to fight Welsh on the same lines when I met him.'

He did, too, and with total success. As the *Mirror* recorded:

He fully realized what a straight left could do to Welsh and he scored with this blow repeatedly and with the greatest of ease. It completely baffled Welsh and put him off his stroke, while when it came down to in-fighting the Welshman had nothing on the Londoner, who knew every trick of the trade and met Fred at his own game.

At the end of twenty rounds Welsh was an ex-champion, and his backer Harry Marks was significantly lighter in the wallet. The result made a considerable impression in America, where Welsh had done most of his boxing since 1905, and Wells immediately cashed in with a profitable and undefeated 12-month tour taking in 10 fights from New York to Boston, Philadelphia and Toronto.

His fourth fight of the tour marked the return of 'official' decisions to New York boxing. The Frawley Law, making points verdicts legal, came into effect in August 1911, and Wells' ten-rounder with the dangerous southpaw puncher Valentine 'KO' Brown was the first main event to be decided by a referee's vote.

Brown was a big local attraction and 10,000 fans packed Madison Square Garden, only to see their man thoroughly outclassed. At the end of the tenth, referee Charlie White immediately raised Wells' glove, and the Englishman had made another little piece of history. Significantly, though, Wells weighed half a pound over 10 stone – the weight problems which eventually pushed him into the welterweight division were already in evidence.

Matt did not believe in taking on soft touches: his other opponents on the tour included Leach Cross and Packey McFarland (who both came close to winning the world lightweight title), and featherweight king Abe Attell. Illness made Wells come home to London, and he could have done without taking on the rugged Australian Hughie Mehegan so soon after his return. They had a riotous brawl at the Ring, Blackfriars, which ended with Wells' first professional defeat, on a fourteenth-round disqualification.

Wells avenged that loss twice in 1913, but by that time he had suffered another, and more serious, setback: Freddie Welsh regained the British title from him on 11 November 1912, on a twenty-round decision which the Londoner's camp hotly disputed.

By now, though, a move into the welterweight class was inevitable. He launched his new career with a seventh-round knockout of Johnny Basham – a future British champion – and then scored the first of his revenge wins over Mehegan. In the 1913–14 period, Australia had suddenly become the centre of activity in the division, with several of the world title claimants campaigning over there, so the ever-adventurous Wells decided to try his luck there, too.

He began well, outpointing Mehegan and Owen Moran, but then lost his way with consecutive defeats by Mehegan, Harry Stone and Herb McCoy. Ray Bronson, an American who had been one of the title claimants, had lost his championship to the Dane Waldemar Holberg in January 1914, and picked Wells as a 'safe' comeback opponent a month later.

Matt knew it was his last chance to make the breakthrough, and he took it with a seventh-round stoppage. Holberg, meanwhile, had lost the title in March to Tom McCormick, an Irishman from Dundalk. (He had squeezed in a defence against Johnny Summers in February as well!)

McCormick gave Wells a crack at his title in Sydney on 21 March 1914, and the Londoner won a convincing verdict over twenty rounds. The unfortunate McCormick won only two of his remaining eight fights, and was killed in action in France in June 1916.

Wells returned to Britain, and beat Young Nipper and Gus Platts in non-title matches. After dropping a fifteen-round verdict to Johnny Basham in a rematch at the Opera House, London, Matt took off for another of his extended American campaigns – and lost his title to Mike Glover in Boston on his first outing, on 31 May 1915.

He stayed on for another 24 fights, the majority of them no-decision affairs, but he was now at the veteran stage and the losses began to mount up. Wells was working on attachment with the US Army as a PT instructor, but got their blessing to return home in late 1917. It was generally assumed that he had retired, but he launched a comeback in 1919, when he was almost thirty-three.

Consecutive losses to Johnny Basham, Ted 'Kid' Lewis and Phil Bloom should have convinced him that it was time to make the retirement permanent, but instead he fought on until 12 May 1922, and managed to win more than he lost.

The fighting edge may have dulled, but the sense of humour which made him such an appealing character had not. He took a fearful beating from Lewis, whom Wells had often served as cornerman during Lewis' long American campaign. The pair were good friends outside the ring, and Lewis pleaded with him in the clinches to quit. Wells refused, and hung on until, in the twelfth round, the referee finally intervened and said, 'That's sufficient.' Wells spat out his bloodied gumshield and said, 'I've been trying to think of that word for the last five rounds.'

His last fight was against Jack Hart, later to become a respected referee, and Wells left the game a winner.

He loved the sport too much to walk away from it, though, and for the rest of his long life he remained involved in one capacity or another. He was instructor to Guy's Hospital, Dulwich College, the Metropolitan Police and, of course, at his beloved Lynn AC, where he taught successive generations of youngsters the virtues of the classic English straight left. He also worked as promoter, referee, cornerman and anything else where his vast experience would be useful.

Wells died in London on 27 June 1953.

CAREER RECORD: 82 fights, 32 wins (8 inside the distance), 2 draws, 19 defeats, 29 no-decisions. According to the *Ring Record Book*, Wells was given the newspaper verdict in 14 of these, lost 9, and drew 3. No verdict could be traced for the other three.

Joe Symonds (1894–1953)

JIMMY WILDE claimed to have had 864 contests, including booth appearances, so he was qualified to recognize a real fighting man when he met one. The Welshman was frequently asked who was the hardest opponent he had ever faced, and he always gave the same answer – Joe Symonds of Plymouth, the man from whom he took the world flyweight title. Coming from arguably the greatest flyweight of all time, that is a compliment that the West Countryman must have cherished.

A good many of the men Symonds faced in his 134-fight career would have endorsed Wilde's opinion. Symonds met the best around, at any weight from flyweight to welterweight, and licked the first three flyweight champions of the world – yet he is rarely mentioned when Britain's world champs are discussed. Maybe Joe was too much of a local boy for his own good: 86 of his fights took place in his home town, and the opportunities to forge a national reputation were therefore limited.

He was born on 28 December 1894. According to Gilbert Odd, the doyen of British boxing historians, his real name was Rupert Harvey, but the American Herb Goldman, whose 1986 edition of the *Ring Record Book* is the most comprehensive of its kind ever published, says it was Hubert Toms. 'Symonds' was probably adopted in honour of his trainer or manager, as was the custom in those days. Teenage boxers were usually billed as, for example, 'Young Symonds', 'Symonds' Nipper', and the like. In fact, 17 of Joe's first 20 opponents had the 'Young' prefix, and he had a well-known Plymouth contemporary called Ernie 'Kid' Symonds, with whom he was often confused.

Symonds had his first fight at the Old Cosmo arena in Plymouth a week after his seventeenth birthday, and he went on to become the most popular performer ever to appear at the Mill Street hall. He was already a Navy man, having joined the Service as soon as he was old enough, after less satisfying spells as a delivery boy and a butcher's helper. The Navy were obliging employers, and as Joe was based in Plymouth anyway there was never any difficulty about getting permission to box.

The Cosmo promoters, a consortium headed by Silas Algar and Bert Dorman, were impressed with Symonds' flair for the game, and kept him busy. He won a 7 st 6 lb competition there after three months as a pro, and was beaten only once in his first 17 fights before they moved him up into fifteen-rounds class. His first venture over the longer distance was disappointing, as Dido Gains outscored him, but six months later Symonds reversed that result and from then on he was an established main-event attraction.

Algar had now taken over Symonds' management, and he persuaded established men such as Alf Mansfield and Bill Kyne to come to Plymouth to test his protégé. On the recommendation of J.T. Hulls, who combined writing for the *Sporting Life* with refereeing at the Old Cosmo, Symonds was given his first NSC date and came through in style with a repeat win over Alf Mansfield.

But then things started to go wrong. He was disqualified for a low blow in the fourth round against Percy Jones, and later in 1913 suffered three bad setbacks. British champion Sid Smith came down to Plymouth for a non-title fifteen-rounder made at 8 st 2 lb to protect his title, and survived a rocky tenth round to win on points. A fortnight later Jones outpointed him in a rematch, flooring him at the end of the fifth round, and although Symonds rallied with a useful stoppage of Joe Wilson, he took a bad beating in a third fight with Jones and was forced to retire in the eighth round.

Wins over Charlie Ward and Sam Kellar put Symonds back on course, and when in March 1914 he fought a twenty-round draw with the recently deposed world champion Bill Ladbury, he was firmly back in contention. Ladbury had lost his title to Percy Jones who, having beaten Joe three out of three already, did not need much persuasion to travel to Plymouth to risk his title on 15 May 1914.

Six thousand fans crammed the Old Cosmo to watch what was billed as a contest for the world, European and British titles. At that time, of course, the NSC claimed the sole right to stage championships and so according to them the British title was not at stake. Since Jones scaled well over the flyweight limit anyway, the match could not really be a championship pairing of any sort, but the Plymouth public was not concerned with such technicalities.

No weights were announced, but reports of Jones' true poundage varied anywhere from 8 st 2½ lb to 8 st 8 lb. Symonds was 7 st 13 lb, and based his subsequent championship claim on the fact that he, at least, had made the stipulated weight.

For fourteen rounds the Welshman outboxed Symonds as comfortably as he had done in their previous encounters, but the rugged little challenger kept ploughing forward and, by the fifteenth, Jones was beginning to crack. Symonds kept up the pressure, and it paid off in the eighteenth. He switched suddenly to southpaw, and fired over a right hook which floored the champion for six. Another right knocked him through the ropes, and when he scrambled back to an upright position Symonds promptly flattened him again, which was the cue for the towel to flutter in from the Welsh corner.

The NSC did not recognize him as champion of anywhere, and no doubt felt vindicated when Jimmy Wilde, whom they regarded as the leading contender, outpointed him over fifteen rounds in November 1914. But Symonds continued to style himself champion, and a long run of wins over class men such as Bill Ladbury, Ike Bradley, Sid Smith, Johnny Best and Johnny Hughes enhanced his credibility.

Scotland's Tancy Lee, meanwhile, had won the 'official' British title by stopping Wilde at the NSC, so when Symonds battered Lee to sixteenth-round defeat in October 1915 no one could any longer dispute his right to the championship. But his was to be a short reign: on 14 February 1916, weakened by a punch to the throat, Symonds was forced to retire at the end of the twelfth round against Wilde, and the world title and Lonsdale Belt were gone.

He still claimed the European championship, but when Tancy Lee stopped him in seventeen rounds at Plymouth in May, his glory days were over. He had been having weight problems for some time, and moved up to bantamweight with immediate success. A run of twelve wins and a draw (including a five-round stoppage against a local welterweight, Ted Bull) earned him a British title chance against Joe Fox, but the Leeds man forced his retirement after eighteen rounds.

He built up another winning run, taking on all comers at all weights. At Grimsby on 1 September 1917 he faced Joe Marks, who scaled 10 st 2 lb, for a £50 side stake, and beat him in ten rounds – ignoring the air raid which was in progress at the time.

The NSC could overlook him no longer, and when the bantamweight title became vacant Symonds was paired with Bermondsey's Tommy Noble in November 1918. It was a great chance for

Joe, as he had already beaten Noble three times, but Noble had learned from the experiences and this time it was the Londoner who got the verdict after twenty thrilling rounds.

Joe was still a serving sailor, and in 1918 conceded weight to win the featherweight championship of the Battle Cruiser Squadron and Grand Fleets. He also won a £25 bet, for the benefit of the local hospital, that he could knock out three opponents in one night during an open-air show at Truro. Young Detain was duly dispatched in the first, George Oates in the second, and Sgt Murphy in the first, although the event does not figure on Symonds' official record.

He quit the Navy in 1919, and spent most of the following two years in Australia, where he proved very popular in his thirteen appearances. He lost five and drew two, but the six wins included defeats of their bantamweight champion, Jerry Sullivan, and the featherweight champ Jack Green. By now his career was tailing off, but he managed one trip to America in December 1922 for a no-decision match with Tommy Gerrard in Trenton.

His thirteen years in the ring ended on 31 October 1924, with a seventh-round loss to Harry 'Bugler' Lake – in the same ring in Plymouth where it had all begun. He never left the town, and died there on 4 March 1953.

CAREER RECORD: 134 fights, 96 wins (45 inside schedule), 11 draws, 2 no-decisions, 25 defeats.

Jimmy Wilde (1892–1969)

SOMEWHERE, probably in Cardiff, lives the last man to knock out the greatest flyweight of them all, Jimmy Wilde – but he would be well advised not to broadcast the fact. Wilde was seventy-two at the time, and he never recovered from the brutal beating he suffered at the hands of a teenage thug who mugged him on a deserted railway platform one night. He lived out his last four years in Cardiff's Whitchurch Hospital, unaware of who he was or the astonishing scale of his achievements in the ring. He deserved so much better.

In his prime he never scaled more than 7 st 4 lb, yet he won 101 of his 151 traceable fights in a twelve-year career by knockout or stoppage, lost only four, and reigned as world champion for nearly seven years between 1916 and 1923. He was the fourth holder of the title, but the credit for establishing the division on an international stage belongs to the skinny little Welshman rather than to his three predecessors.

Wilde himself claimed to have had 854 fights, but he was including the hundreds of battles he had on tour with Jack Scarrott's booth. No one kept records of booth fights, so the real total will never be known, but Wilde's figure may well be near the truth. He once knocked out 17 opponents before 2 p.m., and after a lunch consisting of a bun and a cup of tea flattened another eight.

His appearance ensured that he would never be short of challengers as he stood on the platform outside the booth. He looked almost tubercular, with a pasty complexion, matchstick-thin arms and a chest measurement of only 31½ inches. But the men who fancied their chances of earning a pound for lasting three rounds invariably learned the hard way that the scrawny frame concealed utterly disproportionate hitting power. Wilde was a natural puncher, with the rare gift of perfect timing and coordination. Punch power has little to do with physique, but that simple fact was never more dramatically illustrated than by Wilde.

He was born into a mining family in Tylerstown on 12 May 1892, and as soon as he was old enough he, too, went to work in the pit. He turned to boxing as a means of supplementing the income which he clawed fom the coal-face, where his diminutive size enabled him to crawl into narrow seams and, lying on his back or sides, pick away at the face, thus building abnormally powerful muscles in the back and shoulders. Young Wilde was lodging at that time with David John Davies, known locally as 'Dai Davies Champion'. Dai was a well-known 'mountain fighter', a master of that peculiarly Welsh brand of bare-knuckling.

Dai found Wilde one evening having an argument in his garden with another young miner, and ordered them to meet on the mountain at six o'clock next morning, with himself to keep order. Wilde duly broke his rival's jaw in three places, and had to contribute most of his own meagre wages to the man's keep during the fortnight in which his injuries kept him away from work.

Davies recognized raw talent in the eighteen-year-old Wilde, and started showing him the basics of the game. He encouraged him to join Jack Scarrott's booth, the best known of the many booths which traversed Wales, and the regular five shillings (25p) a night that Wilde earned helped to soften the opposition which Dai's daughter, Elizabeth, had towards Wilde's boxing. He married Elizabeth not long after he came to live in the house, and it was a supremely happy match. She became the driving force behind him, often accompanying him on a bike during his training runs and even, when the budget did not run to sparring partners, donning a crude body-protector of their own invention to do the job herself.

His first taste of semi-professional fighting, as opposed to booth scrapping, came against another Dai Davies, who was known locally as 'Dai Chips'. They had a falling-out at work, and agreed to meet in a twelve-round contest at Scarrott's new marquee in Tonypandy, where he was staging regular programmes of three or four scheduled fights in addition to the usual booth knockabouts. He beat Dai, and brought home a purse of eight gold sovereigns, which was almost double his pit wages for a week.

There is a curious footnote to this story, which Wilde told in his memoirs in the *News of the World* in the 1950s. Wilde wrote that he had stopped Davies in eleven rounds, which provoked an angry letter from Davies' brother the following week. According to Rees Davies, Wilde had won on points, and he also claimed that this was the third time the pair had met in the ring, with a draw and a win apiece. Wilde responded to Mr Davies in print, and corrected his error about the stoppage – but he said nothing about having lost to

Davies previously, which leaves open the question of whether his record should show five losses rather than the generally accepted four.

The day after beating Davies, the Wildes went along to open their first bank account, and Jimmy took the decision to fight for a living. He whizzed through 28 fights in 1911 and won all but one, a draw with George Lake in his fourth outing. Apart from one each in Cardiff and Edinburgh they were all staged in Pontypridd, and 22 were won inside the distance. But despite this electrifying start to his career, Wilde remained so much of an unknown outside Wales that when he turned up at the Blackfriars Ring to seek a match, the promoter, Dick Burge, had never heard of him and was most reluctant to give him a chance.

Finally, and against his better judgement, he paired him with a protégé of lightweight champion Matt Wells, who was billed simply as 'Matt Wells' Nipper'. It took Wilde only 45 seconds to flatten the Nipper, but for some reason Burge was still unconvinced and did not book him for an encore. The National Sporting Club was similarly unimpressed when, after scoring three more wins, Wilde was granted a three-round trial there against title contender Joe Wilson.

So Wilde headed back to Wales, to compile an amazing run of successes – 54 straight wins, 33 by knockout or stoppage. Such a record (82 unbeaten, 55 inside schedule) should have had promoters queueing at his door, but NSC matchmaker Peggy Bettinson was adamant. Wilde, he said, was just too small, and his club members would protest at bad matchmaking if he put him on a bill.

But then, somebody actually found a man who was lighter than Wilde – a French youngster called Eugène Husson, who came in at under 7 stone for their match at the Club on 30 March 1914. Wilde could probably have disposed of him quickly, but instead took the opportunity to show the Club the full range of his skills before knocking Husson out in the sixth. After that, there was no further difficulty about getting bookings at 'headquarters', and when Wilde rounded off 1914 with three major victories in a row over Alf Mansfield, Joe Symonds and Sid Smith, the NSC paired him with the Scottish star Tancy Lee for the British and European titles at the club on 25 January 1915.

Wilde should not have been in the ring that night at all. He was ill and weak with flu (a much more serious ailment then than now), but rather than ask for a postponement and disappoint his public he went through with it, taking a fearful beating before his corner threw in the towel in the seventeenth round.

The porter who carried Lee's bag on his arrival back at Glasgow railway station saw the Lonsdale Belt in it, and asked Lee what he'd won it for. 'Swimmin' the Channel,' Lee replied. The porter, who was no boxing fan, was impressed, and assured Tancy, 'It's no more than you deserve for doing it in January.'

Wilde took five months off, and then bounced back into action with wins over top names such as Johnny Best, Sid Smith and Tommy Noble. Lee in the meantime had lost his title to Joe Symonds, who also claimed the world title, and Wilde and Symonds met to decide both titles at the NSC on 14 February 1916.

Like their first encounter, it was a punishing affair. Wilde recalled that Symonds hit him so hard in the stomach in the fifth round that 'I thought the end of the world had come. My eyes went round and round, and for a moment there was only a red and grey mist in front of me.' But Symonds did not realize how badly he had hurt Wilde, and he never got another chance.

Symonds was still ahead after seven rounds, but in the eighth, as he stepped back and tilted his chin to avoid a punch, the blow caught him full on the Adam's apple. It knocked all the fight out of him; he could not breathe properly, and it was only heart and courage that kept him in there until his corner retired him at the end of the twelfth.

The victory gave Wilde a substantial hold on the world title, but he was well aware that there were several good Americans who disputed his right to the championship. The first, Johnny Rosner, was brought to Liverpool and stopped in eleven rounds, and that left the Italian–American Giuseppe di Melfi, who took his ring name of 'Young Zulu Kid' from his golliwog mascot. While he waited for this match to be made, which all agreed would be for universal recognition as world champion, Wilde squared his account with Tancy Lee, winning again in the eleventh.

Wilde and the Zulu Kid met at Holborn Stadium on 18 December 1916, after a hectic renovation job on the building – which had been used as a stable and store by the haulage firm Carter Paterson – was completed in just 18 days. The taxi Wilde had ordered to take him to the arena failed to arrive, so the unflappable Welshman and his entourage went part of the way by bus and strolled the last few hundred yards through the crowds. The Welshman enjoyed an easy eleventh-round win, and then joined the Army for the duration of the Great War.

He was promoted to sergeant, and although his duties consisted mainly of conducting PT sessions, he managed to fit in the occasional fight, including a world title defence against George Clark and an open-air engagement at Chelsea football ground against the East End featherweight star Joe Conn, whom he floored thirteen times in twelve rounds.

Since Wilde was a serving soldier he was not allowed to be paid in cash for the contest, so instead he accepted a diamond necklace from the promoter as a gift for his wife. It was worth £3000. He sustained his second defeat during this period, a meaningless three-round points loss to the American Pal Moore, in an Inter-Services match at the Albert Hall. When he met Moore again, this time over twenty rounds in July 1919, he left no room for argument, and won easily on points.

Wilde left for a highly paid tour of America and Canada in November 1919, and was gone for most of 1920. When he returned, he decided to try for the world bantamweight title, which was then in the hands of the clever American Pete Herman. Contracts were duly signed for the fight to take place at the Albert Hall on 13 January 1921, with Wilde getting £8000 plus £250 training expenses.

Three weeks before facing Wilde, Herman conveniently lost his title on points to Joe Lynch (and regained it from him as soon as he was back in America). The Wilde fight went ahead anyway, but Jimmy insisted that it remain at the originally stipulated weight of 8 st 6 lb. When he learned that night that the American had weighed 8 st 7½ lb, he let it be known that he was not prepared to go through with the fight.

While the dressing-room arguments were going on, Lord Lonsdale arrived and asked to speak to Wilde. He told him that the Prince of Wales was at ringside, and would be very disappointed if Wilde did not box. Jimmy would have been better advised to tell the Prince that he was out of luck, but instead he got in the ring and, handicapped by a broken right hand sustained in the eighth round, took a bad beating before referee Jack Smith picked him off the floor in the seventeenth round and carried him back to his corner.

Wilde told his wife that he was retiring, and that was how it stayed for over two years. But then an offer was cabled to the Welshman's manager Teddy Lewis, asking him to name a price for Wilde to defend the world title against the Filipino Pancho Villa in New York on 18 June 1923. Wilde told Lewis to ask for an unprecedented £13,000 plus expenses for four, never dreaming that the demand would be accepted, but it was and Wilde went back into training for the last time.

He knew that he probably could not win, but he fought to the bitter end with a courage that has passed into boxing legend. The finish came in the seventh, and the beating that Wilde took almost killed him. Thirty years later he recalled that, 'I was so badly injured that four months passed before I was able to recognize anyone; four months curtained off from the rest of my life and of which I have no knowledge.'

It was too high a price to pay, and he never fought again. He became a respected boxing writer for the *News of the World*, offering his own forthright opinions rather than those of the conventional ghost writer, and stayed active and involved until, at seventy-two, he was battered into the twilight world from which he never emerged for the remaining four years of his life.

He died in Cardiff on 10 March 1969, unaware that his wife Elizabeth, who had been so central to his success and his happiness, had died almost three years earlier.

CAREER RECORD: 151 fights, 132 wins (101 inside schedule), 2 draws, 13 no-decisions, 4 defeats. Wilde was credited with the newspaper verdict in all his no-decision contests.

Freddie Welsh (1886–1927)

FREDDIE WELSH was a freak: a loner who turned his back on a middle-class lifestyle to work at the most menial jobs he could find, on the other side of the world; a fighter who scorned the traditional methods and devised his own, highly individual training routines; an advocate of vegetarianism and healthy eating nearly sixty years before it became fashionable. Many of the great fighters have been eccentrics – perhaps it is that which makes them stand out from the herd – but Welsh took his quirkiness to extremes.

He was born Frederick Hall Thomas in Pontypridd, South Wales, on 5 March 1886. Unlike so many of the other great Welsh boxers, he was not born into the poverty of a coal-mining family. His father was a professional man, an estate agent and surveyor, and young Frederick enjoyed a comfortable upbringing.

His father died while Freddie was in his teens and the youngster, determined to make his way in the world, headed for America. It may well have been the land of opportunity, but for the young Welshman the opportunities were limited to a variety of unrewarding and ill-paid jobs including dish-washing, working as a sandwich-board carrier, and anything else that would provide him with a week's wages and a roof over his head.

For much of his late teens he was a hobo, living as a tramp or riding the rails across the Mid-Western states. It was a harsh environment, but it forced him to learn how to use his fists to look after himself. He finally settled in Philadelphia, and when he was nineteen found a regular job as a salesman and demonstrator of sporting goods in a newly opened department store in the city.

He had told the store manager he was a fully qualified physical culture expert, and in that capacity was invited to give an exhibition of the art of ball-punching. Unfortunately, this was the one aspect of training which, to the very end of his career, he could never master; the man who was one of the most accurate and precise punchers the lightweight division has known invariably ended up in a tangle when he took on the speedball.

Faced with the prospect of unemployment when the deception was discovered, Welsh offered a compromise. He would give a sparring exhibition instead, against two of the best men the store manager could find. Freddie handled the pair of them easily, and was thus encouraged to take up boxing on a more orthodox basis at the Broadway Athletic Club, an establishment run by a colourful character known as 'Diamond Jim Bailey'.

He made his first ring appearance on 21 December 1905, and acquired a new name in the process. The ring announcer asked his name, and the youngster answered 'Freddie Thomas'. The announcer assumed that the boy was so nervous that he had forgotten to add his surname, and so took it on himself to introduce him as 'Freddie Welsh', having taken note of the accent.

Welsh won his debut on a sixth-round knockout, but had to go the distance in 22 of the 25 fights he had in 1906. He was never a big puncher – in fact, one of his great contemporaries, the former champion Battling Nelson, dismissed him contemptuously as a 'snowflake boxer'. Nelson, though, was careful not to risk his title against him, and the pair did not meet until 1917, when both were near the end of their careers. But despite his lack of hitting power, the Philadelphia fans took to him. (Times change; today in Philadelphia, as in Mexico City, fighters run the risk of being booed when they throw a jab instead of a hook.)

A bad experience at the hands of a seasoned veteran called Tim Callahan, who trounced him in a six-rounder, taught him the value of the left jab, and he worked obsessively to master the punch. He even painted a white dot on the punchbag, and practised relentlessly until he could hit the dot with every jab.

It was one of many unconventional training routines that Welsh developed. Between fights he would let his weight go up to around 11 st 2 lb, and would then starve himself for a fortnight, existing only on water, until he was down to 9 st 4 lb – at which stage he would begin his gym work. He ate only one meal a day, usually vegetables and eggs, and would determine the precise time at which the meal would be taken by what he felt his body was telling him after his morning breathing exercises. The meal might be at noon, or at six in the evening, but the day's training routine and timetable would have to be adjusted around it.

In sparring, he worked with three partners – a featherweight for speed, a heavyish lightweight for routine work, and a welter or middle for hard exchanges. The three would often work a minute each, but without any interval while they changed over.

By the end of 1906 he was an established main-event performer, boxing twenty-rounders. His American contests were all no-decision affairs, but the quality of opponents he was meeting soon marked him as a star in the making.

He came home for a working holiday in 1907, and financed it with 13 straight wins, most of them in Wales. The fact that 10 of the 13 were knockouts or stoppages underlined the difference in class between British and American journeymen, but at least the campaign brought his name to the notice of the men who ran the sport in Britain.

Throughout 1908 and the early part of 1909 he fought his way back and forth across America, appearing in Philadelphia, Milwaukee, Los Angeles, New Orleans, New York and Boston. Featherweight champion Abe Attell was considered the fastest man in the American ring, yet Welsh outboxed him comprehensively when they met in November 1908. By the time he returned to Britain in the summer of 1909 he was a contender for the world title as well as the British, and on 8 November 1909 he won the inaugural Lonsdale Belt by outpointing Johnny Summers over twenty rounds at the National Sporting Club.

He was, by his own standards, comparatively inactive in 1910 with only five fights, although he filled in time by appearing in a Drury Lane sporting drama called 'A 33–1 Chance', in which he sparred three rounds with the former featherweight champion Ben Jordan. His five outings brought him four wins and a draw with the classy American Packy McFarland, who had outpointed Welsh in Milwaukee in February 1908 and drawn with him in Los Angeles.

McFarland appeared to have won clearly, and for the first time in the history of the NSC threats were shouted at the referee, Tom Scott. There was a rumour that Scott had been 'bought' after a bet of several thousand pounds had been placed on a McFarland win. He refereed only once more, handling a novice competition a few weeks later, and shortly afterwards was committed to a mental home, where he died.

In December 1910 Welsh faced his great rival for national affection, Jim Driscoll, in defence of the British title in Cardiff. There was bad blood between the pair which went back to an incident in August 1907. Driscoll was working at the time with Frank Guess' booth at St Mary's Hill fair at Bridgend, South Wales, and Welsh – then a virtual unknown – accepted the barker's offer of £1 if he

Right: *Pedlar Palmer's pose is stiff and unnatural, but in reality he was a clever, skilful and inventive performer*

Below: *The pioneer – Ben Jordan was Britain's first world champion of the gloved era*

Above: *Digger Stanley, one of the bantamweight division's most colourful champions, poses with manager Alf Mack*

Left: *Joe Bowker, like so many of Britain's world champions, learned his trade in the booths*

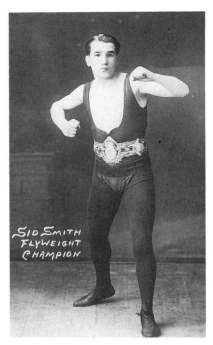

Sid Smith
Flyweight
Champion

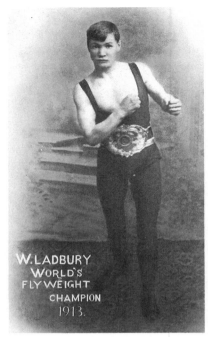

W. Ladbury
World's
Flyweight
Champion
1913.

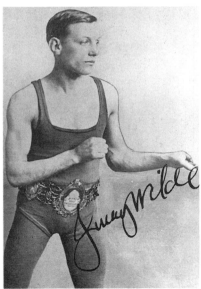

Jimmy Wilde

Above: *The immortal Jimmy Wilde, with the Lonsdale belt which he won outright*

Right: *Freddie Welsh was a master of defensive skills, as his unmarked face showed*

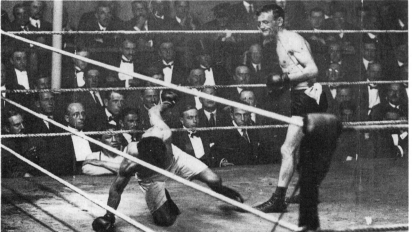

Top left: *The popular Teddy Baldock had a crowd of well-wishers to cheer him on his way to America in 1929*

Opposite top left: *Bermondsey's Sid Smith was the first generally recognized world flyweight champion*

Opposite top right: *Bill Ladbury, the pride of New Cross, in his fighting prime*

Top right: *Jack 'Kid' Berg, the most popular British fighter ever to campaign in America*

Above: *Jim Driscoll, haggard and ill, feints Charles Ledoux off-balance. It was Driscoll's last fight*

Left: *Flyweight rivals Jackie Brown (right) and Valentin Angelmann at Belle Vue, Manchester, in 1934*

Below: *Two Lancashire favourites together: Gracie Fields presents Peter Kane with his world championship belt in 1948*

Opposite bottom left: *The nadir of Benny Lynch's career – untrained and barely sober, he flopped against Len 'Nipper' Hampston*

Opposite bottom right: *Jackie Paterson completes his astonishing one-round demolition of Peter Kane in their 1943 flyweight title clash*

Below: *Three world flyweight champs*

weigh in: *(left to right) Dado Marino, Jackie Paterson and Rinty Monaghan*

Bottom left: *Rinty Monaghan's overhand right finds its mark against Terry Allen, whom he met three times*

Bottom right: *Bitter rivals Walter McGowan (right) and Alan Rudkin shared two British ring classics for a win apiece*

Top: *Typical swarming aggression
from Freddie Mills, as he takes the
light-heavyweight crown from Gus
Lesnevich*

Above: *Sugar Ray Robinson was 41
when he met Terry Downes in 1962,
but was still good enough to take him
the full ten rounds*

Opposite top left: *John Caldwell rips a
left to the body of defending
bantamweight champion Alphonse
Halimi*

Opposite bottom left: *This repeat
points win over Ismael Laguna in New
York was Ken Buchanan's career peak*

Top right: *Howard Winstone takes a low left from Mitsunori Seki in the fight which saw the Welshman become featherweight champ – at the fourth attempt*

Above: *Hedgemon Lewis pitches through the ropes in the final stages of his welterweight title defeat by John Stracey at Wembley*

Above: *The moment of victory for Jim Watt over Alfredo Pitalua*

Top: *The shape of things to come – John Conteh in a publicity shot with Playboy Club Bunnies the day before his world title win over Jorge Ahumada*

could stay six rounds with Driscoll. He did not merely win the money, but gave Driscoll a solid working-over with kidney and rabbit punches, techniques he had mastered in the rough rings of America.

Driscoll never forgave him for taking such liberties, and by the time he got him in the ring again he was ready for war. It began sportingly enough: when Driscoll slipped over in the fourth, Welsh smilingly extended a hand to help him up. But by the fifth Welsh was growing increasingly frustrated as Driscoll, a better jabber even than himself, built up a points lead. Welsh began using his 'American moves', and referee Peggy Bettinson, officiating from outside the ring, ignored Driscoll's appeals and protests.

The exasperated challenger took the law into his own hands, which suited Welsh. The result was one of the dirtiest fights ever seen for a British title as the pair butted, elbowed, gouged and mauled each other for a further five rounds until, in the tenth, Driscoll butted Welsh under the chin so outrageously that Bettinson was finally compelled to leave his seat and enter the ring, where he announced that the challenger had been disqualified. (While he was doing so, somebody stole his new fur coat, which he had left behind on his chair!)

The announcement provoked a punch-up in the ring between Badger O'Brien, one of Driscoll's seconds, and Boyo Driscoll (no relation) in the Welsh corner – a battle which was resumed next day in the street outside Cardiff railway station.

Among the ringsiders that night was Matt Wells, the clever ex-amateur from London who was scheduled to be Welsh's next challenger at the NSC on 27 February 1911. The shrewd Wells learned enough from watching the champion in action to be convinced that he could dethrone him, a point he proved by outboxing Welsh in a big upset.

Welsh headed back to America, scoring a significant win in November 1911 over Willie Ritchie, and spent most of 1912 campaigning in Canada. He came home later in the year, and in a rematch with Wells beat him clearly to reclaim the British title and win the Lonsdale Belt outright. The Belt, incidentally, was stolen in August 1913 but was recovered a week later by a customs officer in Seattle, Washington.

A month later, Welsh outpointed the Australian Hughie Mehegan at the NSC in a match which the Club billed as being for the world title, although in reality only the Empire title was at stake. He rounded off his latest British campaign with a hard-earned twenty-round decision over the Scot Eddie Beattie, at Liverpool. Beattie floored him with a right to the body in the ninth round, but referee J.H. Douglas was undecided about the legitimacy of the blow and delayed for a few crucial seconds before taking up the count.

For the next twelve months Welsh pursued the new world champion Willie Ritchie, whom he had already beaten in 1911. The Americans were keen to stage the fight, but Ritchie's purse demands were considered excessive. Welsh got in touch with the London theatrical impresario C.B. Cochran, who was eager to get involved in big fight promoting, and told him that he would perform for a percentage of the gate, any guarantee, if the match could be made in London.

Cochran duly met with Ritchie at the Hotel Metropole in New York, and the champion opened by demanding a purse of $25,000, (then worth about £5000). He wanted the money to be paid in New York before he would even sign a contract. Cochran agreed to every demand, and Ritchie had the money next morning.

The fight went on at Olympia on 7 July 1914. Eugene Corri refereed, and the MC, unusually, was a clergyman, the Reverend J.H. Boudier, vicar of St Michael's, Islington. For twenty rounds the Californian chased and chased, but could rarely pin the challenger down for long enough to score effectively, and at the end Corri raised the Welshman's hand. It was a wonderful, emotional occasion, but it was also the last time Welsh appeared in Britain.

He returned to the States and embarked on another of his regular coast-to-coast tours, boxing no-decision ten-rounders where his title could not be lost unless he was knocked out. He did make two defences, though, beating former champion Ad Wolgast on an eleventh-round disqualification and outpointing Liverpool-born Charlie White in July and September, respectively, of 1916.

There were two important no-decision affairs in 1916 with the clever New York Jew Benny Leonard. Leonard was content to stand and box with Welsh each time, studying the champion and learning his moves. Since Welsh had come to no grief in their first two encounters, he readily agreed to a third meeting at the Manhattan Casino, New York, in May 1917. By now, though, Welsh's skills were diminishing. Of the seven no-decision contests he had before meeting Leonard, the newspapers gave him the verdict in only one.

Leonard handled him easily this time, flooring him twice in the ninth to force the stoppage and take Welsh's title. The ex-champ retired for three years, and took a commission as captain in the US Army, who assigned him to the rehabilitation of wounded veterans at a Washington Hospital. He had invested his money in a health farm outside New York, but the business flopped and he returned to the ring on 28 December 1920, having six fights between then and April 1922, when he finally quit for good.

He was found dead in his New York apartment on 29 July 1927.

CAREER RECORD: 163 fights, 71 wins (30 inside schedule), 5 draws, 82 no-decisions, 5 defeats. Welsh was credited with the newspaper verdict in 49 of his no-decision fights. He lost 22, and the newspaper verdicts in the other 11 fights were draws.

Jim Driscoll (1880–1925)

JIM DRISCOLL is remembered as the greatest of the Welsh ring heroes, but he was Welsh only by an accident of birth. Everything about him – his name, his appearance, his love of a fight, and his family background – made him as Irish as the parents who bred him. Even the area where he was born, a huddle of streets between the docks and the railway station in Cardiff, was known as 'Irishtown', since this was where the Irish immigrants of the mid-nineteenth century established their own community.

But Driscoll was blessed with an abundance of the Celtic gift that Welsh and Irish alike possess – an unquestioning, open-handed generosity which so endeared him to the public that he became known as the 'King of Cardiff'. The title was well deserved. No boxer in Welsh history, or perhaps even in British history, has commanded such a degree of respect and love, and when he died in 1925 more than 100,000 lined the streets of Cardiff to see him on his way. The funeral procession was led by 100 children from the Nazareth House orphanage which Driscoll had financed and publicized all his working life.

The people loved him because he never forgot his roots in Ellen Street, where he was born on 15 December 1880. His father, a railwayman, was knocked down and killed in the goods yard near their home when Jim was only a few months old, and his mother Elizabeth was left to raise her four young children on Parish Relief of six shillings (30p) a week. The chairman of the Guardians reduced the allowance to four shillings (20p) when he decided that the Driscoll children were so clean, tidily dressed and well nourished that their mother must have some hidden source of income.

She was forced to go to work to feed her family, rising at 4.30 every morning to meet the trawlers as they docked, to buy fish which she sold around the streets. When that income proved inadequate, she laboured instead as a potato loader on England's Wharf, a hard and punishing job normally done by men. One does not have to look far to find the source of the iron will, determination and courage Driscoll so often showed in the ring.

Young Jim attended St Paul's School, where one of his teachers was Nellie Carr, whose daughter went on to music-hall and film fame as Tessie O'Shea. He got into boxing as the result of a street fight in which he went to the rescue of his brother Flurence. That first taste of the exhilaration of physical combat captivated him, and he was soon gathering experience in the highly informal and unorganized world of unpaid scrapping (as opposed to the more genteel 'amateur boxing') that existed in Irishtown.

When he left school he found a job in the composing room of the Cardiff *Evening Express* for 3/6 (17½p) a week, but then Jack Scarrott – who had played such an important role in the development of Jimmy Wilde – invited him to join his booth. It was there that Driscoll studied his craft in countless battles with opponents of all ages and weights, and where he developed his unique defensive ability.

He became virtually impossible to hit, until finally Scarrott made him a featured attraction on the booth. For a silver crown for every performance and a bonus of five shillings (25p) on his weekly wage, Driscoll would spread a handkerchief on the ring floor and stand on it, his hands tied behind his back, while volunteers tried to win the guinea (£1.05) which Scarrott offered to anyone who could hit Driscoll on the nose within 60 seconds. No one ever collected, but the gimmick earned Jim two cauliflower ears, caused by 'near misses'.

By 1901, when he was twenty-one, Driscoll judged that he was ready to graduate from the booth into a proper professional career. For someone whose reputation rested on boxing ability rather than punching power he made a spectacular start, winning 14 of his first 16 inside the distance before Harry Mansfield, a tough featherweight from Bristol, held him to a draw in Cardiff in September 1902.

Mansfield figured prominently in Driscoll's early career. They met twice more in 1903, Driscoll winning both on points, and then on 29 August 1904 Mansfield became the first man in 32 fights to beat the fast-rising Welshman, outpointing him on a controversial ten-round decision at the Badminton Club, Cardiff. They had a fifth meeting, on Boxing Day 1905, and this time Driscoll settled all the arguments by stopping him in the fifteenth of a scheduled twenty-rounder at Wednesbury.

Driscoll had already become a popular performer at the National

Sporting Club; he had outpointed Boss Edwards on his debut there in February 1904, and in December that year scored an important win when he beat Johnny Summers on a second-round disqualification. The Club members appreciated Driscoll's style, and he appeared there regularly in 1906.

Among his victims was Jack Roberts of Drury Lane (then at the end of a decent career), whom he knocked out in seven rounds. In later years, when Jim was in the money and Roberts most definitely was not, the broken old fighter used to hang about outside the club any night when Jim was boxing or was a guest, and buttonhole him for yet another 'loan' as he left. Even Driscoll's patience was tested, until he was moved to remark one night that he had already given Roberts more in loans than he had earned for knocking him out!

Johnny Summers, who had become the British featherweight champion in January 1906, fancied his chances in a rematch with Driscoll and the fight was set for the NSC on 28 May that year. But Summers injured his ankle in training and Joe Bowker, a former champion who still held a valid claim to the world bantamweight title, came in as substitute on condition that the distance was reduced from twenty rounds to fifteen.

Driscoll won comfortably on points, and then knocked Bowker out in seventeen rounds when they were paired again, this time for the vacant British title, on 3 June 1907. He became a dual champion in February 1908 when the New Zealander Charlie Griffin grew so frustrated by his inability to hit Driscoll that he butted him blatantly and was promptly disqualified in the fifteenth round. Charlie Harvey, who specialized in managing British boxers in America, was at ringside that night and persuaded Jim to try his luck in New York, and after a sixth and final meeting with his perennial foe Harry Mansfield, Driscoll left for America in October 1908.

He was an instant sensation, cramming in ten fights in three months and in the process earning the nickname by which he is best remembered – 'Peerless Jim'. The Americans had never seen boxing of such a high order, and not even the ferocious Leach Cross, a leading lightweight, could lay a glove on him. (Cross found Driscoll dozing on the rubbing table in the gym a few days after he had chased him fruitlessly around the ring for ten rounds, and punched the sleeping Welshman lightly on the chest. 'Now,' he announced to the astonished onlookers, 'don't let anyone say that Leach Cross never hit Jim Driscoll!')

The world title was held by Abe Attell, who was generally held to be the cleverest man around in any of the lighter divisions, but Driscoll had so impressed the Americans that a no-decision match was arranged between them to take place at the National Athletic Club, New York, on 19 February 1909 – only nine days after Driscoll had met Cross. A couple of days before the fight Driscoll went down with an attack of pleurisy, but insisted on facing Attell anyway.

Nat Fleischer, the founder of *Ring* magazine, recalled visiting the Welsh dressing room before the fight. Many years later in 1938, he wrote:

Driscoll looked like a ghost. I went over and shook him by the hand. 'Good luck, Jim,' I said. 'Thanks, Mr Fleischer,' Driscoll replied between clenched teeth. His eyes were bright with fever.

When I saw him next I was sitting at the ringside. He staggered rather than climbed through the ropes and slumped down in his seat. To my mind there could only be one result of this unequal contest.

Fleischer was half right – it was an unequal contest, but Attell was the one on the receiving end as Driscoll gave one of the finest exhibitions of pure skill ever seen. At the end of ten rounds there was no doubt who was the best featherweight in the world, even if New York law prohibited a formal decision. 'Driscoll Wins World Feather Title from Attell' was the headline in the New York *Evening Journal*.

Another American paper was even more emphatic:

Abe Attell is no longer the premier featherweight in the world. Jem Driscoll [as the Americans called him] proved to us last night that he, and not the shifty Abe, was entitled to what honours there were to be distributed. At the National Athletic Club the title Welshman opened the eyes of the crowd and closed one of Abe's. He didn't knock the American out, but he had such a lead that there was no question as to which was the better man when the bout was over.

Negotiations were opened immediately for a rematch, but two days later Driscoll packed his bags and went home. His American managers, Harvey and Jimmy Johnson, tried frantically to dissuade him, but Driscoll was adamant. 'I gave the Sisters at Nazareth House my word that I would appear there on St David's Day, and I never break a promise.'

And so he went back to Wales, not even waiting for his pay cheque for the Attell fight, with nothing more than a 'newspaper verdict' to show for an overwhelming defeat of the world champion. But the Welsh welcomed him as a world champion anyway; his carriage was drawn in procession through the streets of Cardiff on his return, and police were needed to control the crowds. His gesture, and the publicity it attracted, helped to raise more than £6000 for Nazareth House. A host of stars gave their services free at the benefit show, which Driscoll presented – great names such as Sam Langford, Joe Bowker, Jimmy Wilde, Tom Thomas, Ted 'Kid' Lewis, Pat O'Keefe, Owen Moran, Matt Wells, Sid Smith, Freddie Welsh and many others.

The nuns presented Driscoll with a scroll which he cherished. It was inscribed:

We can never forget, sir, how in the very zenith of your success, when the fame of your prowess was on every tongue, you generously sacrificed pecuniary advantage and undertook a voyage of some thousands of miles in order to fulfil your promise of assisting Nazareth House.

Our earnest prayers are that He who never forgets a service done in His name, who promises a reward to those who aid even the least of His little ones, may grant you all the temporal blessings in this world and an imperishable, glorious reward hereafter.

It was five days short of a year before he was back in the ring, stopping Seaman Arthur Hayes in six rounds to regain the British featherweight title he had relinquished in 1906, and putting the first notch on the inaugural Lonsdale Belt for the division. The presentation ceremony next day was interrupted by Frank 'Spike' Robson of North Shields, who had been champion earlier in 1906 and wanted to know why Driscoll had been nominated instead of him to contest the vacant title.

Matchmaker Peggy Bettinson agreed to give him a chance to prove his point two months later, on 18 April 1910. Driscoll's preparation had again been interrupted by another attack of pleurisy, and he was far below his best. By the fourth round he was in trouble, his right eye almost closed. In the corner before the fifth his trainer George Bailleau performed some drastic emergency surgery: he burnt a match around the blade of his knife to sterilize it, and then sliced the swelling open and sucked out the congealed blood, thus clearing Driscoll's vision.

As the bell went to start the fifth Robson charged across the ring – and ran full-tilt into the wooden stool that Bailleau was in the act of lifting over the ropes. He went down heavily, and when he rose his face was covered in blood, which was pumping from a deep cut on his forehead. Under today's conditions the fight would have been stopped, but instead the gritty North-Easterner hung on until the twelfth, when Driscoll knocked him out so badly that he was unconscious for over an hour.

Driscoll returned to America in the hope of securing a rematch with Attell, but instead only managed a disappointing six-rounder with Pal Moore in Philadelphia. He came home to learn that his great rival Freddie Welsh had agreed to defend the British lightweight title against him, and was even prepared to come in at 9 st 6 lb – three pounds below the championship limit – to accommodate Driscoll. Further incentive was that the promoters guaranteed to donate a substantial percentage of the proceeds to Nazareth House, and so the fight went ahead on 20 December 1910 at the American Roller Skating Rink in Westgate Street, Cardiff, in front of a packed house of 10,000.

Driscoll by now was in almost constant pain from his damaged lungs and from stomach ulcers, and to add to his misfortunes he developed an abscess over the right ear a few days before the fight. He entered the ring with a plaster over the *left* ear, and Welsh duly made this his prime target. Welsh had learned his trade in America, where the rules carried less weight than in Britain, and what should have been a classic exhibition of skill instead degenerated quickly into one of the most notorious brawls in British ring history before referee Peggy Bettinson finally left his ringside seat to disqualify Driscoll in the tenth.

Fights broke out all over the hall between fiercely partisan groups of spectators, and backstage Driscoll begged Welsh to go back in the ring when the hall had emptied so that they could settle supremacy without the inconvenience of a referee. Welsh declined.

Later that evening the party repaired to the Badminton Club, where Bettinson met Driscoll's formidable mother and started pouring charm over her. 'Mr Bettinson,' she told him, 'you're as false as the teeth in my head.'

Five weeks later Driscoll retained his featherweight title in a rematch with Robson, this time in eleven rounds, and when he did not reappear for over a year it was generally supposed that he had retired. But then Peggy Bettinson tempted him back to face the Frenchman Jean Poésy at the NSC on 3 June 1912 for the European title, and Driscoll stopped him easily in the twelfth – the same round in which Poésy had predicted he would knock out Driscoll.

The old champion was thirty-three, and a desperate struggle against Owen Moran in January 1913, when he needed a supreme effort to see out the final five rounds and earn a twenty-round draw, convinced him that it was time to retire. He joined the Army, and served for the duration of the war as a PT instructor.

But in 1919, foolishly, he came back. A four-round win over another faded veteran, Pedlar Palmer, and a draw with Francis Rossi persuaded him that he still had a future, but the almost forty-year-old Driscoll was brought cruelly down to earth by the young Frenchman Charles Ledoux, who pounded him to sixteenth-round defeat at the NSC. Driscoll, although haggard and drawn, had shown much of his old artistry but no longer had the 'legs' for a distance fight.

This time it really was all over, and the Club members rallied round by launching a national testimonial fund for the former champion. More than £5000 was raised, and was well invested to provide him with an income for the rest of his life. He still had his pub, the Duke of Edinburgh, and worked tirelessly for his favourite charities, including Nazareth House and St Michael's Home.

The pub became an informal social centre for the town's war crippled and unemployed, and few left poorer than when they arrived. And then, suddenly, it ended: pleurisy and pneumonia brought on consumption, and on 30 January 1925 Driscoll died.

His funeral was, and still is, the biggest ever seen in Wales, as the people he had thrilled, cherished and cared for lined the rain-swept streets of Cardiff in final tribute as the man who had come from the poverty of Irishtown went out like a king.

CAREER RECORD: 69 fights, 52 wins (35 inside schedule), 6 draws, 3 defeats, 8 no-decisions. Driscoll was credited with the newspaper verdict in 7 of these, and with a draw in the other.

Teddy Baldock (1908–1971)

THE WORST thing that ever happened to Teddy Baldock was backing the winner of the 1937 Cesarewitch, the aptly named Punch, at odds of 50–1. Baldock collected £5000 and acquired the gambling habit which ruined him financially and cost him his marriage. It is an old, familiar story, which has been echoed a hundred times over in the game's often shameful history.

But for Baldock, the only British boxer to win a world title during the 1920s, life was always a little too fast. The Poplar bantamweight was world champion at twenty, and burnt out at twenty-two. He earned an estimated £20,000 – around a quarter of a million pounds in today's terms – and yet died broke.

Baldock, who was born on 20 May 1908, had boxing in his blood. His grandfather had been a bare-knuckle scrapper, and his father Ted was a regular performer at the old Wonderland arena, so it was hardly surprising that young Teddy showed natural aptitude for the game when he joined the local Boys' Club. He had his first pro fight before his fourteenth birthday, earning 7/6 (37½p) for outpointing Harry Makepeace at Barking Baths. His record, which is probably incomplete, shows only four appearances – all wins – in his first two years in the business, although as Baldock himself claimed a career total of over 200 fights rather than the 80 that are listed, he may well have been busier.

His career got properly under way in 1923, when he was still shy of his fifteenth birthday, and his all-action style soon made him a tremendously popular attraction. Whenever he fought, his east London fans turned out in force to support him, and Teddy never let them down. When he was sixteen the former British featherweight champion Mike Honeyman, a friend of his father's, took him along to see Dan Sullivan, who was then running the Blackfriars Ring. But Sullivan thought the boy was too young and too small, and told Honeyman to bring him back in a couple of years.

Instead, the old champ took Baldock along to Joe Morris, who ran the Ring's main rival, Premierland in Commercial Road. Morris was delighted to use such a popular – and local – performer, and he became a big attraction there.

He won 40 of his first 41 fights, beating top men such as George 'Kid' Socks, Ernie Jarvis and former world title challenger Frankie Ash along the way. His first defeat came in July 1926, when referee Ted 'Kid' Lewis disqualified an ill-prepared and overweight Baldock in the ninth round against George 'Kid' Nicholson from Leeds. But it was a minor setback, and a month later the teenager (barely eighteen) left for America.

He could stay for only six months, the duration of his work permit, but managed to cram in 12 fights of which he won 11 and drew the other to give him an overall record of 54 fights, one draw and one loss. His form was so spectacularly good that a group of four London sportsmen got together under the banner of the International Sports Syndicate to promote him. They booked the Albert Hall and offered Baldock a £1000 three-fight deal, with the third fight to be for the world title – always assuming that he won the first two.

He did so in style. Young Johnny Brown, younger brother of the British bantamweight champion of the same name, was knocked out in three rounds, with the Prince of Wales at ringside, and then Felix Friedmann of Germany was dispatched in the second. The world title was in dispute at the time, and the National Boxing Association nominated Tony Canzoneri (later to become a superb lightweight champion) to meet Bud Taylor for their version of the vacant title. Britain and Europe agreed to recognize the winner of the match between Baldock and the American Archie Bell, which the ISS arranged for the Albert Hall on 5 May 1927.

Baldock was then at the absolute zenith of his popularity, and 52 coaches made the trip across London from Poplar to Kensington to watch the local boy make good. He did, but it wasn't easy. The pair staged a magnificent fifteen-rounder, full of skilful boxing from Baldock and, from Bell, top-quality in-fighting. Baldock was ahead after seven rounds and floored the American briefly in the eighth, but the tide turned slowly against the Londoner as the more experienced American fought his way back into contention.

By the thirteenth there was nothing between them, but with his home crowd urging him on Baldock summoned up the greater reserves and edged home a points winner on referee Sam Russell's card. The promotional syndicate were so delighted with the result that they gave Teddy a £100 bonus. Baldock was back in the ring seven weeks later against the British featherweight champion Johnny Cuthbert. It was only a six-rounder, a supporting titbit on the Olympia show which featured Mickey Walker's world middle-weight title defence against Tommy Milligan. Baldock was not at his best, although he still managed to snatch a draw.

But on 6 October that year, his claim to the world title evaporated. His fifteen-rounder with the former Olympic gold medal winner Willie Smith of South Africa was actually made at 8 st 8 lb to protect Baldock's crown, but Smith scaled 2 oz inside the championship weight of 8 st 6 lb and, after trouncing Baldock by a wide points margin, proclaimed himself the new world champion.

There were no protests from the Londoner; his training had been hampered by an attack of bronchial catarrh, and he fought sluggishly. As *Boxing* reported: 'The Baldock who outpointed Archie Bell would have stopped the Teddy Baldock who opposed Willie Smith inside three rounds.' Teddy tried too hard for a knockout, while the challenger, a clever technician and an extraordinarily accurate puncher, outboxed him in almost every round.

Baldock's reign as world champion had lasted just five months and one day – but Smith did not fare much better. He lost his unbeaten record in his next fight, a ten-rounder in America a month later, and renounced his claim to the title in January 1928 to campaign as a featherweight.

Baldock was still very much in the forefront of the division in Britain, and continued to draw phenomenal crowds. Twelve thousand watched him outpoint Phil Llolsky at Forest Gate Rink, and 15,000 braved an August Bank Holiday downpour to see him stop Bugler Harry Lake in five rounds at Highfield Road Race-course, Blackpool.

The British bantamweight division at that time was in almost as confused a state as the world championship. Johnny Brown of St George's had been champion for five years, winning a Lonsdale Belt outright, but was coming to the end of a long career. The NSC tried to force him to defend against either of the two leading contenders, Baldock or Alf 'Kid' Pattenden of Bethnal Green. But Brown was not interested in the deal they offered, and so the Club announced that he had forfeited the title.

Pattenden and Baldock were matched for the vacant title, but Baldock also considered the NSC's offer to be inadequate and withdrew from the fight. George 'Kid' Nicholson, the man who had spoilt Baldock's unbeaten record, got the job instead. He was comfortably ahead after eleven rounds, but was suddenly crippled by cramp at the end of the eleventh and was an easy target for Pattenden in the twelfth, being counted out as he sat fully conscious on the canvas, groaning, 'Oh, my leg!'

Baldock seemed to be out in the cold, but then his backers, the International Sports Syndicate, stepped in. They hired Clapton Greyhound Stadium and staged what was billed, on shaky grounds, as a world flyweight title fight between British champion Johnny Hill and the American Newsboy Brown. Baldock was paired with the deposed champion Johnny Brown as the chief support, supposedly for the title which Brown had never lost in the ring, and won easily in two rounds. The attendance was 32,000, and it was Baldock rather than the Scot Hill whom they had come to cheer.

A couple of months later Pattenden put the second notch on his Lonsdale Belt by stopping Young Johnny Brown in twelve rounds, to whet the appetite for a championship decider with the Poplar star. It took place at Olympia on 16 May 1929, on a bumper bill which featured Johnny Cuthbert regaining the featherweight title from Harry Corbett, and Len Harvey knocking out Alex Ireland in seven to win the middleweight title. Baldock made it three out of three for the challengers with a hard-earned and bitterly contested points win over his East End rival, but had to survive a desperate final round when Pattenden twice knocked him through the ropes on to the ring apron.

Teddy was a champion again, but he had given his last great performance. He had broken his right hand, and the injury plagued him for what remained of his career. In January 1930 he met the former world flyweight champion Emile Pladner of France, and won on a sixth-round disqualification. Promoter Jeff Dickson accused Baldock of 'acting', and was promptly hit with a libel suit. Baldock won the case, with costs, and Dickson had to publish a humiliating apology. But the promoter had the last word, for Baldock never again appeared at the Albert Hall.

The signs of deterioration were clear in Baldock's work. He lost on points to the clever Geordie Benny Sharkey, and struggled to beat Lew Pinkus and Alf Pattenden in a non-title rematch at the Blackfriars Ring. He had one last chance to recapture lost glories when the great Panamanian world bantamweight champion Al Brown, then on his third European tour, met him in an overweight twelve-rounder at Earl's Court in front of a 12,000 crowd.

Baldock gave everything – he always did – but Panama Al was much too clever for him and at the end of the eleventh referee Owen Moran (the former bantamweight and featherweight star) must have had him in a wide lead. But Brown took no chances, and overwhelmed the fading Londoner with a twelfth-round onslaught which put Baldock on the floor four times before Moran called a halt. Ironically, Baldock was closer to victory than he knew: afterwards, Brown revealed that he had dislocated four bones in his right hand and was in such pain that he could not have lasted another round.

Teddy fought only once more, when Dick Corbett widely outpointed him over twelve rounds. He boxed so badly that night that the London fight crowd, who had idolized him only a few years earlier, jeered him from the ring. It was a painful experience, but it helped him to recognize the inevitable. He returned his Lonsdale Belt, and announced his retirement. He was only twenty-four, but had injured an eyeball in a previous fight and was unwilling to risk further damage.

Baldock later claimed that Jeff Dickson offered him £5000 – a phenomenal sum then – for a three-fight comeback. Two of the fights, according to Baldock, would be 'fixed', the first to take place in France (where Dickson promoted regularly) and the second in England. The third fight would be on the level. Baldock declined. In view of the bad blood which existed between the pair, it might not be advisable to accept Baldock's version of events – although, of course, such unethical arrangements were not exactly unprecedented.

Without the discipline of training to keep him in check, Baldock gave free rein to his taste for the good life, with predictable consequences. His wife left him, taking their daughter Pam, and Baldock's drinking and gambling increased. He took on a pub, but a combination of falling trade caused by the Blitz and Baldock's own financial problems, brought about by his £200 a week gambling habit, forced the brewers to turn him out.

His house was destroyed by a bomb, and he spent the £3000 compensation from the War Damage Commission in less than four months. With his fortune gone he drifted into obscurity, and he died in Rochford Infirmary, Southend, on 15 March 1971.

CAREER RECORD: 80 fights, 72 wins (37 inside schedule), 3 draws, 5 defeats.

Jack 'Kid' Berg (born 1909)

FOR SOMEONE with much to be bitter about, Jack 'Kid' Berg remains a charming and forgiving man. Today, at a sprightly eighty, he is British boxing's elder statesman – President of the London Ex-Boxers Association, and assured of the biggest ovation of the night when he ducks smartly between the ropes to take a bow on big fight nights. He is the country's oldest surviving world champion, the only British fighter to be voted into both the American and British Halls of Fame.

Yet for years he was the game's black sheep, denied recognition in his own country as a world champion although feted and honoured on the other side of the Atlantic. He fought 192 times, earned and spent a fortune, made friends of fans and enemies of officials, and apologized for none of it. Only Ted 'Kid' Lewis matched his achievements, and no one, now, will ever surpass them.

The comparison with Lewis is inevitable, but valid. Both were born into Russian–Jewish families in east London, and had to overcome parental opposition to their chosen career. They each had long and successful campaigns in America, and of course they were both world champions. The same names figure in both their stories, with promoter Harry Jacobs and trainer Zalig Goodman playing prominent roles.

Berg, born Judah Bergman in Whitechapel on 28 June 1909, was destined to become the best of the wave of Jewish fighters who sought to emulate Lewis' achievements in the ring. He never bothered to box as an amateur, although since he was a veteran of hundreds of street scraps this was probably not much of a handicap. His first paid fight, in 1923, earned him 15 shillings (75p); it was also the first time he had ever worn boxing gloves.

Berg never had a boxing lesson in his life, and it showed in the wild, flailing aggression of his early performances. But as he gathered wins and experience in his 'home' venue, Premierland, so he refined and controlled the aggression until he had perfected the disciplined, but no less entertaining, style which carried him on to greatness. He was hugely popular at Premierland, where he had his first 37 fights. They were not all wins – Billy Clarke and Jimmy Wooder both held him to a draw (but were trounced in rematches), and the future British featherweight champion Johnny Cuthbert outsmarted him twice. But the mere fact that Berg, still only fifteen, was facing someone of Cuthbert's quality was a measure of how far and how fast he was progressing.

He avenged the losses to Cuthbert in October 1925, which earned him a non-title match with British champion Johnny Curley a fortnight later. The youngster won widely on points, a result which suggested that he had outgrown Premierland and was ready for promotion. Harry Jacobs booked him for the Albert Hall, but his early appearances there were disappointing. Harry Corbett, a veteran of over 100 fights, outpointed him easily, and then Berg was 'gifted' a points win over André Routis, a Frenchman who went on to win the world featherweight title two years later.

Berg went back to basics for another series of fights at Premierland and the Blackfriars Ring, where he fought a draw with Harry Corbett. He also met Routis again, winning this time on a disqualification, and ran up a string of victories over top Continental lightweights (having outgrown the featherweight class). He rounded off 1927 with a win over Lucien Vinez, recently deposed as European lightweight champion, and in early 1928 Berg and Goodman decided it was time to follow 'Kid' Lewis's example and head for America.

He was an instant sensation. The Americans loved his all-action style, and his breezy personality made good newspaper copy. British fighters were not supposed to fight like that, and Berg's high-living, free-spending habits were more suited to Hollywood than Whitechapel. He was dubbed the 'Whitechapel Whirlwind', and in eight fights on his first tour only the world title contender Billy Petrolle got the better of him – and Berg had battled him to a draw in their first meeting. He came home for a working holiday, beating Alf Mancini at the Albert Hall and Lucien Vinez again, and then returned to America to launch his world title campaign in earnest.

Between May 1929 and January 1930 Berg had 16 fights in New York and won 15 of them, the sole blemish being a draw with former lightweight challenger Stanislau Loayza. He beat the best around, and when he outfought the former featherweight champion Tony Canzoneri in front of a 20,000 crowd in January 1930, he justified promoter Jeff Dickson's decision to match him with the

American champion Mushy Callahan for the junior welterweight (10 stone) championship.

The division was not widely accepted even in America, and Britain did not recognize it at all. While the pre-fight introductions were being made at the Albert Hall on 18 February 1930, the British Boxing Board of Control President, Lord Lonsdale, made a loud and vigorous protest that 'there is no such thing as a junior championship', waving his programme to emphasize the point. But Berg was unconcerned, and so was the London crowd when their man pounded Callahan into retirement at the end of the tenth round. Berg was world champion – or was he?

The National Boxing Association withheld recognition from him until he beat Goldie Hess in January 1931, by which time Berg had already defended the title six times, although only two of them were formally billed as such. On the other occasions, Berg and his opponent both scaled inside the division limit, thereby putting the title automatically at stake. It was a particularly rewarding period for the Londoner; not only did he avenge the loss to Petrolle, and thereby remove the lingering doubts which some American critics still retained about him, but he also snapped the astonishing 160-fight unbeaten record of the fabulous Cuban, Kid Chocolate. It was his finest performance.

The wins over Petrolle and Chocolate earned him a crack at lightweight champion Tony Canzoneri, whom Berg had already beaten. But this time the American was his master, and the third-round knockout that Berg suffered also cost him his junior welterweight title, since both men had scaled under 10 stone.

Berg fought much better in the rematch in September 1931, and the British press were adamant that he was robbed of the decision. (The American papers were equally insistent that Canzoneri, who floored Berg twice in the first round, was a deserving winner.) It was the closest that Berg came to a world title again, although he beat Kid Chocolate for the second time on a split decision in July 1932.

He returned to Britain in 1933, still only twenty-four but already a veteran of 113 fights, and the signs of deterioration were clear. Points defeats by Cleto Locatelli (one in London and the other in New York) and by Tony Falco ruled him out of the world title picture, and when the Liverpudlian Jimmy Stewart knocked him out badly in three rounds in May 1934, even the British championship seemed beyond him.

That title was held by the new Jewish favourite, Harry Mizler, and perversely Berg's loss to Stewart helped to make the match between the two East End rivals. Berg's new manager, Harry Levene, pushed it as a 'grudge fight', and the Stewart loss persuaded Mizler that Berg was not the formidable tearaway he had once been. Jeff Dickson made the match in October 1934, and Berg showed all his old zest and fire as he forced Mizler to retire at the end of the eighth.

But it was a false dawn, and Berg's form nose-dived. He lost two out of three against the Frenchman Gustave Humery, was beaten in South Africa by Laurie Stevens for the Empire title, and left the British title in Liverpool when Jimmy Walsh stopped him in nine rounds. He had twisted his ankle so badly late in the eighth that he could hardly stand – but that was no real excuse, as he had already been floored five times.

He moved up to welterweight, and had a long and generally successful stay in America in 1938–9, winning 18 and drawing one of his 24 fights. But they were low-key, minor engagements; the great days of the 20,000 crowds were gone, and so were the big paydays. Back in Britain he rowed with the Board of Control, was suspended, and started divorce proceedings against his first wife. In the ring, fighting sometimes on shows which were technically unlicensed, he at least managed to stay unbeaten throughout 1940, but losses to Arthur Danahar, Ernie Roderick and George Odwell in 1941 convinced him that it was almost time to go.

He fought twice in 1942 and once in 1943, and made a short-lived comeback in 1945, winning all three fights before his second wife, Morya, put her foot down and ordered him to quit.

Life since then has treated the old champion well. He made a second career in films, working steadily for thirty years before retiring from that as reluctantly as he had left the ring. He resisted the urge to involve himself in boxing again in any professional capacity, but has never lost his love for the game.

In the mid-1960s, when the British Board established the 10-stone division in this country, Berg was at last accorded full recognition as our first world champion at the weight. In the years since, as his career has been reappraised (most notably in John Harding's splendid biography), a new generation of British fans has come to realize what their American counterparts have known all along –

that Britain never sent a finer fighter across the Atlantic than Jack 'Kid' Berg.

CAREER RECORD: 192 fights, 157 wins (57 inside schedule), 9 draws, 26 defeats.

Jackie Brown (1909–1971)

Anyone who manages only one win in his first five fights is entitled to feel that his future in the game is limited, but Jackie Brown's experience proves that it ain't necessarily so. According to the record book – which when dealing with the 1920s and 1930s is far from infallible – the Manchester flyweight won his debut, lost the next three and drew the fifth – yet he went on to lift the world, European and British championships and to challenge for the British bantamweight title as well.

Brown always insisted that the record was wrong, and that he had been a pro for a year before anyone bothered to keep track of his contests. He took up boxing at thirteen, practising his punches with unprotected knuckles on a wet sandbag, and by fifteen he was working regularly on the many booths which operated near his home in Ancoats, where he was born on 29 November 1909.

His first fight, according to Brown, took place at Len Johnson's booth on Albert Croft, Queen's Road, when he was paid 15 shillings (75p) for beating Arthur Evitt. According to the official record, his first opponent was Dick Manning, whom he outpointed in March 1926, eight months before his seventeenth birthday.

There was little glamour about a fighter's life in those days. Jack Bates, who trained Brown for manager Harry Fleming, recalled the conditions in which they worked at the gym in Paley Street, Collyhurst: 'The gym's floor was riddled with holes,' he wrote in *Topical Times* in 1940. 'Our punchbag was a soldier's kit bag, filled with sand, rags and rubbish. Harry Fleming and his brother John, who helped in the gym, made us a wooden footbath. We bathed by standing in this footbath while a mate chucked a bucket of either "hot" or "cold" over us.'

But these were hard times, in Lancashire more than anywhere, and Brown was glad to earn the tiny purses on offer for six-rounders in ramshackle venues. His blinding hand-speed and extrovert nature soon made him a favourite with the fans, and by 1927 he was regularly boxing ten-rounders. Ted Lewis, a well-known Welsh sportsman, recommended him to his promoter friends in South Wales, and Brown appeared frequently throughout 1928 at places such as Pontypridd, Bridgend and Merthyr.

By now he had progressed into the fifteen-round class, and when he beat Tommy Brown of Salford in December 1928 and reversed a previous loss to Phineas John in April 1929, he was accepted as leading contender for the British flyweight title. He was matched with Birmingham's Bert Kirby in a final eliminator, with the winner to face champion Johnny Hill of Scotland for the title.

But then Hill died suddenly, a few weeks before he was due to fight Frankie Genaro for the world title. Promoter Ted Salmon thought he had a ready-made British title fight in Brown v Kirby, having already scheduled the eliminator for the Rink Athletic Club in West Bromwich on Sunday 13 October 1929. But the Board of Control was curiously reluctant to do the obvious and sanction it as a title fight, and the Midlands referee Jack Smith had to make repeated visits to London, lobbying on Salmon's behalf, before the match was approved.

Kirby was a big local attraction whose flat-footed, shuffling style masked his hitting power. The show was held on Sunday morning, with the weigh-in at 7 a.m. It was the most successful promotion Salmon ever staged, and estimates of the attendance varied between eight and twelve thousand. They saw a thriller between two men who, apart from being natural rivals, actively disliked each other.

There was non-stop action, not all of it within the rules, and the ending sparked a riot among the crowd which forced the police to clear the hall. A clash of heads in the third hurt Kirby more than Brown, and as the Brummie staggered back, hands by his side, Brown stepped in with a right which dropped Kirby straight and stiff, the back of his head bouncing off the boards. The disturbances which ensued were so bad that the Board refused to permit any future title fights to be held on a Sunday, a practice to which they adhered until 1971.

They met again at the Stadium Club, Holborn on 3 March 1930, although Brown would have been better advised to seek a postponement after going down with tonsillitis a week before the fight. Joe Bowker, the old bantamweight champion, was among those who pleaded with him to withdraw, but Brown's pride – and the 'needle' that existed between the pair – made him go through with it. After two rounds he was worn out, and Kirby knocked him cold in the third.

Brown worked his way back to earn a third fight with Kirby, and this time he gave a flawless display of pure boxing to outpoint his old rival. The tactics were necessary: Brown had smashed his right hand against a Frenchman, René Challange, three fights earlier and thereafter always had problems with it.

He won the European title from the Romanian Lucien Popescu in his next fight, under odd circumstances. Popescu came in overweight and refused to attempt to shed the excess ounces. The fight went ahead anyway, with Brown a clear winner, and the Englishman claimed the title.

The International Boxing Union, which constituted what passed for a governing body in European boxing at that time, refused to recognize him as champion. But Brown and the British promoters were not greatly concerned with the IBU's views of the matter, and Brown's susbequent wins over Emile Degand, Vincenzo Savo and Jim Maharg were all billed as European title defences. Beating Maharg, which also involved the British title, set up a world title bid against the Tunisian Jew Victor 'Young' Perez at Belle Vue, Manchester, six weeks later on 31 October 1932.

Brown's training was severely disrupted by an attack of boils under his arms, and two days before the fight manager Harry Fleming took him to a doctor in Manchester to have them cut out. The doctor ordered Brown to rest, which ruled out even light training – and that meant a risk of coming in overweight. So poor Brown had to go without food for the last day, making do with sips of brandy-laced milk.

Four rounds into the fight, his right hand 'went' again. It was now a test of raw courage for the challenger, who was already suffering agonies from the effects of the boils. Yet Perez was never given a hint that anything was amiss, as Brown fought head to head with him for thirteen furious rounds before a left to the throat and a right to the jaw dropped the champion for four. He staggered along the ropes when he got up, and then Brown floored him again with another right. The towel came in from the Tunisian corner just as the referee moved to signal the finish.

Brown had a mixed reign as world champion, interspersing brilliant performances with defeats by men such as Dave Crowley, Etienne Mura, Mickey McGuire and Midget Wolgast. He retained the title twice against Valentin Angelmann, who held him to a draw in their second title match, and won the Lonsdale Belt outright by outpointing Ginger Foran of Liverpool in a triple-title fight. The purse for the Foran fight, £2651, was then a record for a European flyweight match.

He kept up a busy schedule of non-title matches, 20 in all, including a repeat win over the ill-fated Young Perez, who was killed in Auschwitz in 1943. But the most significant result was a twelve-round draw with the young Scottish sensation Benny Lynch. Sammy Wilson, the Scot's manager, ordered Lynch to take it easy with Brown, in the hope of convincing the champion that he had nothing to fear by giving him a rematch for the title. The ploy worked. Brown met Lynch for the championship in September 1935, and was butchered. Lynch floored him eight times with body punches, until Brown himself told the referee to stop it in the second round.

Brown moved up to bantamweight, and launched his new career with a win over old foe Bert Kirby. But his path to the British title was blocked by his neighbour and stable-mate Johnny King. They were born within 100 yards of each other and had grown up in the business together. But there was no love lost between them, and their showdown drew 8000 spectators into Belle Vue. For five rounds King allowed Brown to make the running, and then in the sixth Brown's concentration lapsed momentarily and King smashed over a right.

Brown was dazed and defenceless, but the referee hesitated and King landed ten more crushing blows before it was stopped. Harry Fleming could not bear to watch: while his two stars fought, he waited in an office at Blackpool Tower Circus for a phone call to give him the result. Brown battled on, losing only one of his next 15 fights – and that loss, to Johnny Cusick, was avenged within two months.

By 1937 he had qualified for a second crack at Johnny King, this time with King's British title at stake. King knew he had Brown's measure, and again was content to let the speedy challenger wear himself out over the first half of the fight before King went to work from the tenth. The 20,000 crowd – the biggest ever at a Manchester fight – was shocked into silence in the thirteenth when King's right knocked Brown into unconsciousness. He stayed out for a long, worrying time in the ring, and was still dazed and confused next day.

It was Brown's last chance of a major title, although he fought on for another couple of years and won the Northern Area championship. He went into the Army in 1939, and quit the ring in disgust at being overlooked when eliminators were made to find a new challenger for King.

While in the Army he contracted pernicious anaemia, a condition which plagued the rest of his life. Like too many of his peers, Brown's ring earnings – estimated at £90,000 – were soon gone, and although he kept up his dapper and extrovert style to the end, there were recurring reports of financial problems and even eviction from his home.

He spent his last few years in Crumpsall Hospital, Manchester, where he died on 14 March 1971.

CAREER RECORD: 132 fights, 102 wins (39 inside schedule), 7 draws, 23 defeats.

Benny Lynch (1913–1946)

BOXERS, like pop stars, have a dangerous tendency towards self-destruction. Too many of them, unable to cope with sudden wealth and fame, are swamped by their own success. So it was with Benny Lynch, the brilliant Scot who, alone among British flyweights, stands comparison with Jimmy Wilde.

The difference between them was that Wilde competed at top level for more than ten years, while Lynch's day in the sun was tragically brief. Less than a year after he was champion of the world he was back on the boxing booths where his career had begun, penniless and battling hopelessly against alcoholism. At thirty-three, he was found dying in a Glasgow gutter.

Lynch touched the heights and plumbed the depths in the space of a few hectic years, and his disintegration had all the inevitability of a Greek tragedy. He came from the slums of Glasgow, and they remained his emotional and spiritual home. The old cliché about taking the man out of the slums but never the slums out of the man was never more starkly illustrated. He was second-generation Irish – his grandparents had crossed from Inishowen in Donegal to settle in Glasgow – and he possessed all the strengths and weaknesses which the Scots and Irish often share.

He was introduced to boxing by a local priest, Father James Fletcher, who encouraged his young parishoners to spar as a means of keeping them off the streets. Lynch and his cousin, both aged eleven, showed real flair for the sport and at the instigation of one of the priest's helpers the pair were engaged to give exhibitions in a booth run by Tom Berry, who had been British light-heavyweight champion in 1925–7. Benny progressed from that to more orthodox training with an amateur club in Florence Street, Glasgow, but was always keen to earn a pound or two on the booths.

It was there, on Tommy Watson's booth, that Lynch was spotted by the Glasgow bookmaker who was to guide his career, Sammy Wilson. It was an odd alliance, rarer in those times than it would be now, when friendships between Orange and Green are no longer a cause for comment. Lynch turned pro with Wilson in 1931, and the bookie must occasionally have questioned his own judgement in those early months as the eighteen-year-old won only five of his first ten fights.

But Lynch learned well, and fast, supplementing his training and sparring with regular appearances on the many booths around the Glasgow area. There was as much work as he could handle, and in 1932 he fought 29 times, losing just three. The third of those defeats was to his school friend and professional rival Paddy Docherty, whom he met five times in all for two wins apiece and a draw. He was not to lose again until after he had become world champion.

By 1933, the Lynch legend was taking shape. He went through 17 fights unbeaten, and licked rated men such as Jim Brady, Freddie Tennant, Jim Maharg, Billy Warnock and Bert Kirby. But as the successes increased, so did the temptations. Lynch became a familiar figure around the dance halls and social centres of the area, although there was no sign yet that he was drinking to excess.

The fast climb continued in 1934: 17 fights, all wins, among them a pair of decisions over Jim Campbell for the Scottish title – a distinction that meant something in the 1930s, when boxing ranked second only to football as the national sport. He was in world class now, as he proved with wins over the Italian champion Carlo Cavagnoli, Spanish champion Pedrito Ruiz, French star Maurice Huguenin and world title contender Valentin Angelmann. In June, Angelmann had boxed a draw in a world title challenge against Jackie Brown, and two months later Lynch beat him comfortably.

He had arrived, and had a new mentor with the money and contacts to make things happen. Sammy Wilson had been eased aside and George Dingley, a wealthy and smooth-talking bookie, was now in charge. Lynch had also acquired a wife, eloping to Gretna Green with Anne McGuckian, an apprentice hairdresser. They returned to Glasgow to face their families without having taken a honeymoon, which had to wait until they were married in church three weeks later. Four months later, they had separated. Mrs Lynch had learned at first hand what was rapidly becoming common knowledge around the pubs of Glasgow – that her husband's drinking was now a real problem.

But he was still able to disguise it in the ring, and when he fought a draw with world champion Jackie Brown the rematch for the title was assured. It took place at Belle Vue, Manchester, on 9

September 1935, and Lynch gave a brilliant performance to floor the champion eight times before the Mancunian indicated to referee Moss Deyong that he could not continue. It had taken Benny only 4 minutes and 42 seconds to reach the mountain top.

Twenty thousand people packed the concourse of Glasgow's Central Station to welcome him home, and the celebrations went on for three months – with Lynch never far from their centre.

He struggled to get in shape again with three wins in 16 days in December, but in March 1935 Jimmy Warnock, a tough and awkward southpaw from Belfast, beat him in a non-title match in the King's Hall. It was the first time in 85 pro fights that the faithful Sammy Wilson was not in his corner. Lynch had summarily dismissed him, and now Dingley was in full control of his career.

The loss to Warnock shocked Lynch into taking a grip on his life, and for the rest of the year he worked hard on both personal and professional levels. He was reconciled with his wife after the birth of their first son, and in the ring he won six times that year, including a world title defence against the Londoner Pat Palmer, whom he stopped in eight rounds.

There remained one detail to resolve. The world championship was again in dispute, with the Americans recognizing a Filipino called Benjiman Gan, whose ring name was 'Small Montana', as the champion. Montana and Lynch met at Wembley on 19 January 1937 for the undisputed title, in a fifteen-rounder which is still regarded as the finest match ever staged between flyweights. It was an exhibition of all that is best in the sport, fifteen rounds of delightfully skilful boxing and good sportsmanship, and when it was over Lynch got the verdict. What made his performance even more remarkable was that three weeks earlier he had weighed around 10 stone, and had shed the two surplus stones by supplementing his training with huge intakes of the laxative cascara.

Before he won the world title, his ambition to do so had served as some kind of restraint on his drinking habits. Now, with that discipline removed, what had been a problem became an addiction, and it showed. He had a hard time beating Fortunato Ortega, then disgraced himself in a non-title match with the Midlander Len 'Nipper' Hampston. He had been on a non-stop drinking binge for weeks, and was barely sober when he got into the ring at Belle Vue, Manchester – the same ring in which he had become world champion. His condition so appalled his management that they tried to bribe Hampston to take a dive rather than shame the champion, but Hampston insisted that the fight be decided on merit.

He gave Lynch a fearful beating, flooring him six times with body punches before Lynch's second, Nick Cavalli, incurred his man's disqualification in the fifth round by leaping into the ring to save him from further punishment. Somehow, Lynch flogged himself back into shape to stop Hampston in the tenth round of a rematch three weeks later, but then lost again to the tricky Irishman, Warnock. But there was one great performance left in him, and he gave it in front of a 40,000 crowd at Shawfield Park, Glasgow, on 13 October that year against the unbeaten Golborne teenager Peter Kane.

The Englishman had won 46 in a row, and only nine of them had gone the distance. It was Lynch's supreme challenge, and he rose to it unforgettably to knock out Kane in the thirteenth round. He never made flyweight again, for by now the disease had taken an unshakeable grip on him. Today, when alcoholism is a much better understood condition, there are treatments and clinics readily available for people in a similar position, but in the 1930s the only salvation lay in one's own willpower and strength of character. Lynch did his honest best to fight it, but failed.

He paid weight forfeit in his next three fights, two wins against low-grade Continentals and then a disappointing draw in a non-title return with Kane. But he had lost all pride in his championship, and in himself. He was scheduled to defend his world title against the American Jackie Jurich on 29 June 1938, but came in six and a half pounds overweight and lost his title on the scales. He fought Jurich anyway, in an overweight twelve-rounder, and won on points. It was the final victory of his meteoric seven-year career.

'KO' Morgan beat him in September, and this time Lynch scaled more than 9 stone and paid a £500 forfeit. Debts were piling up, and the Inland Revenue were top of the list. His life was in chaos, and his only escape lay in the bottom of a glass.

There was one last, shameful appearance in the ring when, weighing 9 st 5 lb, he was knocked out in three rounds by the former European champion Aurel Toma of Rumania, whose other claim to fame was that he had once served as chauffeur to King Carol. There is a haunting photo of the fallen champion, arms flung out behind him as he lies on the canvas at the Empress Hall in

London, and John Burrowes, in his loving biography of the man, describes what happened next:

They booed when they helped him to his feet and booed even louder and shouted insults and taunts after he had recovered enough to make his way, head bowed beneath the stained towel that cowled his head. 'Drunk' – 'Bum' – 'Has-been' – they vented every abuse they thought appropriate at the man who had been transformed into a grotesque version of the fighter that had held everyone who ever watched him in awe at his grace, tenacity, courage and skill; the man they had called Benny Lynch.

His career was over. No promoter would take a chance on him now, and he had sacrificed his credibility with the public. He made one final, despairing effort to salvage his life, going into retreat at Mount Melleray monastery in Ireland in the hope that the peace there would help him combat the addiction that was destroying him. But, inevitably, he discharged himself and went back to the only life he knew – back to the boxing booths and the bars.

It ended on 8 August 1946, the day after Lynch had been found in a Glasgow gutter, dying of pneumonia. He was thirty-three years and four months old.

CAREER RECORD: 122 fights, 90 wins (34 inside schedule), 17 draws, 15 defeats.

Peter Kane (born 1918)

SOME fighters are fated to be remembered for their defeats rather than their victories, even when those victories include winning the championship of the world. Billy Conn, for example, earned ring immortality by losing to Joe Louis rather than by winning the light-heavyweight championship, and Henry Cooper, similarly, is better known for losing to Muhammad Ali than for winning three Lonsdale Belts outright.

So it is with Peter Kane, the Eddie Cantor lookalike from Golborne, Lancashire. Kane won the world flyweight title and the European bantamweight championship, but his name is inextricably linked with that of Benny Lynch, who knocked him out in thirteen rounds in one of the greatest world title fights of all time. Yet Kane merits a better deal from history. He was, after all, world champion at a time when the flyweight division was at its strongest, and he lost only seven of more than a hundred fights.

He was born at Heywood, Lancashire, on 28 February 1918, but the family moved to Golborne when he was a baby. He started boxing at school and in the Boys' Brigade, and the first title he ever won was the championship of the local branch of the Brigade. Ted Denvir, a Liverpool–Irish manager, spotted him boxing in a charity show at St Helen's and invited him to his Liverpool gym for a trial.

Kane went there with his father, and impressed Denvir sufficiently to be invited back for regular training. Twice a week the youngster made the return trip to Liverpool for coaching, although he was still far from ready for a professional career. He had left school by this time, and was apprenticed to a local blacksmith. The hard work at the anvil helped him develop the prodigious back and arm strength which made him such a formidable hitter, and in any case he enjoyed the work: even when he had won the world title he continued to put in a nine-and-a-half-hour day, every day, for eighteen shillings (90p) a week.

On Denvir's recommendation he started taking part in the unlicensed fighting which was popular in Lancashire in the early 1930s. Shows were usually staged in the back rooms of pubs where the boxers performed for the few coppers or 'nobbins' that would be thrown to them. He also boxed on the booths whenever he got the chance, although, unlike most world champions with a booths background, he was invariably the challenger from the crowd rather than the 'house' fighter on the platform.

He had, by his own reckoning, more than 40 of these unlicensed and unofficial scraps before Denvir judged him ready for his formal pro debut. Kane earned £5 for stopping Joey Jacobs of Manchester in five rounds at Liverpool on 13 December 1934, and in the process acquired a new name. The family surname was properly Cain, but had been wrongly spelt on the posters for the Liverpool show. Denvir considered that the new version had more impact than the old, and the spelling stuck.

He went through a dozen fights in 1935 and won them all by knockout or stoppage, only twice being taken past three rounds. In January 1936 he was matched in his first ten-rounder against the vastly experienced Joe Curran of Liverpool, who went on to challenge for the world title. Curran floored him early in the fight, the first time that Kane had ever been down, and the youngster – still only seventeen – fought five rounds of which he had no recollection whatever afterwards. But he boxed well enough by instinct to earn a comfortable points win, which established him firmly in the front rank of British flyweights.

In May that year he beat the former International Boxing Union champion Praxille Gyde in three rounds. In 18 fights in 1936, only five went the distance. His victims included some significant names: Jim Maharg of Scotland was stopped in three rounds, and the Welshman Pat Warburton, who had taken both Benny Lynch and Jimmy Warnock the distance, went out in 171 seconds. The clever Austrian champion Ernst Weiss gave him the most difficult test so far, stretching him to the limit in each of the twelve rounds.

On 14 December Kane fulfilled one of his more unusual schoolboy ambitions by acquiring a cauliflower ear. It happened against the Belgian champion Gaston Vandenbos, on a National Sporting Club promotion at Earl's Court. He stopped the Belgian in six rounds, but was left with a 'cauli' as a reminder. It was a battle badge the schoolboy Kane had long coveted, but the reality was more painful than he had imagined, particularly as he was contracted to appear again only three days later against Al Hopp of Germany at Liverpool.

Rather than risk a possible breach-of-contract action, he went ahead with the fight. The rules prohibited a boxer from having two ten-rounders less than four days apart, and so the Hopp fight had to be scheduled for nine rounds. But the distance was academic: Kane was in such pain from his ear that he wanted to get rid of Hopp as quickly as possible, and he floored the unfortunate German six times for a second-round stoppage.

Jeff Dickson, who divided his promotional activities between London and Paris, paid Kane £400 for a rematch with Valentin Angelmann in Paris in January 1937. Kane had earned £125 for outscoring Angelmann in Liverpool two months earlier, and was happy to accept. The fight was a big attraction, drawing a record 20,000 spectators to the Palais des Sports, and Kane repeated his earlier points win.

Paul Schaefer, the German champion, was dispatched in 127 seconds in February, and then it was back to Paris in March to earn another £400 by stopping Pierre Louis in seven rounds. The French could not get enough of the wide-eyed Lancashire teenager, and he was booked there again against the European bantamweight title claimant Joseph 'Poppy' Decico on 13 April. Kane knocked him cold in 69 seconds.

His march to the title was unstoppable, and the victories piled up. Phil Milligan was stopped in eleven rounds for the Northern Area title, Ernst Weiss lost again in a rematch, and Jimmy Warnock, who had twice beaten Lynch in overweight matches, was stopped in four sensational rounds at Liverpool to bring Kane's record to 41 consecutive wins, all but eight inside the distance.

He had long been studying Lynch, in readiness for their eventual meeting. Whenever the Scot fought, Kane would be at ringside, and he and trainer Arthur Goodwin would analyse the champion's strengths and weakneses. Lynch invited him to join the camp as a sparmate for his title defence against Pat Palmer, and Kane felt that he had handled Lynch well enough in sparring to satisfy himself that the time was right for a title bid. The pair became good friends during the time he spent in camp, and would often take long walks together, or go off on rabbit-shooting expeditions.

They met for the title in front of a record 40,000 crowd at Shawfield Park, Glasgow, on 13 October 1937. Their battle surpassed all expectations and is still recalled with awe by those who were there. It was, for both men, their finest hour. Although Lynch retained his title by knocking him out in the thirteenth,

Kane's reputation was actually enhanced in defeat. As in the Joe Curran fight, Kane could not remember anything of the seven rounds after Lynch floored him in the first, but had boxed superbly on blind instinct against a magnificent champion who was at the peak of his powers.

There had to be a return fight, and it took place in March 1938. But by this time Lynch had a problem with drinking, and he could no longer make the weight. The fight went ahead anyway, ending in a draw, and when Lynch again came in overweight later that year for a title defence against Jackie Jurich of America, he automatically forfeited the championship on the scales.

Kane was paired with Jurich for the vacant title at Liverpool on 22 September 1938, and the Englishman won a decisive fifteen-round victory. He boxed six times in non-title affairs in 1939, winning them all, including an appearance in Monte Carlo in August on a France v Britain show promoted by the NSC. But increasing weight was becoming a problem, and in August 1939 he announced that he was relinquishing the world title.

Curiously, the record books all show Kane as holding the title throughout the 1938–43 period, but he made his announcement in print and repeated it in many newspaper interviews. Of course, the world had more serious matters to worry about in August 1939 than the destiny of the flyweight championship, which may explain why promoters were able to continue billing Kane as the title-holder during those years.

When war broke out he joined the RAF, in which he served for the duration. In common with all his contemporaries, he was handicapped by lack of opportunities or facilities for training, which accounted for some of his less impressive performances during the war years. By June 1943, however, he had put together enough good wins to justify a match at Hampden Park in Glasgow with the Scot Jackie Paterson, for the world title.

He had boiled himself back down to the flyweight limit, and his wins over Joe Curran (twice), Paddy Ryan and Gus Foran had persuaded him that he could again be a force at 8 stone. Paterson and Kane were long-time friends. They had given many exhibitions together, and were both stationed at RAF Padgate. Paterson even occasionally spent his weekend leaves in Kane's home, but friendship counts for nothing during business hours.

It took Paterson only 61 seconds and two knockdowns to

convince his weight-drained opponent that his future lay in the bantamweight division, if indeed Kane had a future in the game at all. The former champion boxed three times more in 1943, winning them all, but then dropped off the scene for almost three years.

He launched a comeback in August 1946. Few expected it to amount to much, especially after his first venture resulted in a thoroughly unsatisfactory disqualification win over Jackie Hughes in Brighton. But the comeback gathered momentum in 1947 with wins over Theo Medina, the European champion, Bunty Doran, the Irish champion, Belgian title-holder Joe Cornelis, and Dado Marino, who went on to win the world flyweight title.

In September 1947 he took the European title from Medina on a fifteen-round decision in Manchester, and retained it in December against the balding, thirty-year-old Cornelis. But in February 1948 Guido Ferracin dethroned him in Manchester, the first time that Kane had lost in 34 fights against foreign opposition.

There was only one more victory, when Bunty Doran hurt his right hand in the eighth round in April 1948 and asked the referee to stop the fight. Amleto Falcinelli held Kane to a draw in May, and Ferracin beat him in a rematch for the title in July. Kane was badly marked around both eyes, and at the end of the fifth he asked the former featherweight champion Nel Tarleton – who had taken over as his manager – to throw in the towel. In November he was outpointed in a twelve-rounder at Manchester by British bantam-weight champion Stan Rowan, which at last forced him to accept that his ring days were over.

But it was not all gloom for him in 1948. On 26 September he finally received the world championship belt which he had earned ten years earlier. It was presented to him by another great Lancashire entertainer, Gracie Fields, at a charity show for the Sportsmen's Aid Society at the London Casino.

CAREER RECORD: 102 fights, 92 wins, 2 draws, 1 'no contest', 7 defeats.

Jackie Paterson (1920–1966)

IT WAS typical of Jackie Paterson that his first and last fights should both be main events, for throughout his thirteen-year, 91-fight career the colourful and hard-hitting little Scot was never far from centre stage. He won six major titles and fought eleven men who held either world, European, British or Empire championships, and had his career not been hampered by the restrictions of war service he might well have rivalled the immortal Benny Lynch in the affections of Scotland's fight fans.

He was born on 5 September 1920 in Springside, a little village half-way between Kilmarnock and Irvine in Ayrshire. When he was eight the family emigrated to America, spending five years in the mining town of Scranton, Pennsylvania, before returning to Scotland and settling in Glasgow.

Paterson was already a fine all-round sportsman who excelled at soccer, playing centre-forward for his local club, Dreghorn Juveniles. At fifteen he turned to boxing and joined the Anderston Club. Unlike most southpaws he was not naturally left-handed, but simply felt more comfortable boxing from the right-forward stance. Club trainer Pat Collins was sensible enough not to interfere with the boy's natural style, and Paterson was an immediate success. He won his first 11 contests, seven by knockout, and the solitary defeat of his brief amateur career came against Robert Watson of Leith in the final of the 1937 Scottish flyweight championships.

Jackie was working as an apprentice butcher in a shop in Canal Street, Glasgow, but the money was poor and he planned to turn professional as soon as Collins judged him ready. That day came earlier than either of them anticipated. Collins was promoting a show at the Argyll Theatre in Greenock on 26 May 1938, featuring the experienced Irish flyweight Joe Kiely, from Limerick. A few days before the fight Kiely's opponent pulled out, and Collins could not find a replacement.

In desperation he asked Paterson to step in, and after obtaining the boy's parents' approval he made the match. Paterson won on points over ten rounds, and earned a pound a round. At seventeen, he was on his way. The Anderston Club officials were furious with

Collins, feeling that Paterson was much too young and immature for a pro career. Collins was ordered to end his association with the club, and two of its directors resigned in protest.

Collins drew even more criticism for the second match he took for Paterson. Rinty Monaghan was becoming a big attraction in Belfast, and was unbeaten in nearly 30 fights. He was due to meet Tommy Stewart at the Oval soccer ground on 23 July, but Stewart withdrew and once again Paterson was brought in as a short-notice replacement. It was an intimidating prospect for the youngster, but he stunned the Belfast crowd by flooring Monaghan twice and knocking him out in five rounds.

The win gave Paterson a short-cut up the ratings, and before he had been a pro for even twelve months he was beating top men such as Phil Milligan, Freddie Tennant and Raoul Degryse, the Belgian champion. Degryse had made his name by flooring Peter Kane three times in the first round of a non-title match with the world champion, but Paterson put him down six times on the way to a points win.

There were two defeats by Liverpool's Joe Curran, and draws with Tommy Stewart, Tut Whalley and Valentin Angelmann, but when Paterson knocked out Whalley in the first round in June 1939 and then outpointed Curran a month later, the way to the British title was clear. He knocked out Eric Jones inside a round in a final eliminator at Carntyre Race Course, a show promoted by Benny Lynch's old mentor George Dingley, and in September Dingley gave him the chance to become champion when he paired him with Paddy Ryan of Manchester for the vacant title.

The Chief Constable of Glasgow imposed an 8000 limit on the attendance, but this was rescinded at the last minute. But by then the damage had been done, and only 2400 paid to see Paterson knock out Ryan in the thirteenth. It was just over 16 months since his debut.

Paterson became a double champion in March 1940, outpointing Kid Tanner of British Guiana for the vacant Empire title in a fight which the Scot always recalled as the hardest of his career. By now he had left the meat trade and was working as a hammerman in John Brown's shipyard in Glasgow. It was well-paid work, and he felt that the physical exertion it involved served as part of his training.

He had his own somewhat eccentric notions of training. He

preferred to do his heavy gym work late at night, and would often be slogging away at 2 a.m. He hated roadwork, and avoided it whenver he could.

But his methods seemed to suit him, for he built up a 14-fight winning run after the Tanner fight, including an eighth-round stoppage of Paddy Ryan in a championship rematch. In August 1941 he moved up to bantamweight to challenge fellow Scot Jim Brady for the Empire title, but lost on points.

It was a busy period for Paterson: he had joined the RAF, and married his teenage girlfriend, Helen. Their first son died tragically in 1942 when he was only five weeks old, an event which left a deep impression on Paterson and, in the views of many who were close to him, was a major contributory factor to his later drink-related problems.

But he kept fighting, and winning, apart from a freak loss to Frank Bonsor which was quickly and emphatically reversed. By the time he faced Peter Kane for the world title at Hampden Park on 19 June 1943, he had won 42 and drawn three of his 50 fights, and three of his five losses had been avenged. He knew Kane's style inside out, having boxed many exhibitions with him during their shared time in the Services, and had learned more from the sessions than Kane had.

It was all over in 61 seconds. A left hook dropped the champion for five, and he was so dazed and bewildered when he got up that he turned his back on Paterson and faced out over the ropes, staring sightlessly into the 35,000 crowd. Paterson spun him around before referee Moss Deyong could intervene, and knocked him out with one more punch.

Paterson had touched heights he would never again achieve. In fact, he won only 20 of his remaining 40 fights. Service commitments limited his training severely, and it became increasingly difficult for him to make flyweight. By 1944 he was fighting featherweights, without conspicuous success. He lost three of his four fights between October 1944 and August 1945, but that may well have been because a new and dangerous distraction was eating away at his already waning enthusiasm for training.

While stationed at RAF Bishop Briggs, near Glasgow, he had been introduced to greyhound racing. At first, he could not go wrong; he devised a system which involved backing dogs which were well-bred but out of form, so that their odds were longer than their breeding justified. Paterson worked on the principle that sooner or later the breeding would show, and if the dog lost first time he backed it he would simply increase his stake on it next time. Soon he was betting up to £200 on a single race and, as his luck turned, so money problems grew until he was eventually forced to sell the two fruit shops in which he had invested much of his ring earnings.

It now seemed unlikely that he would ever again make flyweight, particularly after he beat Jim Brady for the Empire bantamweight title and then took the European title from the French gypsy Theo Medina, an ex-Resistance fighter who had beaten Paterson in a ten-rounder in Paris in November 1945. But he struggled down to 8 stone to beat his old opponent Joe Curran in a world title defence in July 1946, eight years after Curran had taken away his unbeaten record. He also lost a non-title match with another name from the past, Rinty Monaghan, who forced his retirement with a cut eye after six rounds.

Medina recaptured the European title, stopping Paterson in four rounds in Glasgow in October 1946, but the irrepressible Scot bounced back to take the British bantamweight title from the Manchester veteran Johnny King. Paterson had shared a dressing room with King at Newcastle in January 1939, and he never forgot how charming and helpful King had been to him. King became his idol, and he even had his ring shorts made in the same style that King favoured.

King had spent the war in the Navy, surviving the sinking of the *Prince of Wales* in 1941, but had done very little boxing during those years. When he was discharged he scaled around 11 stone, and he was drained by the effort of shedding more than 30 lb to reach the bantamweight limit. Paterson beat him easily, flooring the gallant old champion six times before referee Moss Deyong counted King out in the seventh.

He signed to defend the flyweight title against Dado Marino of Hawaii, but the fight was doomed from its inception. First Paterson obtained a postponement because of an attack of boils, then had to seek another postponement because of illness. It was scheduled for the third time for 7 July 1947 in Glasgow, but five minutes after the deadline had elapsed for Paterson to go to the scales the Scottish Area BBB of C Secretary, Henry McGrattan, made a dramatic announcement to the crowd that had packed the Astoria

Dance Hall for the weigh-in: 'Gentlemen, I am sorry to say that Jackie Paterson is not here. He has collapsed and is now in bed.'

Paterson had trained until midnight the previous day, watched by the Board's doctor, but was still 3 lb overweight at the end of the session and the doctor certified him as 'unfit to box'. The certificate saved his title, for Marino's manager, Sam Ichinose, had claimed the championship by telegram to the National Boxing Association on the grounds that Marino had made the weight and had beaten the substitute opponent, Rinty Monaghan.

Promoter Jack Solomons, acting on the assumption that Paterson's flyweight days were now definitely over, paired Marino and Monaghan in London on 20 October and billed it as being for the vacant world title. But Paterson was not giving up that easily; he secured a court order restraining the British Board from recognizing anyone else as champion, and from recognizing any contest which did not involve him as being for the world title. The unflappable Solomons merely sought approval elsewhere, and Monaghan's points win made him champion in the eyes of the NBA, the European Boxing Union, and the Irish Board of Control.

Paterson boxed on the same show, retaining his British and Empire bantamweight titles in five rounds against Norman Lewis, and negotiations commenced for a showdown between Britain's two rival 'world champions'. It took place in the King's Hall, Belfast on 23 March 1948, and Paterson, predictably, was counted out in the seventh round. He had been due in Belfast the day before the show, but delayed his arrival until an hour before the weigh-in to allow himself the maximum available time for weight reduction.

It was all downhill after that, and Paterson won only three of his final 12 contests. Stan Rowan took the last of his titles, outpointing him in March 1949, and Paterson announced his retirement. Three months later, he was back to knock out an obscure Algerian and then go the distance with the former world champion Manuel Ortiz.

Paterson stayed in top class until near the end, holding world bantamweight champ Vic Toweel to a ten-round decision in Johannesburg in December 1949. In his only appearance in 1950 he was kayoed in two rounds by Eddie Carson, substituting for the Frenchman Maurice Sandeyron, and when Willie Myles outpointed him at Dundee in February 1951 he quit for good.

Less than two years later, the man who claimed to have earned £100,000 was in the bankruptcy court. He told the hearing that he had gambled away £55,000 and given away another £25,000, and was now working in a pub in Largs. He was earning £7 per week in summer, but got no pay for the rest of the year, only free board and lodgings for his wife and two sons.

He sold his Lonsdale Belt to raise enough cash to take his family to South Africa, where he found a job as a hotel manager, but was sacked for insulting the owner. By now he was drinking heavily, and eventually his wife Helen divorced him after twenty-three years of marriage.

She gave him £1000 for his fare back to London, but Paterson could not settle there and drank his way out of one job after another. In 1965 Helen agreed to give him one last chance, and he returned to South Africa. After a long period of unemployment he found work as a lorry driver, but only a month later, on 19 November 1966, he was stabbed to death with a broken bottle during a brawl in a house in Amanzimtoti, near Durban.

CAREER RECORD: 91 fights, 63 wins (41 inside schedule), 3 draws, 25 defeats.

Rinty Monaghan (1920–1984)

RINTY MONAGHAN'S career spanned fifteen years, but only ten of them were spent in the ring. He was a pro from 1935 until late 1949, yet boxed only once between March 1940 and May 1945. That makes his achievement in becoming world champion in 1947 all the more remarkable; it is, indeed, unparalleled in boxing history.

He was born on 21 August 1920 in Belfast, and was christened John Joseph. His grandmother gave him the nickname by which he became much better known: she originally called him 'Rin Tin Tin' after the film-star dog, because of his childhood fondness for jumping off walls and climbing lamp-posts, and this was inevitably shortened to 'Rinty'.

His father, an ex-Marine, had boxed as a lightweight in the Services and now worked as a foreman in a flax store behind their home in Little Corporation Street, a narrow and shabby district of working-class Belfast. When Monaghan was old enough he, too, went to work there, carrying bales.

He was soon supplementing his wages with the nobbins that he and his friend 'Pimple' McKee – later a successful jockey – earned by giving exhibitions in the regular boxing shows staged at the Belfast Independent Labour Party Hall in York Street. The pair, whose combined weight did not exceed 10 stone, were invariably billed as 'A special heavyweight attraction', and the verdict was always a draw. Monaghan could count on getting a few extra coppers by singing in the ring afterwards, and thus began the tradition for which he is best remembered.

His formal career began in 1935 under the management of Frank McAloran, and the partnership lasted to the end. He probably had many more fights than the record books show; he claimed over 100, although the official list shows barely 60. Most of the early contests were at Chapel Fields in Belfast, where the crowds were hard to please and the pay was derisory. But it was a good learning ground, and apart from a couple of draws in 1936 Monaghan remained undefeated for his first three years in the business.

He had a close call against Paddy O'Toole, who despite his name was actually from Liverpool. Monaghan floored him in the first round of their punch-up in Belfast in October 1937, but was down himself in the second and remembered nothing at all of what happened next. He came to as McAloran was taking him home, and apologized to the bewildered manager for losing a fight he should have won. 'What are you talking about?' McAloran asked. 'You knocked him out in the fourth!'

His first setback came against Jackie Paterson, who was having only his second pro fight. The Scot came in as a substitute for Tommy Stewart, whom Monaghan had been due to face in an eliminator for Jim McStravick's Northern Ireland title. Paterson's only previous fight had been a points win over Joe Kiely of Limerick, and as Monaghan had knocked Kiely out in two rounds a fortnight earlier, flooring him four times in the process, he did not anticipate any problems from the teenager.

Monaghan boxed confidently and cheekily, dropping his hands and clowning. But he took one chance too many in the fifth and Paterson floored him with a fierce left hook to the jaw. He was down twice more, and McAloran threw in the towel just as the referee completed the countout. It was a salutary lesson for Monaghan, who thereafter confined his clowning to before and after a fight.

But it was also a costly setback, as it meant that for the rest of 1939 and 1940 Monaghan was trying to make up lost ground rather than continue his progress towards the title shot he might otherwise have had. A pair of wins over the durable Joe Curran helped considerably, but there were also defeats by Tommy Stewart, Paddy Ryan and Jimmy Gill, who got the ten-round decision despite having been floored twice.

By now the war was on in earnest. Monaghan joined the Merchant Navy, and was shipwrecked. On his discharge he worked as an ambulance driver, serving throughout the worst of the Belfast bombings before he found something much more to his taste. Along with two friends, Jim Hawthorne and Billy York, he formed a group called the Three Hillbillies. They were recruited to entertain the troops for ENSA, and the ENSA assignments kept Monaghan busy throughout the rest of the war. He even gave a concert in Normandy four days after the D-Day Landings.

Monaghan boxed only once between 1940 and 1945, giving a dismal performance to lose on points to Ike Weir at Cliftonville football ground. By May 1945 he was ready to get back in action, and asked McAloran to find him work.

The comeback began at the Ulster Stadium on 4 May, and he could not have returned in better style as he knocked out Joe Meikle in the first round. A fortnight later he was held to a draw by Harry Rodgers of Derry, but then in July he went south to Dublin and trounced Joe 'Boy' Collins, the Irish champion at both flyweight and bantamweight. But the win which let the world know that he was back in the title picture came in November, when he knocked out Eddie 'Bunty' Doran (to whom he was related by marriage) in four sensational rounds at the Ulster Hall in Belfast to win the Northern Ireland title.

It is hard to believe now, when an Area title is virtually meaningless, that Monaghan's fans actually stopped the traffic in Belfast as they carried him shoulder-high through the streets back to his home in Little Corporation Street, where he serenaded them from his upstairs window.

Paterson, who had become world champion in 1943, agreed to meet Monaghan in an overweight match in Belfast in June 1946. It was the Irishman's big chance, and he took it with a sixth-round stoppage. The ending was caused by cuts, but Monaghan had been firmly in command at the finish. Jack Solomons gave him his first chance in London in March 1947, and he took it brilliantly with a first-round blitz of Terry Allen, who would eventually succeed him as world champion.

A win over the rated Frenchman Emile Famechon established him as a contender for the world title, which Paterson was scheduled to defend against Dado Marino of Hawaii at Hampden Park, Glasgow, on 16 July. It was common knowledge that the Scot was having severe weight problems, and Monaghan was engaged to stand by to substitute in the event of Paterson failing the weigh-in. But a few days before the show Monaghan was assured that Paterson was comfortably on schedule, and he left for a few days' holiday with his family, returning to Glasgow to watch the fight.

As he was finishing a heavy lunch in a city-centre restaurant that afternoon, he was tracked down by a search party dispatched by the frantic promoter with the news that Paterson had failed to show up for the weigh-in, and that Monaghan's services would be required after all. He was ill-prepared, and on his own admission he did not make any strenuous efforts to win, being content to use it as a chance to study Marino at close quarters in readiness for a rematch with the title at stake.

The result was a boring, messy encounter, with Monaghan eventually being disqualified for repeated holding in the ninth. Promoter Solomons kept faith with the Irishman, and made the Marino fight in London on 20 October. It was sanctioned only by the National Boxing Association, the European Boxing Union and the Irish Board, after Paterson – who insisted he could still make the weight – secured a court injunction to stop the British Board from recognizing it as a title fight.

Marino met a different Monaghan this time. There was no sign of the hesitant, safety-first tactics the Belfast man had employed in Glasgow, and the Hawaiian was kept on the defensive throughout as Monaghan won comfortably on points to set up his third and most important meeting with Paterson. There would be two versions of the same world title on the line, as well as Paterson's British and Empire titles, which were automatically involved.

Paterson must have known when the match was made for Belfast on 23 March 1948 that he could not win, but he had a champion's pride and was not prepared to let his title go easily. He punished his body in training, dehydrating himself to get down to the flyweight limit. Monaghan floored him in the second, and though Paterson rallied bravely the Irishman always held the edge and earned the undisputed title with two knockdowns in the seventh round. Referee Tommy Little counted Paterson out as the battered champion slumped on his haunches against the ropes, his upper body and head resting on the bottom rope.

Monaghan was poised to cash in on his titles, but the bronchial problems which forced his eventual retirement were already apparent. He fought only once in 11 months, stopping Charlie Squires in seven rounds in Birmingham in June 1948 before returning to action in February 1949 against Terry Allen. Monaghan was badly out of touch, and the Londoner took a deserved points win over eight rounds.

But Rinty was not done yet. In April, in front of his own devoted crowd at the King's Hall Belfast, he retained the world title and won the European championship by outpointing the Frenchman Maurice Sandeyron. It was a hard-earned victory; Monaghan's training had twice been disrupted by bronchitis, and he was so exhausted at the finish that he had to take a swill of brandy in the ring before he could give the crowd his traditional chorus of 'When Irish Eyes Are Smiling'.

He fought only twice more, a non-title win over Otello Belardinelli and a disappointing fifteen-round draw with Terry Allen in the King's Hall. On 25 April 1950 he announced his retirement because of recurring bronchitis. He tried various business ventures, including a showband, but none of them worked out and in 1956 he announced plans to come back as a bantamweight.

He needed the money to keep his wife and four children, one of whom, Colette, was crippled with polio. But the Board of Control refused him a licence, and Monaghan returned to his second love, show business. He made a modest living at that for the rest of his life, and was always a popular and well-received figure at big fight nights in Belfast and Derry, when the crowd would invariably call for his party-piece song.

He died of cancer at his Belfast home on 3 March 1984, and the best tribute was paid by his old opponent Terry Allen: 'Rinty was a fascinating character,' he said. 'We were rivals in the ring, but brothers out of it. He had the secret of eternal youth; he always seemed happy, and he always made everyone he met feel happy too. A great champion, and a great sportsman.'

CAREER RECORD: 56 fights, 44 wins, 4 draws, 8 defeats.

Freddie Mills (1919–1965)

HAD FREDDIE MILLS been a little less brave than the men who made his matches and mishandled his career, the chances are that his life after boxing would have turned out very differently, and would not have ended with a gunshot in a Soho yard in 1965.

The damage that Mills suffered in frightening mismatches against heavyweights Jack London, Joe Baksi and Bruce Woodcock extorted a dreadful price in the years following his retirement, and in the opinion of those who were closest to him, contributed greatly to the mental instability that led him to what seems to have been a lonely suicide.

Mills was always a battler who relied on raw, pure courage to cover up his glaring technical deficiencies. For Mills was one of the crudest fighters ever to hold a world title, a man of minimal technique or finesse, who relied on brawling aggression and a simple inability to know when he had taken enough and was beaten.

Basically, Mills loved to fight, and got enjoyment from it in the way that other men take pleasure in softer recreations. His addiction to the game – never more of a misnomer than when applied to Mills' brutal career – began when his older brother Charlie became a boxer of sorts, performing in unlicensed shows around the Bournemouth area where Freddie was born on 26 June 1919. Later, in his early teens, he used to climb on the glass dome of the Winter Gardens, Bournemouth, for a free, if precarious, view of the regular boxing shows there.

This risky exercise ended when he was caught by Jack Turner, who promoted the shows and whose brother Bob was later to become his manager. Mills' career got formally under way when, aged sixteen, he won a novice competition at Westover Ice Rink. With Bob Turner supervising the training and brother Jack the matching, Mills went through 17 fights before his eighteenth birthday and won 15 of them, drawing the other two. He was boxing twelve-rounders regularly against seasoned professionals, and established quite a local reputation.

He was also an enthusiastic performer on the booths, and

enjoyed the fairground life so much that he returned to it even after he had become a champion. There were plenty of regular bookings to be had as well, and the eager Mills fought as often as the Turners could arrange them. By the end of 1939 he had forced his way into the front ranks of Britain's middleweights, and had lost only eight of his 56 fights.

When war broke out Mills joined the RAF, but his posting as a PT instructor allowed him ample time off for training and boxing. Throughout 1940–1 he consolidated his position as a British title contender with wins over former champions Dave McCleave and Jock McAvoy, as well as rated men such as Ginger Sadd and Jack Hyams. But he was battling the scales by now, and in May 1940 he accepted the inevitable and moved up into the light-heavyweight division.

He acquired a new manager as well: Ted Broadribb, a well-connected London fight figure, bought out Bob Turner's interest and immediately began steering Mills towards a crack at the British title, which was held by Len Harvey. (Broadribb later became Mills' father-in-law when Freddie married his daughter Chrissie. She had formerly been married to the South African heavyweight Don McCorkindale – who accompanied Freddie and his ex-wife on their honeymoon!)

Harvey was one of the heroic figures of British boxing, a fabulous boxer who had been at the top of his profession for nearly twenty years. He had held British titles at middle, light-heavy and heavyweight, and was still recognized by the British Board (though by no one else) as world light-heavyweight champion after beating Jock McAvoy at a time when the world title was vacant. He was serving as a Pilot Officer, and Mills was an NCO, which all helped the publicity along when the pair were matched at Tottenham Hotspurs' football ground on 20 June 1942.

Because of wartime restrictions the fight took place in the afternoon, but around 30,000 were there to see the veteran Harvey, who had not fought for three years, destroyed in two rounds by Mills' swinging, irresistible aggression. Harvey immediately retired, leaving his British heavyweight title vacant, and Broadribb lobbied successfully for Mills to be accepted as a contender for it.

He faced the balding Northern veteran Jack London for the British and Empire titles at Manchester on 15 September 1944, and was outpointed in fifteen punishing rounds. Mills had been ahead after ten rounds, but the 15-stone London ground down his resistance with thumping body punches and sickening, full-blooded blows to the head until, by the fourteenth, the exhausted Mills was functioning on instinct and courage. It was the first of a series of indefensible matches in which Mills' bravery was exploited as a cynical crowd-puller to make money for men who cared more about gate receipts than the fighter's future.

War service restricted Mills to just one appearance in 1945, when he cut the Scottish heavyweight Ken Shaw to defeat in seven rounds – after Shaw had floored him for nine in the fourth with a right to the jaw which lifted Mills clear off his feet. Even in winning fights, he was being hurt.

Mills had been out of the ring for over a year when Ted Broadribb secured him a match for the world title against the American Gus Lesnevich. It was far too soon for him to be facing someone of Lesnevich's calibre, without the benefit of a couple of warm-up fights, and Mills took a fearful beating before the fight was stopped in the tenth. Mills was floored four times in the second round, and although he rallied to inflict considerable facial damage on the champion, he fought himself to a standstill and took three more counts before referee Eugene Henderson stopped it four seconds from the end of the tenth.

It had been the kind of fight which can end a man's career – Mills later admitted that, 'For a week afterwards I found my speech slurred at odd times, and every morning I used to be wakened from a sleep which was more like a deep coma.'

Yet, unbelievably, Broadribb and promoter Jack Solomons had him back in the ring only three weeks later against the heavyweight champion Bruce Woodcock. Again Mills was far too courageous for his own good; he lasted the twelve-round course, but absorbed another pounding.

It was painfully evident that Mills did not have a future as a heavyweight, but that was where the money was and so, in a reversal of the fighter's customary nightmare, he struggled to put on weight, even drinking a pint of Guinness every day on Broadribb's instructions. A one-round knockout over an obscure Swedish heavyweight persuaded him that he could still make the grade in that division, so Solomons imported the imposing, world-ranked Joe Baksi to test him again.

The American had lost only four of 68 fights, and at 6 feet 1 inch and over 15 stone he was two stone heavier and three inches taller than his opponent. It was a brutally one-sided affair, and it ended in an undignified argument in the corner at the end of the sixth round between Broadribb, who wanted Mills to continue, and the referee, who proposed – belatedly – stopping the fight.

Three consecutive knockouts in early 1947 restored Mills' confidence, but then in June he took another savage beating from the classy black American Lloyd Marshall, who put him down four times in five humiliating rounds. But once again the astonishingly resilient Mills regrouped and came back for more. He won and defended the European light-heavyweight title and beat heavyweights Stefan Olek and Ken Shaw, and the renewed run of form persuaded Solomons to try for a rematch with Lesnevich.

He succeeded, and 46,000 packed into White City in London on 26 July 1948 to watch Mills outbox the faded American. It was an uncharacteristically cautious performance, and the result was a fairly dull affair, but when it was over Mills was champion of the world.

Despite all that had happened, he still harboured heavyweight ambitions, and when he knocked out Johnny Ralph in front of a 30,000 crowd in Johannesburg, he qualified for a crack at Bruce Woodcock's British and Empire titles. Few gave him a realistic chance of reversing the result of their first fight, but 46,000 paid to watch him try. Predictably, it ended in painful and one-sided defeat, with a dejected and demoralized Mills being counted out on one knee in the fourteenth round.

Mills fought only once more, when Joey Maxim knocked him out in ten rounds and took his world title – knocking out three of his front teeth in the process. He retired to run his restaurant in Soho, and carved out a second career as an entertainer and radio personality. He also dabbled in management, and, guided by Solomons, became moderately successful as a promoter.

But, gradually, it began to unravel. The restaurant failed, and he reopened it as a nightclub instead. Money problems mounted, and he was forced to sell off the property he had bought during the good years to meet his debts. Business at the club was hurt by a newspaper exposé which revealed that – unknown to Mills – it was being used for prostitution, and when the Government abolished tax-free entertainment allowances for businessmen, the situation became ever more desperate.

Mills was suffering recurring headaches and bouts of depression, which were not helped by the way in which the stars who had formerly sought his company now shunned him. Finally it all became too much for him, and on 24 July 1965 he sat in his car in the yard behind his club and shot himself with a fairground rifle – or so the inquest decided. The full extent of his financial problems became known when his will was published, revealing that the man who had earned £100,000 in the ring was worth exactly £387 when he died.

Rumours persist that his death was murder, not suicide, and certainly there are aspects of the case which have never been satisfactorily explained. But even if it was suicide, the blame was not all his own: the fearful and accumulative punishment that he took in fifteen years in the ring, and the men who profited from it, must share the responsibility.

CAREER RECORD: 97 fights, 74 wins (52 inside schedule), 6 draws, 17 defeats.

Terry Allen (1924–1987)

THE only thing angelic about the teenage Terry Allen was his address. The Angel, Islington is now a trendy place to live, but when Allen – whose real name was Edward Govier – was growing up there it was a tough working-class area where street gangs ran wild and villains were heroes to the local youngsters.

Allen was the product of a broken home, and was reared by his blind grandmother. Given that background and environment, it is hardly surprising that he drifted easily into the world of petty crime and small-time thieving. He could always fight, despite his size, and had plenty of street battles before a sympathetic teacher encouraged the thirteen-year-old to join the Belle Isle boxing club and channel his aggression into a more legitimate form.

There was a long-standing tradition of boxing in Allen's family: his father had fought professionally as Johnny Coppin of Islington, and his uncle, Fred Govier, ran a gym in Grant Street.

Terry had served time in an approved school in Battersea, where he had been sent for six months after being caught on a modest smash-and-grab raid on a shop in Islington. He enjoyed boxing, and reached the final of the Boys' Club championships, but he relished his 'Dead End Kid' lifestyle as well, progressing from shop-lifting to running a small-scale protection racket.

By the time he was seventeen he was the acknowledged leader of his group of tearaways, and had a three-month spell in a young offenders' prison behind him. It seemed that he was doomed to the life of an habitual criminal, with short spells of freedom being followed by ever-longer jail sentences. But then a friendly local priest, Father Johnson from St Silas's, took an interest in him and, under the priest's influence, Allen began to spend more time in the gym and less on the streets. It was a reformation worthy of a Spencer Tracy/James Cagney film, and it lasted.

He found a job tarring the tops of street air-raid shelters; the Blitz was in progress, and there was no shortage of well-paid work. He drifted away from boxing, and had not even trained for over a year when a local promoter, knowing of his amateur record of 102 wins in 107 contests, offered him £6 for a professional engagement at

Caledonian Road Baths against a Scot, Joe Thomas of Dundee. Allen accepted, and won the six-rounder on points.

But before his new career could get properly under way, he was called up into the Navy. The discipline was irksome to a teenager who had grown up running wild, and he deserted within weeks. A change of identity became imperative, and he swapped ID cards with a newspaper boy he knew called Terry Allen. Thus Edward Govier vanished, and Terry Allen, professional fighter, was born.

He acquired a manager, Johnny Sharpe (who had beaten Ted 'Kid' Lewis on the Kid's pro debut), and was kept busy with regular bookings in London and Liverpool, where he was particularly popular. He stayed unbeaten in 16 fights, but eventually the law caught up with him and he was sent back to the Navy.

He was posted to Alexandria, where he was lucky enough to have a commanding officer who was keen on boxing. Allen – or Stoker Govier, as he was officially known – was happy to fight as an alternative to Service chores, and packed in 14 semi-pro bouts during his 18 months in Egypt.

Back in civilian life, Allen resumed his career under Johnny Sharpe in 1946. It was not an auspicious return: Alec Murphy, a tough little Scot who later died after fighting Emile Famechon, knocked him out in six rounds. But by the end of the year he was back on course with wins over Welsh champion Billy Davies and the Northern star Billy Hazelgrove. Soon after beating Hazelgrove, Allen was taken ill, and had not completely recovered when he foolishly agreed to meet the hard-punching Irishman Rinty Monaghan in March 1947.

Monaghan, soon to become world champion, hammered him to humiliating defeat in less than a round, flooring him four times before the referee rescued the Londoner. It was a shocking setback, but Allen put it behind him with a run of 15 wins in 16 fights, including a pair of victories over his Islington schoolmate Dickie O'Sullivan for the Southern Area title.

Monaghan was now the world champion, and met Allen in a non-title eight-rounder at Haringey on 7 February 1949. It was Allen's chance to reverse that one-round disaster, and he took it brilliantly. The champion was floored three times and decisively outpointed, and Allen was now a contender. Honoré Pratesi, a clever Frenchman, outpointed him two fights later, but then Allen outscored Norman Tennant in a final eliminator for the British title, which was also held by Monaghan, and the way was clear for a world title chance.

He had to travel to Belfast and brave the intimidatingly hostile atmosphere of the King's Hall on 30 September 1949. Allen made a great start, dropping Monaghan for nine in the second round, but could never repeat that success and had to settle for a fifteen-round draw. When Monaghan surprisingly retired a few months later, promoter Jack Solomons matched Allen with Pratesi for the vacant world and European titles, and on 25 April 1950 the one-time Dead End Kid became champion. It was a close-run thing, with Allen just getting the verdict on the strength of a good last round.

Next morning he was back at work on the greengrocer's stall he ran in Chapel Market, Islington; flyweights did not command big purses, even for world title fights, and Allen had opened the stall to help keep his wife and their two young children, Terry and Annette.

Allen was not allowed to enjoy his title for long. He was under pressure to defend against the leading contender, Dado Marino of Hawaii, who had already been outpointed in world title challenges by Monaghan and by Manuel Ortiz (for the bantamweight championship). It seemed a relatively safe defence, even though Allen had to travel to Honolulu for the fight, but Marino snatched a close verdict and ended Allen's short reign after just 98 days.

Two months after that, on 30 October 1950, the European title was lost as well, when the Belgian Jean Sneyers won a very unpopular decision at Nottingham. Wins over Jimmy Pearce and Henry Carpenter moved Allen quickly back into contention, and he won the vacant British title against the Scot Vic Herman in June 1951. A rematch with Marino in November meant another long trek to Honolulu, and an identical result, and when in quick succession he was outpointed by Maurice Sandeyron in a ten-rounder and by Teddy Gardner for the European and British titles, his future looked bleak.

But the irrepressible Allen bounced back yet again. Gardner relinquished the British title and, in October 1952, Allen regained it with a peculiar sixth-round win over Eric Marsden, who twisted his sciatic nerve after taking a blow to the ribs and could not continue.

He boxed only twice in 1953, and lost both fights. Gaetano Annaloro, a Tunisian bantamweight, beat him at Earl's Court and

Yoshio Shirai, who had taken the world title from Dado Marino, outpointed him in a dull world title bid in Tokyo. It was Allen's fourth unsuccessful challenge.

There was only one victory to come, and it was an undistinguished affair. Eric Marsden hit him low in the fifth round of a rematch for the British title, and Allen won his Lonsdale Belt outright on his hands and knees on the canvas as referee Ike Powell disqualified the Northener.

His career ended in scandal. On 23 March 1954 he faced the unbeaten young Welshman Dai Dower in a non-title fight, and, according to Allen's published memoirs, he took a dive. The plan – to which Dower was not party – was to set up a big-money rematch for the British title. Allen let the light-punching Welshman catch him on the chin with a right in the second round and went down to be counted out, crawling around on the canvas, while the fans booed and whistled.

Despite that dismal performance, he managed to land one last title fight, but when Nazzareno Giannelli outpointed him in Milan for the vacant European title, he quit. The modest ring earnings were long gone, and he took whatever jobs he could find. He was a lorry driver for a while, and in later years I used to see him in Bouverie Street on Saturday nights working as a casual van loader for the *News of the World*.

The publication of his memoirs did not endear him to the British boxing establishment, but Terry was such a likeable and cheerful man that he was soon forgiven. He became a prominent and active member of the London Ex-Boxers Association, and maintained his interest in the game until his death, from cancer, on 8 April 1987.

CAREER RECORD: 76 fights, 62 wins (18 inside schedule), 1 draw, 13 defeats.

Randolph Turpin (1928–1966)

RANDOLPH TURPIN'S life went into a tail-spin the night he won the middleweight championship of the world from Sugar Ray Robinson, and what happened to him after that makes the semi-literate, hard-of-hearing half-caste the most tragic figure in the history of British professional boxing. The business used him and abused him, bankrupted and rejected him, and in terms of ultimate responsibility there were many fingers other than Turpin's own on the trigger when he shot and killed himself on 17 May 1966.

He was potentially a great champion, yet he ruled the world for only 64 days and everything thereafter was an anti-climax with which he could not cope. It is hard at this distance in time to appreciate the impact that Turpin's win over Robinson had on the British people, not merely on boxing fans. It was 1951, rationing was still in force, and life in general was dull and grey. And then into this dreary world came the flamboyant, extravagant, unbelievably glamorous figure of Sugar Ray Robinson. He was already accepted as the greatest fighter in history, and he travelled with a retinue of camp followers like some medieval potentate.

He had that aura of invincibility that only the truly superlative champions possess, and his fight with Turpin dominated the nation's attention for weeks. Most saw the British champion in the role of 'straight man', there to make up the numbers to allow Robinson the chance to display his extraordinary talents to a new and appreciative audience. But when Turpin achieved the unthinkable by beating the unbeatable, it was as if everyone's life had been somehow brightened by his success.

The quiet man from Leamington Spa became, briefly, a symbol of hope, a reminder that however depressing life seemed there was always room for optimism. He was thrust into the role of national idol, but it was one he was singularly ill-equipped to fill. His hearing difficulty made him a withdrawn and reserved man, ill at ease with the money men, publicists and 'advisers' who took over his life and his finances.

Catastrophe was inevitable, but even with hindsight it is difficult to see how the poorly educated and unsophisticated Turpin could have organized his life differently. He was the product of a mixed marriage between Lionel Fitzherbert Turpin, an immigrant from British Guiana, and Beatrice Whitehouse, a local girl whose father, Thomas, had been a bare-knuckle fighter around Warwickshire. Lionel, the first black man to settle in Leamington, had been wounded and gassed on the Somme while serving with the King's Royal Rifles. He never fully recovered, and died three months after Randolph's birth on 7 June 1928. His wife worked as a cleaner to support the family, while her mother and an aunt helped care for the children.

Given his family background, there was probably nothing that Turpin could have done except become a fighter and accept the risks that went with the job. He was born into a boxing family and it was always assumed that he, too, would make his living in the ring. Brother Dick had broken the racial barrier which stained the sport for so long by becoming the first black man to win a British title (he took the middleweight title in 1948), and his other brother, Jackie, was a good-class featherweight who had a long career of well over 100 fights, spent mostly at eight-round and area championship level.

But while his brothers were good fighters, Randolph had the mark of greatness. He started boxing at nine, performing 'exhibitions' with Jackie on bills on which Dick was featured, and also appeared on local booths. Had the Leamington amateur club been fully aware of all this when the fourteen-year-old Turpin applied for membership, they may not have been too inclined to take him on, but they did and he became the most successful competitor in the club's history. His first title was the Midlands junior ABA flyweight title, and he followed that with three national junior titles.

He made history by winning junior and senior ABA welterweight titles in the same season – 1945 – and completed an ABA double at middleweight a year later, while serving as a cook in the Royal Navy. His 1945 title came just 23 days after his seventeenth birthday, making him the youngest ever ABA champion and, significantly, the first black ABA winner. But the highlight of his amateur career was a dramatic one-punch knockout of the fancied American Marine Harold Anspach at Wembley in an ABA v USA match, two days before Randolph's eighteenth birthday. Anspach was regarded as the pick of the American side, but Turpin flattened him with a single right hook inside 90 seconds. In all, he won 95 of his 100 amateur contests before joining his brothers in George Middleton's pro stable in September 1946.

Within a year he was beating good second-division middle-weights such as Jimmy Davis, Bert Sanders, Mark Hart and Jimmy Ingle, although he also had to get off the floor to outpoint a Frenchman with the quaint ring name of Jury VII, whom he always nominated as the hardest man he ever fought. His first two losses came in 1948, and brought with them an ominous hint of what was to come.

Turpin had made a disastrous marriage when he was eighteen, and at the time of his points loss to Albert Finch and his retirement against Jean Stock, was engaged in bitter divorce proceedings. In fact, he learned on the day of the Stock fight that his wife had been given custody of their son, Randolph Jr, and admitted that he had no heart for boxing that night. It was to become a familiar feature of Turpin's career; so many of his defeats were at a time of emotional upset, as though he was incapable of coping with more than one pressure at a time.

Albert Finch featured prominently in the story of the Turpin family. He had a three-fight series with Dick, from whom he took the British title in April 1950, and also met Randolph twice.

Throughout 1949 and 1950 Turpin continued to progess against quality opposition, and by mid-1950 his wins over Doug Miller, Pete Mead, Cyrille Delannoit and Gilbert Stock had long erased the memory of the two defeats. He won the British title from Finch in five rounds in October 1950, a particularly satisfying result for both the brothers, and five months later added the European title with a dynamic 48-second destruction of the Dutchman Luc van Dam. A month later he avenged the Jean Stock loss by stopping him in five rounds, an exact reversal of their first meeting, and further victories over Billy Brown, Jan de Bruin and Jackie Keough set him up for the challenge to Robinson.

Only the wildest optimists gave him any real chance of ending Robinson's fabulous reign when promoter Jack Solomons secured the match for Earl's Court on 10 July 1951. Robinson had lost only one of 133 fights, and seemed invincible. He was rounding off a hugely successful and lucrative European tour which had brought him to Paris, Zurich, Antwerp, Liège, Berlin and Turin for six fights between 21 May and 1 July. But Robinson had also indulged to the full his considerable appetite for the good life, and the Englishman made him pay for his lack of condition with a comprehensive points beating. The packed crowd of 18,000 sang Turpin home with 'For He's a Jolly Good Fellow', and the beaten champion had no complaints about referee Eugene Henderson's decision.

The cynics said that Robinson 'had left his legs in Paris', but that would be an unfair assessment of what Turpin had achieved. Robinson acknowledged that the challenger had been infinitely more difficult and awkward than expected, and the fact that Turpin was battling on level terms after nine rounds of the rematch indicates that he might well have won the title anyway, without the help of the various mesdemoiselles and frauleins who had made Robinson's European jaunt so pleasurable.

The week after becoming world champion, Turpin kept a promise to a friend by boxing on his booth in Kenilworth, doing 30 rounds in four days.

The return was made for New York 64 days later, with Turpin earning $207,075.99. It drew 61,370 spectators, an outdoor record for a non-heavyweight match, but the fight itself was a disappointment. Nothing much happened for nine rounds, with the referee Ruby Goldstein scoring them level at the end of the ninth, while the two judges – both American – had Robinson ahead by one and two rounds. But then in the tenth Robinson sustained a shocking cut over the left eye, and he knew he could not survive another round.

He feinted a jab, and as Turpin jerked his head back to avoid it Robinson stepped in with a smashing right to floor the champion for seven. Turpin was still groggy when he rose, and retreated to the ropes where he half-sat on the middle rope. Robinson opened up with a dazzling barrage of hooks and uppercuts, until finally Turpin's hands dropped and he bent over double, at which point Goldstein intervened. There were protests from the English camp, who argued that with only eight seconds left in the round Turpin should have been given the chance to recuperate between rounds, but Goldstein had acted properly: Turpin was defenceless, and even in eight seconds could have taken blows which might have had lasting effects.

Turpin was never quite the same again, although he picked up the British and Empire light-heavyweight titles by stopping Don Cockell and then moved back to middleweight to beat George Angelo for the Empire title in that division. In 1953 he had another chance to scale the heights. Robinson retired, and the European

Boxing Union recognized the winner of a match between Turpin and the Frenchman Charles Humez as being for the title. The Americans disagreed, and proclaimed a balding Hawaiian, Carl 'Bobo' Olson, as champion after his win over Paddy Young.

Turpin duly beat Humez in a dull fifteen-rounder, and went to New York to face Olson in the decider. It was a nightmare from the start. There were rows and upsets in the training camp, domestic problems, tax demands, and a scandal involving an American showgirl which resulted in Turpin being arrested for alleged assault. As if that were not enough, he was then cited by a Lancashire policeman as co-respondent in his divorce case.

Turpin fought like a man whose mind was elsewhere, and was floored twice on the way to a unanimous fifteen-round defeat. Even his mother told a journalist that her son had fought 'as if he didn't want to win'.

The erratic Turpin carried on for a further five years, but by now a pattern had been established of good wins followed by crushing defeats – three steps forward, four steps back. Tiberio Mitri annihilated him in 65 seconds for the European title, but Turpin bounced back to regain the British light-heavyweight title from Alex Buxton. There was talk of a world title bid against Archie Moore, but then a crude Canadian slugger called Gordon Wallace removed that hope with a fourth-round knockout of the former champion.

But still Turpin fought on, and when he battered Buxton to fifth-round defeat in defence of the British title, the world championship hopes flickered again. Lainson Wood, writing in the *Daily Telegraph*, reported that, 'it was the old, fierce-hitting Turpin of his middleweight championship days, and he has not given a better exhibition in the last six or seven years.' The win over Buxton gave Turpin outright ownership of the Lonsdale Belt, which was the last of the original gold trophies still in competition.

He stayed unbeaten in his next seven fights, but when Yolande Pompey, a heavy-fisted West Indian, knocked him out in two rounds at Birmingham on 9 September 1958, he had to accept that this time there could be no comeback.

By now, only seven short years since he had been world champion, the money was gone. There had been a series of disastrous investments, including the purchase of the castle in Wales where he used to train. Driven by debts, he was reduced to joining the professional wrestling circus and trading on his lost glories for £25 a time.

He fought, if such is the word, twice more in unlicensed shows, but no matter what he did he could not escape the mass of debts which engulfed him. Finally, on 17 May 1966, he shot himself in the upstairs room of the transport café that his second wife Gwen ran in Leamington. He was thirty-eight, fifteen years and a lifetime away from the night when he had shocked the world at Earl's Court.

He left his own epitaph, a sensitive, bitter and angry poem which concluded:

> So we'll leave this game, which was hard and cruel
> And down at the show, on a ringside stool
> We'll watch the next man – just one more fool.

CAREER RECORD: 73 fights, 64 wins (43 inside schedule), 1 draw, 8 defeats.

Terry Downes (born 1936)

THE GREAT weakness of the British Honours system is that it so often rewards the wrong people. A captain of industry, having grown rich by underpaying his workers and fiddling his taxes, can make a whopping donation to Party funds and, surprise surprise, find himself knighted, while someone else who devotes twenty years to raising over a million pounds for his favourite charity goes unrecognized. Or maybe just the thought of *Sir* Terry Downes, former world middleweight champion and fund-raiser extraordinaire, makes the faceless figures who compile these lists choke on their cucumber sandwiches?

Downes has always been loud, brash, and occasionally vulgar, but the public are invariably ready to forgive him, firstly because he was such a prodigiously brave and entertaining fighter and latterly because, like that other unconventional folk hero Bob Geldof, while others wring their hands and twitter about the world's injustices Downes actually goes out and does something about it. In the 25 years since he quit the ring he has worked tirelessly for charity, most notably in raising funds to buy 'Sunshine Coaches' for handicapped children.

He travels up and down Britain to attend any function where there is a chance to rattle a collection box. His own efforts have raised, at last count, over a million pounds, and a lot of children have had their lives enhanced by the rough diamond from Paddington. Downes is not fussy where the cash comes from; he has rubbed shoulders for the cause with businessman, entertainers, politicians, club owners, gangsters and bishops alike, and he shows them all the same face. But then, that is an essential part of his appeal. He is a real man of the people, uncomplicated, straightforward, and totally honest with himself and everyone else.

Those were the qualities he brought into the ring from the day he started boxing in the London Schools championships for St Augustine's in Paddington, and then for the Pembroke Club in North Kensington, in whose colours he reached the ABA junior finals. But it was a family catastrophe which put Downes firmly on the road to the world title. His sister Sylvie, a dancer with the

Ringling Circus in America, lost an arm in a coach accident in Baltimore and the family went over there *en masse* to be with her.

Terry joined the Baltimore YMCA and won the State novice championships, but his trainer withdrew him from the senior event because, at sixteen, he considered him too young to compete with grown men. Instead, Downes continued to gather experience in various representative matches, and it was one of these, against the US Marines, which proved a turning point in his life. He liked what he saw and heard of the Marine life, and enlisted at seventeen. It can't have been easy for an English teenager to survive the harshest training of any American Army unit – in fact, two members of his draft killed themselves during basic training – but the Marines soon learned that they breed them just as tough in Paddington as in Philadelphia.

Downes won Marine and Inter-Services titles during his three years in the Corps, and was even short-listed for the Olympic trials in 1956 before the authorities realized that, as a British subject, he was ineligible to represent America. What made it even more galling for Downes was that he had beaten three of the four final trialists, including the eventual winner, Pearce Lane.

When he had completed his Service time Downes came home for a holiday, prior to launching a pro career in the States, and on the recommendation of Tim Riley, then editor of *Boxing News*, he joined the Fisher Catholic Club in Bermondsey to keep in trim. (Downes was a Protestant, but never one to worry about details.) He stopped Sugar Bill Robinson, later to win an ABA title and box in the Olympics, but then lost his second contest with a cut forehead. The club wanted him to enter the ABA championships, but Downes had had enough of amateur boxing.

He went to see Jack Solomons, the country's major promoter, who advised him that his future lay in Britain rather than America, where he would be just another struggling prelim fighter. Over here, Solomons argued, his swashbuckling style and fast-talking, wise-cracking personality had already established him as a star in the making, with great potential as a crowd-puller. Downes was convinced, and on Solomons' recommendation took on Jarvis Astaire as his manager. Solomons and Astaire would, ironically, later become bitter rivals.

Downes got off to a flying start, but the 'Paddington Express', as he was inevitably billed, was derailed in his third fight by an obscure Nigerian journeyman called Dick Tiger, who floored and stopped him in the compact, atmospheric Shoreditch Town Hall in May 1957. Tiger's record was spotted with losses – five in his eleven British appearances – and there was not a hint that he would blossom into one of the greatest African fighters of all, winning world titles at middleweight and light-heavyweight. Downes was paid £125, Tiger £75 – and five years later they were both world champions.

Downes soon put the loss behind him, coming back with a win three weeks later, and over the next twelve months he worked his way steadily up the rankings. There were a couple of minor setbacks: the cagey veteran Les Allen outpointed him and Freddie Cross stopped him on a cut. But when Downes sent British champion Pat McAteer into retirement by trouncing him in a non-title eight-rounder in June 1958, he had arrived in the big-time.

He stopped Phil Edwards, a handsome, neat-boxing Welshman, to take the title which McAteer had vacated, but then stepped out of his class and took a painful beating from the world-ranked American Spider Webb. Webb was one of a dozen classy middleweights of that generation who would certainly have lifted one of today's devalued and diluted championships. He had beaten Tiger, Holly Mims, Rory Calhoun, Pat McAteer, Randy Sandy, and a host of other rated men. It was a disastrous match for Downes, but even though he was stopped in the eighth the courage he showed in defeat enhanced his image.

It was the start of a bad spell for the popular Londoner. He lost his next fight, to Michel Diouf on a cut, and in September 1959 lost his British title in farcical circumstances to the lanky Scottish southpaw John McCormack, who was floored ten times, nine of them from body punches, before referee Ike Powell disqualified Downes in the eighth. McCormack was so embarrassed that he did not even take his Lonsdale Belt home. Forty-nine days later, Downes had his Belt back; this time, he survived a wicked split on his nose and a closed left eye to drop the Scot five times and stop him in the eighth.

The bad times were over, and Downes scored five straight wins in 1960 to earn a New Year title shot against Paul Pender, the Boston ex-fireman who had ended Sugar Ray Robinson's reign. Two of the wins were particularly significant: beating Phil Edwards again, this time in twelve rounds, gave him the Lonsdale Belt outright, while

Top: *Alan Minter (right) erased any doubts about his supremacy over Vito Antuofermo with this decisive eighth-round stoppage in their rematch*

Above: *Maurice Hope's jab falls short here against Rocky Mattioli, but the elegant Antiguan rarely wasted a punch*

Right: *This kind of brawling almost cost Terry Marsh his IBF light-welterweight title against Akio Kameda, when a clash of heads left him with a bad cut*

Below: *Cornelius Boza-Edwards goes to war with Bazooka Limon in the style which made him an American TV favourite*

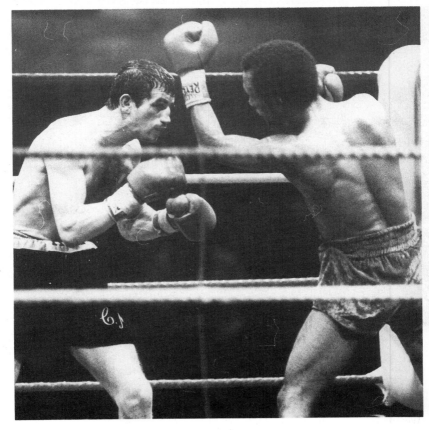

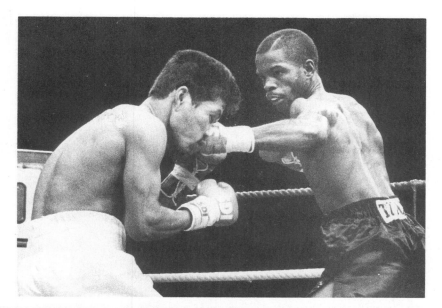

Left: *Charlie Magri (left) on the way to victory over Eloncio Mercedes*

Top: *Duke McKenzie spears Rolando Bohol with a perfect left jab as he takes the Filipino's IBF flyweight title at Wembley*

Above: *No, Dennis Andries is not about to kick Tony Sibson in the head – he's just tripped over him in their world light-heavyweight title fight in 1986*

Top: *Dave McAuley bridges a 40-year gap by bringing the world flyweight title back to Ireland – or at least the IBF version of the championship*

Above: *That winning look – it would have taken more than Patrick Lumumba could offer to stop Glenn McCrory becoming cruiserweight champion in front of his home-town fans*

his ten-round points defeat of the American veteran Joey Giardello was, with hindsight, one of the best results of his career.

Giardello had been a contender for the most part of a decade, and was regarded as one of the finest craftsmen in the game. Yet Downes, supposedly an unsophisticated brawler, outjabbed him in round after round to win at a canter. Giardello went on to take the world title from Dick Tiger a couple of years later.

Downes went to Boston to face Pender on 14 January 1960, but nothing went right for him. He was harassed before the fight with writs relating to agreements he had allegedly made with two American managers before opting instead for a career in Britain, and when Pender floored him with a sneak right in the first round it was clear that this was not going to be Terry's night. He was cut over the eye in the second, and his nose split open in the third. His corner could not stop the bleeding, and the referee finally called a halt in the seventh. To round off a dismal venture, Downes' £6000 purse was frozen pending settlement of the legal action.

Pender accepted a £35,000 offer from Harry Levene to give Downes another chance at Wembley on 11 July, and this time it was the American who had the pre-fight problems. He came down with a heavy cold which affected his breathing, but with a return clause written into the contract he felt confident enough to go ahead with the defence. It was a disappointing affair, with few highlights until Pender finally opened up in the ninth when it looked as though he was at last going to show why he was world champion – but instead his corner called over referee Ike Powell and retired their man.

Downes was not able to enjoy his new status for long. The third fight took place on 7 April 1962 in Boston, and Pender won a narrow decision in a mauling and uninspired fifteen rounds. Downes marked time for the rest of the year with three solid wins over American opposition, including the forty-one-year-old Sugar Ray Robinson, but all attempts to land another middleweight title chance came to nothing. By this time the betting shops Downes had opened along with Astaire's managerial partner Sam Burns were flourishing, and it might have been a good time for him to retire.

But the old hunger was still there, and with the middleweight door seemingly shut he put on a few extra pounds and started a second career as a light-heavy. A few wins over nondescript Americans at least established some credibility in the heavier division, and guaranteed a good house when Willie Pastrano came to Manchester to defend his 12 st 7 lb title against him in November 1964. Pastrano was a regular visitor to Britain, where the fans had always appreciated his text-book boxing more than their American counterparts.

But he was off form against Downes, and boxed sluggishly as the challenger piled up a points lead. Coming out for the eleventh Downes seemed well on his way to the title, but then Pastrano turned the fight around with a desperation rally. Two knockdowns later, the fight was over – and so was Downes' colourful career. He claimed that referee Andy Smythe had acted hastily, and that he was fully aware of what he was doing when he dropped for the second count, and he may well have been right.

But at least it was defeat with glory, and after such a blood-and-thunder career his public would have settled for no less. In retirement, he has prospered. He eventually sold out his betting shops, and shrewd investment of the proceeds has ensured that he, unlike so many other former champions, will never need a benefit night. He has been happily married to Barbara for over thirty years, and their children (three sons and a daughter) were educated at public school.

Downes has never been able to tear himself away from the sport. After dabbling in management, he now contents himself with a ringside seat at small halls and championship bills alike, where his vivid, noisy and enthusiastic presence is a constant reminder of the colour and excitement that he generated in the days when he was on top of the world.

CAREER RECORD: 44 fights, 35 wins (28 inside schedule), 9 defeats.

John Caldwell (born 1938)

JOHN CALDWELL had gunfighter's eyes: ice-blue, cold and expressionless. They earned him the not particularly tasteful nickname of the 'Cold-eyed Killer', and his ring performances justified the hype.

He was a destructive flyweight, good enough to have been world champion in the division. But he had the misfortune to reach the top as a bantamweight when the rival claimant was Eder Jofre, one of the division's outstanding champions. Had the brilliant Brazilian not been his contemporary, the Belfast man's tenure of his share of the world title would have been much longer and his place in ring history more secure.

Caldwell, who was born on 7 May 1938, began boxing at ten and was an instant success, winning Schoolboy, Juvenile and Youth titles. As a member of the Immaculata Club, he lifted the Ulster and Irish junior and senior titles in the same season, 1955–6, a four-timer which had never been achieved before, and won for Ireland in America and Canada.

Caldwell went to the 1956 Olympic Games with perhaps the finest international side Ireland has ever sent into action. (The Northern Irish are dual nationals, and thus have the choice of competing for either Ireland or Britain in the Olympics. Caldwell, like his fellow townsman Freddie Gilroy, opted to represent Ireland, although both won British titles as professionals.)

The Melbourne Games were Ireland's best ever Olympics. Welterweight Freddie Tiedt reached the final against Nicola Linca of Romania, but lost a decision which even after the excesses of Seoul still ranks with the worst the tournament has produced. Lightweight Tony Byrne, Caldwell, and bantamweight Freddie Gilroy (Caldwell's room-mate and future professional opponent) earned bronze medals, while on the track Ronnie Delaney took the only gold medal the country has ever won when he surged to victory in a thrilling 1500 metres final.

Caldwell turned professional in February 1958 under his former amateur trainer Jack McCusker, after repeating his Irish title success in 1957 and losing a bad decision in the Prague European championships. He had won a remarkable 243 out of 250 contests, including 22 in the Irish singlet.

The relationship with McCusker soon became strained, and Caldwell moved to Glasgow where he came under the guidance of a bookmaker and occasional promoter, Sammy Docherty. Docherty wanted to take over his management, but when McCusker refused to release him there was a suggestion that Caldwell might emigrate to America and continue his career there. But an arrangement was eventually reached with McCusker, and Docherty took over, with Joe Aitchison as trainer.

John had served his apprenticeship as a plumber in Belfast, but seemed destined for a much more exciting future than sinks and drains could offer as he quickly made his mark in championship class. British Empire champion Dennis Adams of South Africa was brilliantly outscored in a non-title eight-rounder in only the Irishman's fifth fight, and throughout 1958 and 1959 he built up an unbeaten run of 14, mainly over Continental opposition.

The former European champion Young Martin of Spain, who had fought for the world title and had destroyed the clever little Welshman Dai Dower, was imported to London in February 1960 as supposedly the acid test of the Irishman's worth, but was floored seven times on the way to a third-round knockout defeat.

Only a fortnight later Caldwell was at Wembley to face the Finn who had taken Martin's European title, Risto Luukkonen. But it was only a ten-rounder; the Finn had no intention of risking his championship, a decision which proved wise as Caldwell coasted to an easy points win. Only three of his 17 wins so far had been in Belfast, but Caldwell made it up to his home-town fans by taking the British title from Frankie Jones of Scotland with a clinically executed third-round knockout at the King's Hall on 8 October 1960. He was on the way to a world title – but not the one he anticipated.

It was increasingly difficult for him to maintain the flyweight limit, and a move into the bantamweight division looked inevitable. His old team-mate, Freddie Gilroy, was European and British champion at the weight, and was regularly filling the King's Hall. A meeting between the friendly rivals was an intriguing possibility, but then the position at world level in the division changed suddenly. The champion, a destructive Mexican called Jose Becerra, quit the ring in despair after fatally injuring an opponent for the second time in his career.

Wembley promoter Jack Solomons moved quickly to fill at least one half of the vacant world title, pairing Gilroy with Alphonse Halimi, a hard, square-cut, French-Algerian Jew from whom Becerra had taken the world title in 1959. Halimi won a bitterly disputed decision over the Belfast southpaw at Wembley on 25 October 1960 – I can still recall the shattering disappointment I felt when, as a thirteen-year-old in boarding school, I listened to the fight on a smuggled transistor radio in the dormitory. Gilroy was my hero, and his photo (autographed!) jostled for space with Howard Winstone and Cassius Clay on the inside flap of my desk in the study hall.

The National Boxing Association, forerunner of the modern World Boxing Association, recognized the dazzling Brazilian Eder Jofre as their champion after he had knocked out Eloy Sanchez in six rounds a month after the Halimi–Gilroy encounter. Solomons, who had presumably taken promotional options on Halimi, then had a brainwave: why not match the Algerian with Caldwell? After all, there was the 'national revenge' factor to help sell the fight – not that Caldwell needed any persuasion when the proposition was put to him.

Solomons' judgement, as usual, proved impeccable. Caldwell boxed superbly to score a runaway points win, and even abandoned his boxing in the fifteenth and final round to have a toe-to-toe trade with the bleeding and desperate champion. For an awful moment it seemed that the Irishman was going to throw away the title for the sake of a show of reckless bravado, but then he floored Halimi for five in the dying seconds of the round to clinch the championship. It was the peak of Caldwell's career, although it held the promise of so much more and better to come.

Backstage, the pair entered the shower-room at the same time, but Halimi stepped aside and said to Caldwell: 'You are the champion now – you go first.' *Toujours la politesse.*

There was a rematch – there invariably was in those days – but this time Caldwell won even more decisively in a dull and listless fifteen-rounder. Jofre, meanwhile, had consolidated his position with defences against Piero Rollo and Ramon Arias, and was beginning to earn recognition as an outstanding champion. He was, by boxing's standards, an eccentric: a vegetarian who was exceptionally well read, articulate and intelligent far above the norm for professional sport. (When he finally retired from the ring after winning the featherweight title a couple of times, he entered politics, where he has had a second successful career.)

Solomons promoted the unification match in the Ibirapeura Stadium in Sao Paulo on 18 January 1962, and drew a capacity crowd of around 18,000. The Brazilian had an intimidating record of 40 wins and 3 draws in 43 fights, 30 of them won by the short route, and he swept the Irishman aside with contemptuous ease. Caldwell never had a chance, and his cause was not aided by the weight problems which brought him in a pound overweight at the first attempt. He had to run around the stadium, fully dressed, for twenty minutes before trying again. This time he was half a pound over the limit, and a further run, followed by strenuous skipping, was needed before he finally made the weight.

He was as good as beaten before he got in the ring, having been jostled and abused by the fans as he made his way through the crowd. Jofre floored him in the fifth, and gave him a sustained beating thereafter. Caldwell fought with courage and skill, but simply did not have the tools for the job and was put down again before the one-sided affair was belatedly halted by referee Willie Pep, the former featherweight champion, with 15 seconds left in the tenth.

There was a return bout clause in the contract, but Jofre was so obviously the better man than there was no point in attempting to enforce it. Instead, Caldwell lowered his sights to domestic level, and a Belfast showdown with Freddie Gilroy. The ubiquitous Solomons was again involved, as co-promoter with George Connell, when the pair met at the King's Hall on 20 October.

Their battle surpassed all expectations – nine rounds of pulsating, punch-for-punch action with never a moment's let-up. Caldwell was floored in the opening seconds, but roared back to take the initiative away from Gilroy in the second. And so it went on, for round after round. Gilroy was cut in the sixth, and then in the eighth a couple of head clashes split open cuts on both Caldwell's eyebrows.

Southpaw Gilroy was a shade in front when Danny Holland, the famous cuts man in Caldwell's corner, indicated to referee Andy Smythe that he could do nothing with the wounds and retired his man at the end of the ninth. This time everybody wanted to see a return, but it was not to be. Gilroy retired without boxing again, after a dispute with the Board of Control, while Caldwell was stopped again with a cut in his next fight, against Michel Atlan of

France in February 1963, and stayed inactive for the rest of the year. It was more than twenty years before the King's Hall, one of the world's great fight arenas, was used again for boxing, when Barney Eastwood and Barry McGuigan revived the game in Ireland.

Caldwell came back to win the British bantamweight title against George Bowes in the ABC cinema in Belfast, but lost it on his first defence to Alan Rudkin. Rows with his manager, and growing disenchantment with the business in general, sapped what little enthusiasm he had left for boxing and he quit after Monty Laud, a youngster with only a handful of fights behind him, outpointed him in Brighton.

As with so many ex-fighters, life has not been kind to Caldwell in the years since retirement. His money soon vanished, and for a while he worked as a taxi driver in Belfast. He emigrated to Canada, but that did not work out either and, his marriage broken, he returned home. In 1984, when *Boxing News* held a banquet to mark its 75th birthday, one former world champion from each of the four home countries was invited to sit at the top table. Caldwell was Ireland's representative, and he clearly relished the opportunity to be at centre-stage again.

Boxing soon forgets its heroes, and it had been many years since Caldwell had been acknowledged by the sport in which he was once, however briefly, supreme.

CAREER RECORD: 35 fights, 29 wins (14 inside schedule), 1 draw, 5 defeats.

Walter McGowan (born 1942)

WHO WAS the only British boxer never to have lost a single round in two world title fights against the same man – and yet been beaten in both of them? The answer is Scottish flyweight Walter McGowan, and the opponent was a strong but limited Thai, Chartchai Chionoi, who was widely outboxed each time he met the dazzling little Scot, but stopped him twice on cuts.

Had it not been for his tender skin, McGowan would undoubtedly have established himself as one of Britain's best and longest-reigning world champions. Instead, he held the flyweight title for only six months in 1966, and that, in terms of the talent he had in such glorious abundance, was a cruel injustice.

McGowan was born into the game. His father Thomas had fought professionally under the ring name Joe Gans, after the turn of the century lightweight champion, and he needed to be a hard and busy performer to provide for a family of ten children. Walter, the second youngest of five sons and five daughters, made his first ring appearance at nine and had won three titles before his sixteenth birthday.

His fleet-footed, fast-jabbing style was ideally suited to the three-round sprint course of amateur boxing, and in 124 contests with the Royal Albert Club, Larkhall, he lost only twice. McGowan won the 1961 ABA flyweight title and was unbeaten in nine internationals for Scotland. Two of those amateur wins were over Alan Rudkin, the Liverpudlian with whom he would later share a memorable professional rivalry.

The Scots wanted him to box in the Belgrade European championships in 1961, but he declined. Instead he turned pro, with his father as manager, at a time when the flyweight division in Britain was at its weakest for years. He was working as a trainee mechanic in a garage in his home town of Burnbank, having declined an apprenticeship as a jockey, and no doubt the extra money to be earned from the ring was a factor in his decision to bypass the European championships.

McGowan was in top class from the start: in only his third fight he lost a tight decision to the reigning British champion, Jackie

Brown of Edinburgh. His early victims included Danny Lee, one of the only two men to beat him as an amateur, and by the time he had completed his first year in the business he was recognized as the leading contender for the British title. He got his chance on 2 May 1963, after the Board of Control had bent their rules to allow him to box for a title before his twenty-first birthday.

Brown did not surrender easily, and McGowan (who was seconded by former British flyweight champion Frankie Jones) had to wait until the twelfth round before knocking him out. The crowd at Paisley Ice Rink knew they were seeing something special, and the winner – the youngest British champion to be crowned since the war – was carried shoulder-high to his dressing room. Two fights later, still a month away from his twenty-first birthday and in only his twelfth fight, McGowan became a double champion by stopping a Fijian, Kid Solomon, in nine rounds for the vacant Empire title.

The European champion was Salvatore Burruni, a Sardinian veteran of almost a hundred fights, and McGowan was matched with him for the title in Rome on 24 April 1964. It is a measure of the Scot's precocious talent that he picked the European bantamweight champion Risto Luukkonen of Finland as his warm-up opponent, and won a tough ten-round verdict over the Helsinki customs officer at Paisley a month before meeting Burruni. It was McGowan's severest test so far, and it hinted that Burruni might well be a little too knowledgeable for him.

So it proved: after fifteen brisk rounds, the Sardinian – a teetotaller who kept a bar in his home town, Alghero – had retained his title by a close but fair margin. Burruni had not got off lightly, though. He was cut over both eyes, under the right eye and on the bridge of the nose, and McGowan had proved that he could compete with the best in the world.

London promoter Jack Solomons, who was heavily involved in McGowan's career, began thinking in terms of a bantamweight campaign for the Scot, and after a couple of minor victories at the new weight McGowan made his London debut at the Albert Hall against Felix Brami, a Tunisian Jew who was ranked number eight in the world bantamweight ratings. McGowan's performance was dazzling; he drew rave reviews from the London writers, and when he shone again on a live TV broadcast from Rome, beating Benny Lee of Ghana, Solomons was convinced that he had made the right move. The win over Lee was a supporting match on a show headlined by Burruni's world title win over Pone Kingpetch of Thailand.

Solomons decided that McGowan was ready for the best, and on 3 May 1965 signed contracts with him for a bantamweight title challenge against the brilliant Brazilian Eder Jofre at Wembley on 21 September. But then, in a moment of lunacy, McGowan was matched at Wembley with the lethal Mexican Joe Medel.

Medel faced world champions Joe Becerra, Eder Jofre, Fighting Harada, Chucho Castillo, Efren Torres, Lionel Rose and Ruben Olivares, and only narrowly missed becoming champion himself. He was a man to avoid, not to take on in a warm-up match, and he was far too strong for the Scot. McGowan was on the floor in the first, and although he recovered to box superbly for the next four rounds, Medel had the punch to cancel out any size of points lead. In the sixth, McGowan went down again and was stopped, protesting, moments later.

Ronnie Jones, a clever black American, stopped him again – also in six rounds – next time out, and the world title contract was torn up. Instead, he lowered his sights and aimed for the European title, then held by a moderate Italian, Tommaso Galli. They fought in Rome on 3 December, and the drawn verdict rendered by Belgian referee Jean Deswerts still rankles as one of the worst suffered by a British challenger abroad.

With his bantamweight aspirations thwarted, McGowan switched back to the flyweights, and Solomons managed to persuade Burruni to risk his title at Wembley on 14 June 1966. The championship had split by this time – Burruni was, in fact, the last man to hold the undisputed world title, until the WBA stripped him of their half of it in November 1965. Solomons paid dearly for the privilege, losing over £12,000 on the show, but at least he had the winner as McGowan, ignoring a shocking cut over the right eye and another on the bridge of his nose, danced his way to the championship with an unforgettable display.

There were no big paydays on the immediate horizon, so McGowan once again tried his luck as a bantamweight. Alan Rudkin, whom he had beaten twice in ABA quarter-finals, held the British and Empire titles and was an attractive option. The Liverpudlian was one of the best British fighters never to win a world title, and was unlucky in two of his three challenges. He travelled to Tokyo to hold Fighting Harada to a close verdict in the first, lost a split decision to Lionel Rose in Australia in the second, and was knocked out by Ruben Olivares, the heaviest hitter in the division's history, on his third attempt.

He and McGowan renewed their rivalry at Wembley on 6 September 1966, and the fight surpassed all expectations. McGowan got the verdict after fifteen magnificent, sprint-paced rounds, but it was close enough to warrant a rematch. In the meantime, though, McGowan accepted a £10,000 offer to make the long trip to Bangkok and defend against a fairly obscure Thai, Chartchai Chionoi, who was not even champion of his own country.

They fought on 30 December, in the presence of Thailand's King and Queen, and Chionoi ruined the Scot's Hogmanay by stopping him in nine rounds, after McGowan had suffered a four-inch gash on his nose. It was a heart-breaking way to lose a world title, especially as McGowan had been in command of the exchanges all the way.

While Solomons worked to secure a rematch, McGowan kept busy with three points wins, including one against Osamu Miyashita, who was one of the few Japanese to box in a British ring. The Chionoi fight took place at Wembley on 19 September 1967, and it was a bad night for both McGowan and Solomons, who once more lost heavily and never again promoted a show there. McGowan won every one of the six completed rounds, but had boxed from the fifth with a dreadful cut over the left eye. He knew that he could not possibly survive another ten rounds, and threw everything at the Thai in a blistering, brilliant assault.

Chionoi was hammered around the ring, and the relentless onslaught continued throughout the sixth as McGowan, fighting with reckless and desperate courage, tried to salvage the fight. But he did not punch quite hard enough to worry the square-cut, sturdy champion, and at the end of the sixth referee Ike Powell, handling his 1170th bout, told the Scottish corner that he could allow only one more round.

But he could not even give him that much time: a minute into the seventh, with McGowan's face a sickening mask of blood, he led the brave challenger back to his corner in defeat. McGowan had not taken a worthwhile punch, and had won every round, but his world title days were history.

Alan Rudkin reclaimed the bantamweight titles from him on

another wafer-thin verdict at Manchester (Rudkin told me once that he thought he had won the fight he lost, and lost the one he won!), and after that McGowan's interest in the game waned. He stayed unbeaten in six fights against Continental opposition, but when a promised European bantamweight title fight with Italy's Franco Zurlo fell through, he suddenly announced his retirement early in 1970.

There were no comebacks. He went into the licensed trade, and now runs the 'Walter McGowan Bar and Grill' in Carluke, Lanarkshire – the only one of Scotland's world flyweight champions to remain firmly, and happily, on the proprietor's side of the bar counter.

CAREER RECORD: 40 fights, 32 wins (14 inside schedule), 1 draw, 7 defeats.

Howard Winstone (born 1939)

SOMETIMES great fighters are doomed to spend their peak years like theatrical understudies, waiting for the summons to centre-stage which can come only when the star drops out. So it was with Howard Winstone from Merthyr Tydfil, a featherweight who possessed the most immaculate ring skills I have ever seen but who had the misfortune to be a contemporary of one of the division's legendary champions, Vicente Saldivar.

In any other era Winstone would have ruled the world. It is one of history's injustices that when he was finally able to call himself 'world champion' he held only a fragment of the title, which he had won too late in his career to stamp his mark as indelibly on the history of world boxing as he did on the annals of the game in this country.

Winstone refined the craft of boxing to its purest degree. He was a consummate ring artist, and if world titles in his day had been decided over the modern distance of twelve rounds instead of the traditional fifteen, he would have beaten Saldivar in two of their three meetings. Each time, it was the last three rounds that did for Howard, as the Mexican southpaw, a man of phenomenal, almost freakish stamina, kept coming at him until, finally, the Welshman wilted.

And yet it was surprising that Winstone was a boxer at all. When he was seventeen he had trapped his right hand in a machine at the toy factory where he worked, and lost the tips of three fingers. The handicap was severe enough to secure his discharge from National Service after a couple of weeks, when the authorities realized that a soldier who could not hold a rifle would not be a lot of use in the infantry. But his boxing was only slightly affected, although had the injury been to that fabulous left hand his effectiveness would have been greatly impaired.

There was no tradition of boxing on either side of Winstone's family, and in fact he took no significant interest in the sport until his father bought him a set of gloves when he was ten. Like all the boys in Merthyr, of course, he knew all about the achievements of the town's best-known sports figure, Eddie Thomas, the former

European and British welterweight champion. He even ran home one evening to tell his father how Thomas had bought a paper from the stall where Howard sometimes helped out, and had told him to keep the change from the shilling with which he paid.

When Winstone eventually decided to try amateur boxing, he joined the same club, Dowlais ABC, with which Thomas had won his ABA title in 1946, and worked with the same trainer, Ephraim Hamer. By the time he was fifteen he had collected three Welsh and one British Schools titles, and in 1958 he completed the double of ABA and Empire Games championships at bantamweight. The Empire gold medal was particularly pleasing for him, since the Games were held in Cardiff that year. In all, Winstone lost only two of his 82 amateur contests, and the last defeat came when he was still only fourteen.

Had his financial circumstances been better he might have been persuaded to stay on and try for an Olympic medal in 1960 – and who, over three rounds, could ever have outboxed Winstone? But he had a family to keep; he had married Benita when he was seventeen and she sixteen, and they already had two sons, Wayne and Roy. It was time to start turning his skills into hard cash, and his choice of manager was easy.

If ever a boxer–manager 'marriage' was made in heaven, it was that between Winstone and Eddie Thomas. The older man had been retired for less than a decade, so was still young enough to identify with his charge. Like Winstone, he had always favoured science over slugging, and Howard was his ideal pupil – just as, a boxing generation later, was Ken Buchanan.

Under Thomas' guidance, Winstone was soon high in the British featherweight rankings. He won all ten fights in his first year, 1959, and was unbeaten in 13 in 1960. They were not all walkovers, though: fellow Welshman Gordon Blakey gave him a cauliflowered left ear in his fifteenth fight, and Billy Calvert, a bow-legged scrapper from Sheffield, inflicted the first knockdown of his career at Aberdare in 1959.

In January 1961 he outpointed the Empire champion Floyd Robertson so easily in a non-title match that Robertson could not be persuaded to face him again for the title, and instead, on 2 May, Winstone made his bid for the British title. The champion was Londoner Terry Spinks, who had won the 1956 Olympic gold medal at flyweight. Their clash at Wembley Pool was, inevitably, billed as the 'Battle of the Golden Boys', and the purse – then a record for the division of £12, 055 – justified the description. But the fight was not the anticipated classic: Winstone boxed superbly and dominated the champion so thoroughly that the battered, exhausted Englishman reeled back to his corner at the end of the tenth after taking a sustained pounding to the body, and told his seconds, 'I'm finished – I can't go on.'

Stoppages of Derry Treanor and Harry Carroll gave Winstone outright ownership of a Lonsdale Belt in the span of 393 days – the first Welshman to win one since before the First World War. The win over Carroll came on Benita's birthday, eight months after she had presented him with twin daughters, Benita and Faye (named for Jack Solomons' wife).

By now the Welshman, unbeaten in 34 fights, was the leading contender for the European title – but then, inexplicably, it all went wrong. Leroy Jeffrey, a twenty-five-year-old black American from Saginaw, floored him three times and stopped him in the second round at the Queen's Hall, Leeds. It was a bad setback. Jeffrey was a competent but hardly world-class performer; in fact, he lost to Billy Calvert three weeks later, and so far as I know never boxed again.

Thomas took Winstone back over old ground, defending the British title three more times to earn a second Belt in 313 days and, in July 1963, winning the European title from Alberto Serti of Italy. After the bad experience with Jeffrey, there was no rush to challenge for the world title, which was then in the keeping of the fierce-hitting Cuban Sugar Ramos. Instead, Winstone kept busy with a string of fine performances whose quality proved that the Jeffrey result had been merely an aberration.

He lost only once, on a shockingly bad verdict to the Californian Don Johnson in January 1964. Johnson appeared to have won only the last of the ten rounds, and referee Jack Hart's verdict was so controversial that he was invited to explain his scoring to the Board of Control. When Winstone met Johnson again, in front of 4000 Welshmen at Carmarthen Market Hall 15 months later, he won at a canter.

There was a nasty moment against the Nigerian Rafiu King, who floored him for eight but lost on points, but otherwise the 1964–5 period was one of unbroken triumphs. He even drew a crowd of 15,000 in Rome to watch him retain his European title – against a

Frenchman. Winstone's skills transcended national barriers, and the Continentals could appreciate him as much as his home crowd.

In September 1965 Winstone's world title chance finally arrived, when Vicente Saldivar (who had dethroned Ramos a year earlier) accepted an offer of £23,000 from promoter Harry Levene to risk his title at Earl's Court. (Thomas believed in taking the best offer regardless of its source, and so Winstone worked equally readily for both the rival promoters, Levene and Solomons.) It was, coincidentally, the first world title fight I attended, and it remains one of my most vivid memories, a night full of Welsh fire, emotion and passion.

It was one of those rare occasions when an exceptional champion meets an outstanding challenger, each at the absolute zenith of his ability. Winstone's performance was breath-taking. He had never jabbed faster or more accurately, and he moved around the ring with the grace of a ballet dancer as the stocky, moustachioed Mexican stalked him relentlessly.

For twelve rounds it was Winstone's fight – but all the time, Saldivar's persistence had been hacking away at the Welshman's resilience, and his sustained attacks to the body were draining Howard's stamina. Finally, in the fourteenth, Winstone almost folded. He was under fierce fire throughout the round, and although he punched back defiantly at Saldivar in the fifteenth, the champion's big effort in the previous round proved the difference between victory and defeat.

Winstone's work in the earlier rounds had put so much credit in the bank that there was still a flicker of hope that he could hang on for a points win, but referee Bill Williams unhesitatingly raised Saldivar's hand at the final bell. It reflects the changed times to recall that the decision was greeted with nothing but heartfelt applause for two superb combatants. Today, there would probably have been a riot.

The fight had been so good that there had to be an encore, but it took nearly two years to arrange. While he waited, Winstone won six out of six, including three European defences, one of them in Sicily. His old nemesis Don Johnson was beaten for the second time, on a fourth-round foul, and the only man to take him the distance was the Chinese–American Richie Sue, who lost a brilliant ten-rounder at the Albert Hall.

Winstone got his second chance on home ground, at Ninian Park,

Cardiff, on 15 June 1967. It seemed impossible that the pair could match their first fight, but they actually surpassed it. Heartbreakingly, the outcome was the same: Winstone built an early lead with flawless boxing which had the 25,000 crowd enthralled, but was ground down in the last three rounds by Saldivar's unending pressure.

This time Winstone was down once, for eight in the fourteenth, but rallied to share the final round. At the bell there were plenty who thought he had made it, but referee Wally Thom – an old ring adversary of Eddie Thomas' – was not among them. He gave it to Saldivar by 73¾ to 73¼, and Thomas exploded in fury and disappointment. 'It's the most diabolical decision I've known in boxing,' he raged, but, as at Earl's Court, the sporting Welsh fans rose in tribute to the magnificent Mexican.

They met for the third time four months later, in Mexico City. It was a hopeless venture for Winstone: if he could not beat Saldivar with home advantage, what chance could he have at altitude in Mexico City? He had other problems, too – his marriage was crumbling, and later that month Benita left him for another man, saying that she 'could not stand the lonely and frustrating life of the wife of a professional boxer'.

Winstone did the best he could, as always, but this time Saldivar was clearly his master and pounded him to defeat in the twelfth round. Immediately afterwards, the Mexican stunned the crowd by taking the ring mike to announce his retirement. The championship split, and has remained so ever since. The Californian Commission recognized Raul Rojas as the new champion, and the WBA endorsed Rojas three months later. Britain and the European Boxing Union nominated Winstone to meet Japan's Mitsunori Seki for their version of the title, and the WBC eventually concurred. The pair were well matched, with a combined record of only 15 defeats in 136 fights, eight of the losses being to world champions.

Mike Barrett made the match at the Albert Hall on 23 January 1968, and his first world title promotion cost him around £20,000. Saldivar himself signified that he regarded this as the rightful pairing by coming to London to present the championship trophy to the winner. He knew Seki almost as well as he knew Winstone, having defended against him twice. (Seki, who had won 62 of his 72 fights, had also challenged Sugar Ramos for the title, and had lost to Pone Kingpetch in an earlier flyweight title bid.)

By Winstone's own high standards it was a disappointing

performance, ending in controversy when referee Roland Dakin (handling his first world championship) intervened in the ninth round when Seki sustained what appeared to be an innocuous cut over the right eye. The Japanese was a round in front at the finish, although Winstone was coming on strongly and looked set to take control. Seki was furious: 'Does the referee know anything about boxing?' he asked plaintively. But the Welsh were delighted, and it was appropriate that Winstone should be crowned champion in the same ring where, sixteen years earlier, he had become national Schools champion. He was Britain's first world featherweight title claimant since Ben Jordan, a lifetime earlier.

Success had come too late in Howard's career, however. He fought only twice more, coming off the floor in the first to outpoint the heavy-handed British junior lightweight champion Jimmy Anderson in an overweight match and then, on 24 July 1968, losing the title at Porthcawl to Jose Legra. Legra was a flashy Cuban expatriate, based in Spain. Winstone had outpointed him in a ten-rounder at Blackpool in 1965, the only defeat the Cuban had suffered in 82 fights leading up to the rematch.

It was a strange occasion. Winstone was floored by a looping bolo punch in the first round, and his left eye closed like a fist as we watched. He clearly could not survive fifteen rounds with such an injury, but he boxed on as best he could while Legra simply moved around, as if unwilling to hit him again. The fight was conducted in an eerie, funereal silence which I have never encountered since. Even from my cheap seat some 40 rows from the ring I could hear the scuffle and squeak of the boxers' boots on the canvas, as if they were boxing in a sporting club.

Howard battled on for four and a half rounds, but it was a lost cause and there was general relief when referee Harry Gibbs sent him to his corner. Winstone delayed the formal announcement of his retirement for nine months, although it was widely known before then that he would not box again.

He has enjoyed mixed fortunes in the twenty years since then. He remarried, more happily this time, although his financial ventures have been less rewarding. But if you judge a man's worth by the number of his friends and admirers rather than his bank balance, Winstone is a millionaire.

CAREER RECORD: 67 fights, 61 wins (27 inside schedule), 6 defeats.

Ken Buchanan (born 1945)

THE PEOPLE who called Ken Buchanan arrogant or cold were invariably those who did not share the boxer's own entirely justified assessment of his worth. For Buchanan was a man of exceptional qualities, and only the Jack 'Kid' Berg loyalists would dispute the taciturn Scot's right to be regarded as the finest lightweight Britain ever produced.

Buchanan was a winner, who refused ever to acknowledge that there was a better man than himself alive, and who insisted on being treated and paid accordingly. For that, some disliked him, but their opinions remained a matter of supreme indifference to Buchanan. So long as his worth was acknowledged, Ken never cared what anybody thought or said about him.

He was a complex man, and I suspect at the root of it all a shy one. He found it difficult to act the part of the superstar, although in terms of quality he truly was one. In the opinion of those who knew him well, he was driven as much by the fear of failure, of discovering his own inadequacies, as by any other motivation.

Buchanan was a thrilling amateur champion, who won the ABA featherweight title in 1965 and competed in two European championships. He was a regular performer for Scotland: I can still recall him scoring one of the most spectacular stoppages I have ever seen, in a televised Scotland *v* France international. He hit his opponent with a left hook which knocked him out on his feet, and then kept him upright with a blindingly fast burst of hooks and uppercuts that carried the unfortunate Frenchman across the ring, like a man bouncing a table-tennis ball on his bat.

There was understandable competition for his signature on a pro contract. Bobby Neill, a fellow townsman of his from Edinburgh, had been British featherweight champion and now headed one of the country's brightest young stables. But Neill wanted him to move to London, while the other front-runner, Eddie Thomas of Merthyr, was content to let him stay in Edinburgh and come to Wales only for training. That settled the issue in Thomas' favour, although the success which Thomas had enjoyed with Howard Winstone was another telling point in his favour.

Buchanan got his pro career under way on 20 September 1965, when he stopped Swindon's Brian Tonks in two rounds at the National Sporting Club, the spiritual heir to the old NSC. The Club's power and influence in British boxing was history, but it was still the busiest promoter in the country, staging weekly shows at the Café Royal in Lower Regent Street. Buchanan became a regular there, and nine of his first ten fights took place in that unique atmosphere, where absolute silence during boxing was the rigid rule, with applause permitted only during the intervals.

With hindsight, it is a pity that Thomas allowed Buchanan to appear there so many times during those early years. The exclusivity of the dinner-suited, members-only club denied him the chance to build a popular following on the scale which he would certainly have achieved had he been boxing regularly at the major commercial venues. Thus, the hottest amateur of 1965 became the pro game's best-kept secret, while his career stagnated behind closed doors. The wins were impressive and plentiful, but they did not make the impression they would have done on a wider audience.

Buchanan was partly a victim of circumstances, of boxing's political conflicts. By this time Jack Solomons had virtually given up big-time promoting, leaving the Wembley–Albert Hall axis of Mickey Duff, Harry Levene, Jarvis Astaire and Mike Barrett with an effective monopoly on the staging of major shows. Thomas had fallen out with them, and consequently his boxers were rarely seen on their shows.

(Duff, curiously, had been scheduled to be Thomas's opponent when the Welshman made his professional debut in 1946. Thomas used to say, wryly, that it was a shame Duff had pulled out, as it would have been at least one occasion when he would surely have got the better of that clever mover.)

By the end of 1966 Buchanan had worked his way through the ranks of the British lightweight division, and started to gain international experience against American, Italian and French opposition as well as beating John McMillan, one of five boxing brothers, for the vacant Scottish lightweight title. A points win over the cagey Belfast veteran Jim 'Spike' McCormick in October 1967 earned him the right to challenge the Shotton stylist Maurice Cullen for the British title.

Inevitably, it took place in a sporting club, this time the Anglo-

American in Park Lane, London. Cullen was thirty, a seasoned pro who was reputed to have the fastest left jab in the business. But Buchanan, eight years his junior, was too young and forceful, and Cullen was on the floor five times before being counted out in the eleventh.

Buchanan fought on through 1968 and 1969 moving higher in the world rankings but still denied national exposure. A brilliant points defeat of the tough Puerto Rican Frankie Narvaez on 2 January 1969 was screened live by the BBC, and served to give the country's fans a glimpse of what boxing politics were denying them.

His frustration boiled over in July that year when the former world champion Carlos Cruz pulled out of a scheduled world title eliminator at Nottingham. Buchanan worked off his fury on the hapless substitute Jerry Graci, who was stopped inside a round, and then shocked the sport by announcing his retirement and returning his Lonsdale Belt to the Board of Control. He was twenty-four and unbeaten in 34 fights, but felt that his career was going nowhere. Money problems were accumulating; he was married by now, with mortgage payments to meet, and so he returned to his old trade and worked as a joiner.

In October his mother, Cathie, died, and he and Thomas were reconciled when the Welshman travelled to Edinburgh for the funeral. Three months later, Buchanan was fighting for the European title in Madrid against the Spaniard, Miguel Velasquez. The fight was televised live to Britain, and proved to be one of those contests where the ringsiders reached one conclusion and the televiewers another. Most of the British press supported Buchanan's view that the 15-rounds decision in the Spaniard's favour was an outrage, but a very different impression was given by the television film.

But the setback was only temporary, and a run of three wins between February and May quickly repaired the damage. The last of these, on 12 May, saw the Scot make a rare appearance at Wembley, where he knocked out the former amateur champion Brian Hudson in five rounds to retain the British title.

Negotiations were started for a world title fight with the elegant Panamanian Ismael Laguna. The champion's American agent, Dewey Fregatta, had been instructed to 'find someone Laguna would be sure to beat', and Buchanan seemed to fit the bill. When the Scot was compelled to make his challenge in the searing afternoon heat in a San Juan stadium, the odds against him appeared insurmountable – but Buchanan, fighting with total self-belief, pulled off one of the great British results of all time by taking a split decision.

Ironically, he found himself a prophet without honour in his own land. The British Board, along with the World Boxing Council, had previously withdrawn recognition from Laguna and so Buchanan's victory made him world champion only in the eyes of the rival World Boxing Association and the New York Commission. Buchanan was irritated and hurt by the British Board's refusal to back down, but they could hardly have done so without forfeiting credibility. Anyway, the question of who recognized him as champion was a pedantic irrelevance: what mattered was that Buchanan had suddenly become a major attraction in America.

Like the two Kids, Lewis and Berg, Buchanan took his talents to New York in search of the recognition that was denied him at home, and he astounded the Americans with the sheer hard quality of his fighting. He could not have picked a tougher opponent for his debut there, on the undercard in Madison Square Garden on the night when Muhammad Ali continued his comeback against Oscar Bonavena.

Donato Paduano was a handsome Canadian welterweight who outweighed the Scot by a full stone, and who was unbeaten in 24 fights. But Buchanan showed him the difference between world-class and the level of opponents against whom he had compiled that record with a dazzling points win which clinched him the American Boxing Writers Association selection as Fighter of the Year for 1970. It was a rare honour for a European boxer, particularly as the two runners-up were Joe Frazier and Muhammad Ali.

Now, at last, Buchanan had the platform on which to display his talents, and a fresh and adoring public who were only too eager to give him the acclaim he was denied at home. He trounced the Californian–Mexican Ruben Navarro in Los Angeles to clinch universal recognition as champion, stopped the former world light-welterweight king Carlos Hernandez in six rounds at Wembley, and survived shocking cuts to retain his title in a Madison Square Garden rematch with Ismael Laguna. By then, though, he had already lost half his title: the WBC stripped him for signing for the Laguna rematch, but this time the British Board stayed loyal to the

Scot and continued to recognize him as champion.

On the undercard that night was a rock-fisted young Panamanian, Roberto Duran, who destroyed Benny Huertas inside a round. It was Duran's 25th consecutive win, and he was rapidly establishing himself as Buchanan's leading contender. Ken, meantime, kept busy with non-title appearances in London and Johannesburg. At Wembley he trounced the twenty-one-year old Canadian champion Al Ford, who had lost only once in more than 42 fights. It was his first appearance without Thomas in the corner, after the partnership had ended acrimoniously.

When he defended against Duran in New York on 26 June 1972 Gil Clancy was in Thomas' place, but probably not even the Welshman's expertise could have helped Ken against the unstoppable Panamanian. Buchanan boxed as well as he ever did, but Duran poured punches in from all angles and of all degrees of legality, finally bringing the Scot to his knees with a viciously low blow which landed after the bell to end the thirteenth round – and which Duran followed with a knee to the groin. He should have been disqualified, but instead Buchanan, unable to answer the bell for the fourteenth, found himself an ex-champion.

It was an injustice which still rankles with Buchanan, but at least he has the twin consolations that Duran thought he was the hardest man he had ever faced, and that the new champion never dared to risk his title against him in a rematch.

His world title was gone, but Buchanan's popularity in New York was undiminished and he fought there three more times over the next year, as well as regaining the British title from Jim Watt. The Danish promoter Mogens Palle became increasingly influential in his career around this time, and Buchanan fought regularly in Copenhagen in 1973–74. He won the European title in Cagliari and defended it in Paris. Then, almost three years after losing to Duran, he got a second chance at the world title, when he went to Tokyo to challenge Guts Ishimatsu for the WBC version.

He sustained an injury to his left eye early in the fight and, boxing virtually one-eyed, lost a unanimous decision. There would never be another chance, and after retaining his European title with a difficult twelfth-round stoppage of Giancarlo Usai, Buchanan retired because of recurring double vision.

Inevitably, there was a comeback nearly four years later. His marriage had failed, and bad investments had accounted for most of his ring earnings. He linked up again with Mogens Palle, who steered him through a couple of easy wins into a European title bid against Charlie Nash. They fought in Copenhagen, a curious place for a Scot to fight an Irishman, and Nash won a tight decision.

Buchanan had six more fights, winning two and losing the last four, and then ended his career where it had begun – in the National Sporting Club. It was a neat way to complete the circle . . . but then recurring financial problems forced him back into the ring again, this time on the unlicensed circuit. The NSC, to its credit, offered to stage a benefit night to raise cash for him and thereby spare him the humiliation – and the physical risk – of boxing on unlicensed shows, but Buchanan's pride demanded that he earn the cash himself in the only way he knew how, with his fists. For once, the shady and tawdry world of unlicensed fighting was vested with a dignity it did not deserve.

He made two appearances on those knockabout tournaments, winning both, and then quit. But he could find neither happiness nor success outside the ring. His second marriage also failed, as did a spell as a pub manager in Dagenham. Today he is back in Edinburgh, still without the recognition which is rightfully his. It is ironic that the Americans should have long since accepted what the British seem so slow to acknowledge – that we have never had a finer lightweight than the hard, unyielding Buchanan.

CAREER RECORD: 69 fights, 61 wins (27 inside the distance), 8 defeats.

John H. Stracey (born 1950)

FEW of us, mercifully, will ever see our worst nightmares come true. But John H. Stracey was not so lucky. It happened to him in a Mexico City bull-ring on 6 December 1975, when the twenty-five-year-old Londoner was 12,000 miles from home and challenging one of the all-time greats of the welterweight division, the Cuban José Napoles, for the world title. The odds seemed to be overwhelmingly against Stracey from the start: the Mexican-based Napoles had ruled the division, with one brief hiccough, for six years and 13 successful defences, and had the advantage of a partisan and noisy crowd of around 30,000 to urge him on and intimidate his opponent.

Within two minutes of the opening round, the young Londoner found himself on the floor from a Napoles left hook. He was dazed and hurt, and had to cope with the sickening knowledge that what had always been a difficult assignment now looked an impossibility. It says everything one needs to know about Stracey's self-confidence and character, as much as his ability, that he survived that nightmare start, clawed his way back into the fight, and finally halted the fading Napoles in the sixth round to record one of the great upset victories in British boxing history.

Stracey, though, always had the look of a winner. He was born in Bethnal Green on 22 September 1950, and grew up in a block of council flats just off the Whitechapel Road, the 'home manor' of that other great welterweight champion Ted 'Kid' Lewis. Boxing was always part of his life; his father Dave was a passionate and knowledgeable fan, and like so many boxing fathers became obsessed with his son's career when the schoolboy Stracey took up the sport with the famous Repton Club in Bethnal Green.

I recall being astonished at the extent of Dave's devotion when I visited the family home in 1968. He insisted that I inspect every item of his son's equipment, and showed me how he even ironed the laces with which John threaded his boxing boots!

Dave, of course, had much to be obsessive about. The young Stracey had precocious, natural ability, and he learned fast, although in the early stages boxing was still battling for his affections with swimming and soccer (he had a trial with Millwall). In Tony Burns, the former Welsh amateur international, he had one of the finest coaches in the game, and there was a pool of quality sparring available at the club.

With such resources, success was inevitable. He won four national titles (a National Schools title, a Boys' Club championship, and a pair of junior ABA titles) and caused the sensation of the 1968 London championships when, in his first senior season and only his thirteenth contest, he trounced the defending ABA champion Terry Waller in the lightweight final at the Albert Hall. (The defeat did Waller no lasting damage: the south London stylist went on to win four more ABA championships, three at welterweight and one at light-welter.)

It was victory at a price for Stracey, though – that weekend he had a letter from the City stockbroking firm where he worked as a clerk, telling him not to bother coming back because 'boxing appears to come before your firm's interests.' But John had other things on his mind. Beating Waller had made him favourite for the ABA title, and this was Olympic year.

He got there, too – but not by the route he had anticipated. In the semi-finals at Belle Vue, Manchester, he came up against a southpaw Scot called Jim Watt, and 45 seconds later (including the count) his Olympic dream seemed dead. A perfect short right hook did the damage. Who could have imagined that night that both winner and loser would become world champions, and for the same manager?

Watt won the ABA title, and a place in the Olympic squad. The inclusion of Stracey – still only seventeen – as the reserve raised a few eyebrows. A week later, Stracey was in the team. Watt had announced that he was pulling out as he had been 'starving himself' to make lightweight, and could not hope to keep it up until the Games, which were nearly five months away.

Stracey had never boxed before at international level, and his record of exactly 100 bouts (83 wins) incuded only 16 at senior level. But he performed better in Mexico than might have been expected, outscoring a Canadian before going down on a 4–1 vote to the southpaw American Ronnie Harris, who went on to win the gold medal.

He could have turned professional on his return from the Games, but wisely opted for another season in the amateurs (now as a light-welterweight) in the hope that he might make up for his disappointment in the 1968 ABA championships. He injured a leg at the London semi-finals stage of the 1969 title chase, and I vividly recall him hobbling around the Albert Hall ring – wearing his Olympic vest – against Tony Senior. The damage was not severe, and this time he made it all the way to the ABA title.

It was time to turn pro, and he opted to join the east London stable of Tony Burns' great friend Terry Lawless, who was rapidly establishing himself as the brightest and best connected of the younger managers. The Lawless mould was already firmly in place, a recipe for success which has not altered in the twenty years since then. After all, why change a formula which has produced four world champions and a roomful of European and British title-holders?

Stracey was fed a selection of carefully chosen opponents, who were designed to enhance the youngster's confidence and give him experience, without at the same time jeopardizing his record. Lawless and his promotional associate Mickey Duff have always been masters of the art of picking the right opponent at the right time, and the skill was never better exhibited than in the development of John Stracey.

Of course, Stracey was good enough to make the grade without their meticulous stage-management, but Duff's expertise and contacts, allied with Lawless' enthusiasm and skills as trainer and motivator, combined to form powerful assets for a young man seeking a short-cut to the top.

Stracey ran up an impressive string of 25 wins and a draw in 27 fights, with the sole loss coming on a disputed eight-round decision at the Albert Hall against the smart young Canadian Marshall Butler (of whom, curiously, nothing further was ever heard). That run earned him a match with the Coventry stylist Bobby Arthur for the British welterweight title that Stracey's stable-mate Ralph Charles had vacated.

They met at the Albert Hall on 31 October 1972, and Alan Minter, later to become world middleweight champion, opened the show on his professional debut by stopping a Bradford-based Antiguan, Maurice Thomas, in six rounds. Stracey started as 7–2 favourite, and looked it for six and a half rounds. Then Arthur suddenly sank to the floor, clutching his groin, and for a while chaos and confusion reigned. Referee James Brimmell twice asked him to get up, then signalled the finish.

Some thought that he had counted Arthur out, others that he had disqualified Stracey for a low blow. The latter were nearer the mark: in fact, the heart-broken Stracey had been thrown out for hitting on the break. The referee may well have been technically correct, but the result was a travesty of justice and Stracey quickly put it right in the rematch on 5 June 1973, flattening the Midlander in the fourth round with a right hand driven straight and hard through the guard.

Now Duff's international clout really began to pay off, as he manoeuvred and manipulated Stracey up the rankings. A succession of middle-grade Americans, including the once-rated Jackie Tillman, were imported for Stracey to beat, while negotiations went on for him to meet European champion Roger Menetrey.

The veteran was one of the twin pillars of French boxing, the other being middleweight champion Jean-Claude Bouttier, and the pair were eventually signed to meet British champions Stracey and Kevin Finnegan in the same show in Paris on 27 May 1974. It was a bleak night for the French: Finnegan outpointed Bouttier, Stracey stopped Menetrey in the eighth round, and neither of the ex-champs ever boxed again.

The respected American veteran Ernie 'Red' Lopez was engaged to face Stracey at the Albert Hall on 29 October that year, in a fight designed to project the twenty-four-year-old Londoner as a world title contender. Lopez, whose younger brother Danny would become one of the most exciting featherweight punchers in history, had challenged Jose Napoles twice for the world title but had been inactive since July 1973.

It was yet another illustration of how to make the right match at the right time. Stracey hammered the ring-worn and rusty Lopez into retirement, and the long process of negotiation, haggling and wrangling to secure the world title match with Napoles began. Stracey's eventual purse was £25,000, easily the best of his career up to then, but it was generally felt (even in Britain) that his was a lost cause.

Instead, John shocked us all with a wonderfully courageous, battling performance to bridge sixty years of history and bring the world title back to London. The result made him an overnight star, in areas beyond boxing. Shrewd marketing men created a 'British Bulldog' image for him, to the point where Stracey seemed to have claimed the Union Jack as his personal symbol. Hedgemon Lewis, once an outstanding contender, was hired for a showcase defence at Wembley on 20 March 1976, and Stracey draped himself in the flag as he stood triumphantly on the ropes in the corner after sending Lewis into permanent retirement with a tenth-round stoppage.

But the party ended abruptly two months later when Carlos Palomino, picked as a 'safe' opponent, wrecked the listless champion with body punches to stop him in the twelfth. Stracey fought without fire or ambition, as if he had been overwhelmed by the events of the last six months. The defeat broke the close relationship with Terry Lawless and, although they worked together for Stracey's brave but losing battle with the new welterweight star Dave Green at Wembley in John's only fight of 1977, the partnership finally dissolved in bitter recriminations.

The recently married Stracey opened a hotel in Bayswater, but decided to give the game one last try and, on 23 May 1978, struggled to beat a moderate Frenchman called Georges Warusfel. That was enough to convince him that his best days were gone, and he quit to concentrate on his business.

Sadly, Stracey has not enjoyed the same success in either his personal or commercial life as he did in the ring – but nobody can ever take away from him the memory of that marvellous achievement in Mexico City.

CAREER RECORD: 51 fights, 45 wins (37 inside the distance), 1 draw, 5 defeats.

John Conteh (born 1951)

JOHN CONTEH had the world in his hands – and let it slip through his fingers. He was the fighter with everything – skill, glamour, class and charisma – but through a combinaton of bad luck, bad advice, bad investments and erratic performances he finished up with nothing.

As this chapter was being written, a sad four-paragraph story in a Sunday paper recorded that the former world light-heavyweight champion was battling to keep his house out of a bankruptcy settlement forced on him by the Inland Revenue. It should have been so very different. Bob Arum was not overstating the case when he described Conteh as potentially the greatest British fighter since Randolph Turpin.

That potential was always very apparent, but so too were the flaws which would ultimately drag him down. The class was there as he won the ABA and Commonwealth Games titles at middleweight in 1970 and took the ABA light-heavyweight title the following year. But the faults were worryingly evident when he flopped in the European championships in Madrid six weeks later.

He went there as England's brightest hope for a gold medal, and came home in humiliation after being eliminated by a balding, flabby Austrian southpaw called Richard Kolleritsh. The twenty-eight-year-old Kolleritsh should have been the easiest possible draw for Conteh, but the whole occasion overwhelmed the twenty-year-old from Kirkby, and he froze. He was to do the same many years later, with the world championship at stake. The gold medal, incidentally, was won by Mate Parlov of Yugoslavia, with whom Conteh had a fiercely contested world title fight seven years later.

Boxing's money-men were prepared to write that off as a fluke, a freak bad performance which would surely never be repeated. In October Conteh duly made his pro debut, under the management of Londoner George Francis, in front of a dinner-suited audience at the World Sporting Club in Mayfair. It was a perfect start: Conteh needed only 56 seconds to dismiss an Algerian substitute called Okacha Boubekeur, the first of a string of obscure imports who were lined up for him.

He won 11 in a row, 10 inside the distance, and only the slippery Liverpool spoiler Billy Aird gave him trouble. But in his twelfth fight he gave another of those sluggish performances that punctuated his career and was outpointed by a Philadelphia journeyman called Eddie Duncan. That was written off as part of the learning process, and with Mickey Duff doing the matchmaking and George Francis the conditioning, the Conteh bandwagon was soon rolling again – but on an altered course. Conteh's early fights had been against heavyweights, but by 1973 it was clear that he lacked the size to handle the big men impressively so he was switched back to his natural division.

The British champion at the time was Chris Finnegan, elder of the two brothers whose skill, courage and humour graced British boxing in the 1970s. Southpaw Finnegan won the 1968 Olympic gold medal, and had successfully adapted his safety-first amateur style to one more suited to the demands of the professional market. He had fought heroically for fourteen rounds in an unforgettable bid for Bob Foster's world title (Conteh lost to Duncan on the undercard), and a match between the old campaigner and the new golden boy was a certain crowd-puller.

But Duff made it even more appealing by first matching Conteh with the German Rudiger Schmidtke, who had stopped Finnegan on cuts to take the European title. Conteh performed brilliantly, and the champion had not won a round when he was rescued in the twelfth. Finnegan boxed on the same bill, retaining his British and Commonwealth titles against the durable Welshman Roy John.

The winners met at Wembley on 22 May and provided one of the decade's greatest battles. Conteh edged it on points, although there were plenty at ringside – myself included – who thought the verdict might have gone the other way. The case for a rematch was unanswerable, but it took a day short of a year to materialize. In the meantime, Conteh kept busy with defences of his European and Commonwealth titles, and a 'thank you' appearance at Liverpool Stadium to show his appreciation of the home-town fans who had followed him since the day when, as a nervous eleven-year-old, he had lost his first amateur contest as a novice with Kirkby Boxing Club.

The Finnegan rematch was again at Wembley, on 21 May 1975, and it left the arguments unsettled. Finnegan's boxing was inspired, and he was in a good lead after five rounds. Conteh looked increasingly anxious as the rounds passed with him no nearer to establishing any kind of grip on the fight, and in the sixth round the frustration showed as his head cracked against Finnegan's, with drastic results. Blood pumped down the side of Finnegan's head from a deep cut in the scalp, above the right ear, and he turned away in confusion as it flowed into his eye.

Referee Roland Dakin inspected the damage, and then signalled the finish. It was not the first time, nor the last, that Conteh was guilty of careless headwork – but he could counter that boxing is a tough and brutal business, in which nice guys generally finish down the field. John had grown up in a mixed-race family of ten, in an environment which steered many of his contemporaries – including a few of his brothers – into a life of crime. Kirkby is a long way from the playing fields of Eton, and different ethics apply.

The result confirmed Conteh's position as challenger to world champion Bob Foster, and when Foster retired following a disappointing draw against Jorge Ahumada, Conteh and Ahumada were paired for the vacant WBC version of the title. Ahumada's Argentinian compatriot Victor Galindez won the WBA version. (In those happy days there were only two 'governing bodies' instead of the four which clutter the scene today.)

I recall spending a day with Conteh a fortnight before he met Ahumada at Wembley on 1 October 1974, and I have never known a fighter more certain of himself, and his destiny. As I wrote in *Boxing News* at the time, with more than a hint of wistful envy: 'It must be good to run high in the hills, with London spread out beneath you, and know that in two weeks you will be the light-heavyweight champion of the world.'

Conteh justified this confidence with a masterful display. The Argentinian resisted bitterly, contesting every point, but Conteh that night touched the heights. Typically, the post-fight photos were of Conteh in the Playboy Club, drinking champagne and sur-rounded by Bunny Girls. He had always had a taste for the good life, although his dedication in training was inflexible. But now he had the status, and the cash, to indulge himself, and he did it with enthusiasm.

He was poised to earn a fortune, but somehow it all went wrong. He had an easy defence against an American veteran, Lonnie Bennett, and then stunned the trade by launching a bitter court action against George Francis and the Board of Control, on the grounds that his earning capacity would be greater if he managed himself and was not tied to one particular promoter. He also initiated actions against Mickey Duff and the Wembley promoter Harry Levene. But he was tilting at windmills, and learned the expensive lesson that, whatever the merits of the case, the only people who profit from legal actions are usually the lawyers who handle them.

To stay busy, and to earn some ready cash, he took a non-title ten-rounder in Scranton, Pennsylvania against the unranked Willie Taylor, and smashed his right hand. It was a bad break, and his right-hand hitting was never so venomous again. When he resumed training he broke the hand again in sparring, and lost more precious time from what should have been his peak earning period.

A proposed fight in Kampala in April 1976 came to nothing, and instead he made his solitary ring appearance of the year in Copenhagen, outpointing the Californian Alvaro Lopez, who made five unsuccessful title challanges in his long career. It had been a costly year, but there was worse to come. In March 1977 he retained the title in Liverpool, stopping Len Hutchins in three rounds, but then the latest in his series of battles with authority cost him his championship.

He signed a contract to defend against another of the production-line Argentinian light-heavies, Miguel Cuello, in Monte Carlo, but claimed that he did so under duress. He argued that the British Board's rule prohibiting the live televising of a world title fight had cost him £35,000, which was the difference between a British offer to stage the same fight and the £117,000 on offer from Monte Carlo.

His court action failed, but he refused as a matter of principle to go through with the fight and was duly stripped by the WBC. Cuello, a crude brawler, knocked out the substitute challenger, Jesse Burnett, to win the vacant title, which he lost in his first defence to Mate Parlov of Yugoslavia.

Conteh's representative was Bobby Naidoo, a man with close connections to the WBC (he is now their Press Officer). Naidoo was instrumental in securing Conteh a fight with Parlov in Belgrade on 17 June 1978, and Conteh came heart-breakingly close to recapturing the title he had never lost in the ring. Controversy always seemed to swirl around Conteh, and this time it focused on the protective substance that Parlov, in direct contravention of the WBC rules, was allowed to wear on his vulnerable eyebrows.

It was a split decision, and the two points Conteh had deducted for butting in the eighth and elbowing in the fifteenth were enough to get Parlov home. But Conteh had proved himself the better man, and came within a couple of punches of victory in the last round as he battered the exhausted champion against the ropes. The roar that went up from the 40,000 crowd in the Red Star Stadium was of relief rather than acclaim.

Conteh's performance had been good enough to earn another chance, but in the meantime Parlov was dethroned by Matthew Saad Muhammad, a hard Philadelphian who had begun his career as Matthew Franklin before becoming a Muslim. While manoeuvring went on to land a chance at Muhammad, Conteh kept busy with three rather uncertain displays.

He had made his peace with Mickey Duff, and on his first Wembley appearance for three and a half years he knocked out a difficult southpaw, Leo Rodgers, in seven rounds. He followed that with a rocky ten-round draw with Jesse Burnett, the American who had replaced him against Miguel Cuello, and this time Conteh had to come off the floor twice. When he struggled to outpoint the obscure Ivy Brown in June, his prospects of beating Muhammad in Atlantic City on 18 August looked bleak indeed.

But Conteh, ever unpredictable, fought magnificently. Muhammad, like Parlov, was allowed to break the rules by using a banned substance to treat cuts which would otherwise have forced him out of the fight. The champion was bleeding by the fifth round from an appalling cut which ran the length of his left eyebrow. Time and again, Conteh had him in dire trouble, following perfect jabs with smashing hooks to the head.

But the fight slipped away from him as the remarkable Muhammad, a fighter who made a career out of coming back from the brink of defeat, rallied heroically. Conteh was battered throughout the thirteenth, floored twice in the fourteenth, and badly cut in the last round. The decision for Muhammad was unanimous, but the closeness of the fight and the row about the treatment of Muhammad's cuts earned Conteh a rematch.

It took place in March 1980, again in Atlantic City, but Conteh was unrecognizable as the man who had fought so well last time. He was destroyed in four humiliating rounds, and later confessed that he had not even tried to win. 'The vision of being stretched out at another man's feet with television cameras and news photographers recording my humiliation for the waiting world was almost too much for me to bear,' he wrote afterwards.

It was a sad and unworthy exit from the championship stage he had graced for so long, and it meant that this time there could be no further chances from the ever-obliging WBC. He boxed only once more, stopping James Dixon in Liverpool on 31 May 1980, and then drifted off into a nightmare world of cocaine, alcohol and tranquillizers.

Psychiatric care, a new-found faith in God and the loyalty of his long-suffering wife Veronica helped him back to normality, and he is now an inspiring example to others. The money, sadly, is all gone – hangers-on, high living and the tax man saw to that – but what Conteh has left is something infinitely more valuable: his self-respect, and the affection of a generation of boxing fans for whom he remains the finest fighter of his time.

CAREER RECORD: 39 fights, 34 wins (24 inside schedule), 1 draw, 4 defeats.

Jim Watt (born 1948)

THE SEVENTIES was a bad time to be a lightweight contender. Roberto Duran, the ferocious Panamanian, had ruled the division since 1972, although the WBC insisted on recognizing various lesser men as champion until Duran finally cleared up the confusion by knocking out their representative, Esteban de Jesus, in 1978.

Fighters like Jim Watt must have despaired of ever becoming world champion with the formidable Duran on the scene, but in· Watt's case the daydream seemed more futile than most. He was an unglamorous Scottish southpaw, lacking the connections or the charisma to move him up the ladder. His ability was unquestioned, and those in the trade had long appreciated his worth. But it looked as though he would have to resign himself to collecting a Lonsdale Belt, and the very occasional five-figure purse, before drifting out of the game at thirty and going back to working for a living.

But one phone call changed his career, and his life. The call was to London manager Terry Lawless, and it set Watt on the road to the world championship.

His is an encouraging tale of quality rewarded, and happily the success story did not end with his retirement. Today, with his ring earnings soundly invested in a flourishing business, Watt is a wealthy man. His lucid, articulate and perceptive commentaries on ITV fight shows have also made him one of the most respected voices in the media world.

Watt, to his lasting credit, has never forgotten how and where it all began – with an eccentric, off-beat character called Jim Murray. The balding, slightly built bachelor ran the Cardowan ABC in Maryhill, Glasgow, which Watt joined at fifteen at the prompting of a friend, Joe Glencross. Murray was an unusual and, in his own way, an inspiring man, and Watt – whose father had died when the boy was only five – responded to him. Murray saw his responsibilities towards his protégé as extending beyond the narrow confines of boxing, and he proceeded to enlighten him equally on the virtues of socialism, yoga and vegetarianism.

Under Murray's guidance and coaching, Watt became an outstandingly successful amateur whose career was crowned in

1968 by a dramatic, one-punch knockout of John H. Stracey in the ABA semi-finals. Stracey, who went on to win the world welter-weight title, was the championship's golden boy, while Watt, in a role that was to become all too familiar, was the unglamorous outsider. That one punch marked Watt as a man to watch, and his subsequent victory in the final was an anti-climax. It was his 33rd win in 37 amateur contests.

He was selected to go to the Olympic Games in Mexico City, but even then Watt was very much his own man. He knew that he was not ready for the severe competition he would face there, and was determined to be a winner or nothing. And so he turned down the invitation, on the pretext that he could not hold his weight down during the gap between the ABAs and the Games.

Instead, he turned professional, with Murray as his manager. Theirs was not an easy road: Murray lacked the connections with the established London promoters, and he also lacked the financial resources to promote Watt's career on his own. The Scot's early years in the business were therefore spent on the sporting club circuit, since at that time there were very few commercial promotions outside the major London shows. The pay was poor, and the exposure minimal.

But the sheer hard quality of the man shone through, and eventually he earned a crack at the vacant British title. The opponent was another Scot, Willie Reilly, whom Watt had beaten on a cut eye in a final eliminator five months earlier, in September 1971. This time Watt was the victim, as a cut forced him out of the fight in the tenth round. But then he had a rare stroke of luck: Reilly threw in the title over a purse dispute, and Watt was matched again for the vacant championship with the stylish Midlander Tony Riley.

He made the most of his second chance, stopping Riley in the twelfth round at Solihull, but he was not destined to have a long reign. The marvellous Ken Buchanan was rebuilding his career, and saw the British title as a worthwhile step along the road back towards another world title challenge. The St Andrew's Sporting Club in Glasgow secured the match as their opening-night attraction, and were rewarded for their initiative with a magnificent fifteen rounds of skilful, earnest boxing. Buchanan got the decision, deservedly, but the young Glaswegian's performance against a man who had been world champion less than a year earlier was a revelation.

Watt came away with his reputation enhanced rather than dented by the defeat, and with the admiration of his conqueror. There had been attempts to whip up rivalry and bitterness between the pair, but they were both much too professional to allow the hype to blind them to the other's worth. Buchanan said afterwards that Watt had the potential to become a world champion. Few at the time believed him, regarding it as a routine pat on the back, a word of comfort for a beaten opponent, but Buchanan knew what he was talking about.

Watt and Murray went back to the clubs, taking the purses where they could find them. Watt also won twice in Johannesburg, and lost a third fight there on a dubious decision to Anthony Morodi in the first black *v* white contest ever staged in the country. In January 1975 he became British champion again when he stopped another Scot, the gifted but ill-disciplined Johnny Cheshire, for the vacant British title.

He failed to make it a double when Jonathan Dele outpointed him in Lagos for the vacant Commonwealth title and, after Andre Holyk was given a shockingly bad decision over him in a European eliminator in October, Watt decided that he and Murray had come to the end of their road together. Sixteen of Watt's 29 fights under Murray's management had been in club shows, and he had only appeared once on a major London bill. It was time for a change – and a call to Terry Lawless.

Lawless and Watt had an instant rapport. Unlike most of the young fighters in Lawless' Canning Town gym, the quiet and thoughtful Scot was a mature man who was well able to make his own decisions. Their relationship was thus on a subtly different plane from that which Lawless enjoyed with Watt's gym-mates, and it worked from the start.

There were no instant bonanzas, just progressively better exposure and more significant fights. Their first season together in 1976 was a marking-time affair, but the partnership began to pay off in 1977. Watt won a Lonsdale Belt outright against Johnny Claydon, and then relinquished the title after he had been ordered to defend it in Derry against his great Irish rival Charlie Nash. Lawless convinced him that it would not be wise for a Scots Protestant to fight an Irish Catholic in Derry at that time, and in any case he had a shrewd idea that the pair would eventually meet anyway, under more favourable conditions.

Instead, Watt faced Holyk again for the vacant European title, and won it without landing a worthwhile punch. Their heads cracked together in the second minute, and Holyk was cut on the right eyebrow. (Watt insists that the cut was caused by a punch, but if so I missed it at ringside.) Three defences followed, against two Spaniards and an Italian, and it was the second which showed that Watt had the character to go all the way to the world title.

The challenger was Perico Fernandez, the former world light-welterweight champion, and he had home advantage in Madrid. Watt was floored in the opening round, but fought back so effectively that Fernandez had to take three standing counts and failed to win another round on any of the three official scorecards. It was the most decisive points win ever secured by a British boxer in a Continental title fight, and it moved Watt a significant notch up the world ratings.

Equally significant, for a different reason, was Watt's third European defence against the Italian Antonio Guinaldo (who later won the European light-welterweight title). Duff and his promotional partner Mike Barrett gambled by booking the Kelvin Hall, which had not been used for boxing for many years, and drew a near-capacity crowd despite the fight being screened live by the BBC. It proved that Watt – whatever had been said about him in the past – could put bums on seats, and the success of that show was crucial to what followed.

While the Scot was moving unobtrusively up the rankings, Roberto Duran was fighting a losing battle to keep down to the lightweight limit. Lawless and his shrewd partner, Mickey Duff, were well aware of Duran's difficulties, and when the Panamanian finally conceded defeat and relinquished the title, Watt, as the number two contender, was matched with Alfredo Pitalua of Colombia for the vacant WBC version of the title.

Mickey Duff won the right to stage it, and Watt himself enlisted the cooperation of Glasgow City Council and the Glasgow Sports Promotion Council to ensure that it took place in the Kelvin Hall. Six thousand extra seats were installed to expand the capacity, and some masterly publicity and salesmanship ensured a sell-out on fight night, 17 April 1979.

Pitalua, half-brother to the former WBC middleweight champion Rodrigo Valdes, was a worthy number one. But on this night he was fighting not only Watt but the crowd of around 10,000 as well. The atmosphere (and the decibel level) was unforgettable. There were flags, banners, chants and even bagpipes to fan the ardour, and it says much for the Colombian's courage that he defied all that hostile pressure to last into the twelfth round before referee Arthur Mercante rescued him.

Now it was time to make up for the hard years and the low purses. There was no sense in taking a risky defence first time out, so instead Watt hammered an intimidated and overwhelmed Tex–Mex named Roberto Vasquez to fifth-round defeat in the Kelvin Hall.

His next challenger, though, was rather more formidable. Charlie Nash, a sharp-hitting southpaw from Derry, had succeeded Watt as British and European champion, and had been trying for years to get him in the ring. They were matched three times, but each time Watt withdrew, prompting silly speculation that he did not fancy his chances against the Irishman. The truth, of course, was that Watt wanted to face him on his own terms, and on home ground, and as world champion he was now in a position to dictate the conditions.

The sectarian rivalry which has scarred Glasgow almost as much as Belfast over the years was scarcely in evidence when they entered the Kelvin Hall ring on 14 March 1980, although the atmosphere there was just as intense as it had been for the two previous world title fights. Nash began brilliantly, dumping the champion for a short count in the opening round. But as he had done against Perico Fernandez, the cool Scot merely got up, wiped his gloves, and got on with the job of dismantling a brave but fragile challenger. Nash was on the floor three times in the fourth before referee Sid Nathan stopped it.

Watt's mandatory challenger was Howard Davis, the dazzling American who had won the Olympic gold medal in the 1976 Olympics and was unbeaten in 13 fights as a pro. Duff won the purse bidding, although Watt agreed to take much less than the published purse of £500,000. The fight went on at Ibrox Park, home of Glasgow Rangers, on 7 June 1980. It was Scotland's first open-air show for twenty years, on a cold, rain-soaked evening.

Davis and the American media regarded Watt as a manufactured champion, and saw Davis' coronation as a tiresome formality. The challenger did not endear himself by referring to his opponent as 'Jim Who?', and predicting the round in which he would become champion. But Watt knew that the gap in experience worked hugely in his favour, and won the battle of pre-fight barbs by pointing out to the challenger that, 'This will be my fourteenth fifteen-rounder. You've not even had that many fights.' It was a crucial point, and the decisive factor in Watt's unanimous points win.

Watt boxed superbly in the finest performance of his life, and Davis' subsequent bleats about being intimidated by the crowd did him little credit. Nobody had been there to hold Watt's hand when Perico Fernandez had floored him in Madrid, in an atmosphere just as intimidating as that at Ibrox.

Watt's next challenger, Sean O'Grady, sounded like another Irish Catholic but was in fact an American Baptist from Oklahoma City. His father Pat was an exuberant, larger-than-life character who had engineered Sean's world ranking with a long run of knockover wins – 73 in 74 fights, with 65 stopped or knocked out since he had turned pro five years earlier, at sixteen. Most of the fights had been promoted by Pat, who hand-picked the opponents, but on the few occasions when Sean had faced 'real' fighters he had shown that he could look after himself in good company.

O'Grady and Watt had a bloody, thrilling and evenly matched battle. Both were more cut-prone than the average fighter, and both were bleeding long before the half-way stage. In the ninth Watt sustained a really bad cut, and it seemed for a moment that his title might be gone as referee Raymond Balderou called for a doctor's inspection. But Watt was allowed to continue, and in the eleventh a terrible clash of heads split open a gash on the American's forehead.

The doctor was called twice to look at O'Grady's wound, in the eleventh and again in the twelfth, and by now even the fight-hardened Kelvin Hall crowd was screaming for it to end. Coins and a rolled-up programme were thrown into the ring in protest as Watt pounded a challenger who was blinded by his own blood, but the referee even ignored a towel thrown in from O'Grady's corner. Finally he signalled the finish, and gave Watt the last victory of his career.

There were bitter recriminations from the American camp and from American TV viewers. They argued that Watt should have been disqualified for a deliberate butt, and O'Grady Sr lobbied hard for a rematch, but it never materialized. Instead, O'Grady proved his worth again by winning the WBA version of the title, which he never lost in the ring. Today he, like Watt, works as a TV commentator, and, still only twenty-nine, talks of a comeback.

The O'Grady win was the last of the glory nights. Alexis Arguello, the fabulous Nicaraguan, moved up from junior lightweight (also known as super-featherweight) to outscore the Scot at Wembley on 20 June 1981. Watt was professional enough to know that he probably could not beat Arguello, but nobody could fault his courage and pride as he survived a knockdown to battle on with stoic determination to the last bell. When it was over, Watt quit the ring, although the official announcement was not made until some time later.

He left with the knowledge that no British world champion since Jack 'Kid' Berg had defended a world title more often, and, perhaps more comfortingly for a Scot, that no British world champion – including his arch-rival Ken Buchanan – had ever been better paid for doing so.

CAREER RECORD: 46 fights, 38 wins (27 inside schedule), 8 defeats.

Maurice Hope (born 1951)

IF MAURICE HOPE had not enjoyed living in Britain quite so much, the chances are that the country's tax inspectors would not have had to bankrupt him only five years after he had reigned as light-middleweight champion of the world. Hope was granted land by the Antiguan Government to mark his world title win in 1979, which would have entitled him to tax-exempt status had he chosen to uproot his family from east London and return to live in his native country. The tax he would have saved by doing so would have been more than enough to meet the financial crisis which eventually engulfed him in the mid-1980s. Bankruptcy seems a poor reward for a man who, in his own quiet way, did so much to fight racism and better the lot of the black boxer in Britain.

Hope was the first black British world champion, as distinct from mixed-race men such as Randolph Turpin and John Conteh, and his success did much to enable boxers to be judged on their ring ability rather than their colour. Without Hope, the likelihood is that Dennis Andries and Duke McKenzie would have found it even harder than they did to reach the top, and Frank Bruno, too, should feel eternally grateful to his one-time stable-mate.

Hope came here from Antigua when he was nine and, inspired by his elder half-brother, Lex Hunter (a fine professional light-weight), he joined the Repton Club in Bethnal Green when he was eleven. Maurice was only the fourth black member of the club, and racism was part of his experience from the start. He was faced with racist remarks and jibes, and was even spat on in the showers after training.

But slowly he fought and overcame it, with a mixture of quiet dignity and iron-hard resolve. It was a difficult apprenticeship for the pro game, but there, similarly, he used the same weapons to combat hostility. By the time Hope turned professional, having competed for Britain in the 1972 Olympic Games, a black face in the Repton colours was no longer a cause for comment. Maurice followed a good many of his Repton club-mates into the Terry Lawless camp, and quickly became a contender in the recently established light-middleweight division, one weight up from that in which he had competed as an amateur.

After ten fights (nine wins) he travelled up the motorway to challenge Larry Paul for the British title on the Midlander's home ground, Wolverhampton Civic Hall. It set the pattern for Hope's future career, when so many of his major fights took place far from home. Hope was a revelation: he boxed brilliantly against the gifted but erratic Paul, wearing him down gradually before knocking him out in the eighth round.

Three quick wins over imported opponents persuaded Hope to step up a division and face Bunny Sterling, the former European champion, for the vacant British middleweight title. It was a foolish move, which was rumoured to have had its roots in a confrontation between the two in a black club in Croydon. Whatever the truth of that tale, Lawless and Hope convinced themselves that he could handle the vastly experienced Sterling, but Bunny pointed out their mistake with a painfully one-sided beating. Hope simply could not get going, and Sterling dominated the exchanges before the fight was halted in the eighth.

The lesson was well learned, and Hope did not lose again for six years. Concentrating on his own division, he retained his British title against Paul, this time in four rounds, and added the vacant Commonwealth title with a gruelling twelfth-round stoppage of the gallant Tony Poole from Northampton. Six months later, in October 1976, he went to Rome and took the European title from Vito Antuofermo, later to become world middleweight champion. It was a clinical performance by the challenger, who defied the crowd's antagonism to wear down and stop the hard-as-nails Antuofermo in the fifteenth and final round.

That result moved him into position to challenge Germany's Eckhard Dagge for the WBC version of the world title, and once again that meant an away trip, to Berlin. Hope looked to have won clearly, but the judges saved the German's title with a draw. Any expectations of a speedy rematch were soon crushed as Dagge gave him the runaround, and the fact that he had to wait two years for a second chance reflects no credit at all on the WBC.

Hope knew that one defeat would sabotage his chances of another world title chance. But he was a professional fighter with a living to earn, so he kept busy with two European defences (one a risky match in Hamburg against an unbeaten young German, Frank Wissenbach) and four routine ten-rounders. The opponents were not outstanding, but Hope's number one ranking was at stake every time he entered the ring and the pressure on him must have been intense.

Dagge in the meantime had lost the title to Rocky Mattioli, a rugged Italian who had made his name in Australian rings before returning home. Mattioli would probably have preferred a couple of safe defences before facing Hope, but at last the WBC acted to protect Hope's interests and he got his second chance, on 4 March 1979 in a circus tent in the Italian seaside resort of San Remo.

Mattioli was a typical Italian brawler in the Vito Antuofermo/ Rocky Graziano mould, yet it turned out to be as easy a job as Maurice ever had. Mattioli was floored in the opening round and fell awkwardly, breaking his thumb as he sat down heavily on it. He must have been in considerable pain, but plodded on until his corner signalled surrender at the end of the eighth.

Hope, understandably, looked for an easy option in his first defence. Promoter–matchmaker Mickey Duff settled on Mike Baker, a white American with a moderate record. Baker probably owed his place in the world rankings, and his title opportunity, to the fact that the famous American lawyer Edward Bennett Williams (whose clients included many leading Mafiosi as well as the WBC itself) was closely involved in his management. Certainly he had done little to earn his position on merit, and his performance against Hope confirmed that he was little more than a club fighter who had no business being in a world title ring.

He was warned for holding in the first minute, and that set the tone for a woefully inadequate challenge. Hope was embarrass-ingly superior, and coasted through seven rounds before the referee stopped it.

All kinds of big-money fights were mooted for Maurice: Wilfred Benitez, Roberto Duran, Sugar Ray Leonard. But one after the other they drifted away like wisps of smoke. Instead he had to face Mattioli again, fifteen months after taking the title from him. At least, for a change, Hope got home advantage, as the fight headed a late-night televised show from Wembley Conference Centre. This time there were no excuses Mattioli could offer, as Hope took him apart with a near-flawless exhibition of southpaw punch-picking. The Italian lasted until the eleventh, but scarcely won a round.

Then came the cruellest blow of Hope's career: an eye examination disclosed a loose retina, and it seemed that he would be forced into retirement without having earned a fraction of his potential. With nothing to lose, Hope gambled on a revolutionary laser-technique operation, and it worked. Within months of the original diagnosis, he was back in the Wembley ring defending his title against Carlos Herrera, a dour and formidably strong Argentinian. Herrera gave him the toughest fifteen rounds of his career, and it took real character for Hope to survive some rocky spells and fire back to win a close but merited decision.

And now, at last, Hope got his payoff – a date in Las Vegas against the precociously gifted Wilfred Benitez, who was bidding to become a three-weight world champion. It was not quite the financial bonanza Hope had anticipated, but it was still a huge step up from his previous purses.

Hope fought well and held his own with the brilliant young Puerto Rican for two-thirds of the distance, but Benitez drew away from the tenth and finished the fight in the twelfth with a single, stunning right hand. Hope was pole-axed, and it was a few minutes before he had recovered sufficiently to leave the ring. He was taken to hospital for observation, but happily no lasting damage had been done.

The next day he legitimized his long-standing union with Pat, a beautiful and elegant hairdresser who was the mother of his two daughters, in a Las Vegas hotel wedding chapel. Even though his career was in decline, these were good times for Hope. The family lived in a large and impressive home in Stoke Newington, and his children were being educated at private school, to which he ferried them in an expensive car. But when the boxing stopped, so too did the earnings, and Hope did not adjust his lifestyle in time. He became a victim of the wealth trap, and the crash was inevitable.

Hope boxed only once more, when he attempted to regain his European title from Luigi Minchillo of Italy at Wembley and lost a punishing fight on a split decision. He was still a world-class performer, but clearly not the force he had been two years earlier, and his retirement announcement shortly afterwards was well timed.

He took out a manager's licence and had some success, notably when Prince Rodney won his old British light-middleweight title, but his heart was never in that side of the business and he drifted away from it. He subsequently divided his time between Britain and Antigua, whose Government engaged him to coach the national side, but his business interests in Britain did not prosper and in 1986 he was declared bankrupt.

Hope was never a high-profile world champion like his contemporaries Alan Minter and Jim Watt, but the courage and class which hallmarked his career earned him the respect and affection of everyone who appreciates a true fighting man.

CAREER RECORD: 35 fights, 30 wins (24 inside schedule), 1 draw, 4 defeats.

Alan Minter (born 1951)

SOME years ago an American boxing magazine published its ratings list of the men who have claimed the middleweight championship of the world. The last name on the list was the Crawley southpaw Alan Minter. It was a grossly unfair assessment, which probably owed more to the fact that Minter had committed the unforgivable sin of winning a world title in America than it did to any dispassionate critique of his accomplishments. After all, English fighters are not supposed to do that sort of thing.

Minter does not belong with the Robinsons, Zales, Walkers and Grebs of the division, nor did he ever claim to, but he was infinitely better than pedestrian performers such as Al McCoy and George Chip whom the magazine rated above him. Minter had the bad luck to straddle the reigns of two of the greatest of all middleweights, Carlos Monzon and Marvin Hagler, and inevitably he suffers by comparison. But he deserves to be judged on the basis of the men he beat, and there were enough quality names there to establish Minter as one of our better world champions.

He was born on 17 August 1951, of an English father and German mother – and ironically it was in Germany that the young Minter suffered the biggest disappointment of his amateur career. It came in the semi-finals of the 1972 Olympic Games in Munich. Minter had been a cut-eye loser in the ABA championships that year after winning the title in 1971, but the selectors decided that he merited a place on the team anyway. In fact, they offered him two, at light-middle and middle, and allowed him to pick his own poundage.

He went as a light-middleweight, and won three times to qualify for the semi-finals where he faced the home favourite, Dieter Kottysch. Minter appeared to have outboxed the German easily, and the decision in Kottysch's favour brought howls of protest from home fans and British supporters alike. To his credit, Kottysch made it clear that he, too, thought Minter had won, and even sent him a Christmas card that year!

Minter turned pro on his return under the management of his amateur mentor Doug Bidwell, who later became his father-in-law. The London promoter Mike Barrett was also heavily involved with

Minter's career, and it was in a Barrett–Duff promotion at the Albert Hall on 31 October 1972 that Alan made his pro debut, stopping Maurice Thomas in six rounds.

In those early days he was known as 'Boom Boom' Minter, which derived from his habit of snorting twice as he threw his punches. Professional coaching soon eradicated the habit, but the nickname lingered. He progressed smoothly up the ratings, and within six months was beating well-regarded pros such as Ronnie Hough, Pat Dwyer, Harry Scott, Pat Brogan and Frank Young. There was one minor setback: Scottish veteran Don McMillan stopped him on a cut eye. But generally everything was proceeding to plan.

But then, between 30 October 1973 and 29 October 1974, it all went horribly wrong. Jan Magdziarz, a rugged brawler whose daytime job was as a lab technician at Southampton University, stopped him twice on cuts, in October and December. Minter managed a win in March, outscoring Tony Byrne, but then his fragile eyebrows let him down again when Ricky Ortiz of Puerto Rico cut and stopped him in three rounds at Wembley. Three losses in his last four fights was disheartening form, but the British Board was sympathetic and matched him with Magdziarz again, this time in a final eliminator for the British title.

It was the lowest point of Minter's career; neither man made an aggressive move for three and a half rounds, and finally referee Harry Gibbs imposed the professional game's ultimate sanction and disqualified both men for 'not giving of their best', declaring it a 'no contest'. It was a humiliating experience for a young fighter accustomed only to victories and acclaim, but it was a salutary lesson. One of the signs of a good fighter is the ability to learn from setbacks, and Minter was certainly a much better fighter after the Magdziarz fiasco than he had been before that dreadful evening in October 1974.

He rebuilt his image with four solid wins in 1975, and then in November that year met Kevin Finnegan, the younger of the two formidable brothers from Iver, for the British title which Bunny Sterling had vacated. Finnegan was, in my view, the best British champion never to win a world title. He was certainly the unluckiest: he lost to Minter three times, always by the minimum half-point margin, and when he did finally get to within one fight of a world title challenge he suffered a broken jaw in a meaningless ten-rounder and never again got close to the chance that his talent merited.

Their first meeting was at Wembley on 4 November 1975, and the two young middleweights put on a marvellous battle. I was in the minority who felt that Finnegan had just got home, but the decision was really too close for argument. They fought again ten months later, after Minter in the meantime had added a second notch on the Lonsdale Belt with a devastating two-round win over the ex-amateur star Billy Knight. This time, Finnegan looked to have won beyond any dispute, as he twice had Minter on the very edge of a knockout, with only the southpaw's heart and will keeping him upright. But referee Roland Dakin, who was to be at the centre of another scoring row when Minter won the world title, thought otherwise.

The ubiquitous Mickey Duff, who made virtually all of Minter's matches, judged the time was right to move him into major international class (Minter had, of course, already beaten his share of the foreign cannon-fodder on which today's rising young stars are invariably fed). He imported former world title challengers Tony Licata and Sugar Ray Seales, the one-time Olympic gold medal winner who went on to have quite a few fights too many, and who is now blind as a result. Minter whacked them both, surviving a hideous swelling on the forehead – almost as if a tennis ball had been inserted under the skin – to stop Seales in the fifth.

A trip to Milan brought him a knockout of Germano Valsecchi for the European title, but then Minter took an ill-judged match against the awkward American southpaw Ronnie Harris – another former Olympic champion – and referee Sid Nathan had to rescue him in the eighth, bleeding from a cut mouth and from cuts over both eyes. Typically, Minter wanted to fight on, but it was a lost cause.

He added a distinguished name to his record by ending the career of five-time world champion Emile Griffith in July, but then came another setback. Gratien Tonna, an erratic but murderous-hitting Frenchman, stopped him on a cut in Milan and the European title was gone. And so it was back over old ground again, to face Finnegan for the third time. It was the clearest win of the three, although the margin again was only half a point.

The European title was vacant, and Minter was paired with the lanky Italian Angelo Jacopucci in the seaside town of Bellaria. Jacopucci did not really belong in Minter's class, but was fighting for pride as much as for the title after accusations of cowardice had been made against him. He ended those rumours, but at a terrible price. When lesser men would have surrendered, Jacopucci hung on in the face of severe punishment until, at last, he could take no more and was counted out in the twelfth round.

I was in Minter's dressing room afterwards when Jacopucci came in to congratulate him, and the smiling Italian seemed to have made a full recovery. But later that night he collapsed at a restaurant, and never came out of his subsequent coma. His death was a test of Minter's character, but he put it behind him and, by stopping Tonna in a rematch four months later, confirmed his status as official contender for the world title.

It proved an elusive target, and Minter spent the whole of 1979 in marking-time fights against middle-grade opponents before he eventually landed his world title chance, in the Sports Pavilion at Caesars Palace, Las Vegas, on 16 March 1980. The champion was Vito Antuofermo, a squat, powerful, Italian-born brawler who had once held the European light-middleweight title, losing it to Maurice Hope. His propensity to bleed was, if anything, even worse than Minter's, and a blood-bath was expected when the division's two most cut-prone fighters met.

In fact, though, there was very little blood in evidence. Minter boxed a careful, competent fight and outsmarted the predictable Italian at every turn. The scoring caused a furore when it was announced that British judge Roland Dakin had given Minter a 12-point margin, but, reporting at ringside, I noted that the judge whose competence should be questioned was Adaslad Sanchez of Venezuela, who gave Minter only five of the fifteen rounds; Dakin's card was not so outrageous. This was one of those fights where the scoreline might suggest an overwhelming victory, but where each round might have been won by only a couple of punches.

Dakin's scoring helped to create the myth that Antuofermo had been robbed, and probably because of that Minter has never been given the credit he deserved in America. To settle the doubts, he gave Antuofermo a rematch at Wembley in June, and this time the brave Italian was outclassed and had to retire, bleeding, at the end of the eighth.

A threatening black cloud had hung over the championship reigns of both Antuofermo and Minter: the shaven-skulled south-paw from Brockton, Marvin Hagler. Many had regarded Hagler as the world's best middleweight for a couple of years, and indeed, had it not been for some peculiar scoring which allowed

Antuofermo to snatch a draw with him in Las Vegas, he might well have made his status official a year before he did.

Minter might have been able to avoid him for a while, but grasped the nettle by agreeing to defend against him at Wembley on 27 September. The Englishman chose a singularly unfortunate phrase when he told a press conference that 'there was no way he was going to lose his title to a black man'. He may well have regretted it the moment he said it, but the remark was seized upon by Britain's extreme right, who interpreted it as proof that Minter was 'their' man.

It created the ugliest atmosphere I have ever experienced at a title fight. Wembley was awash with flag-waving, beer-swilling, racist yobs, who went berserk when Minter was cut to defeat in the third round of a fiercely fought battle. Hagler was winning anyway, but Minter was a long way from disgraced. The same could not be said for those who claimed to be his supporters: beer cans were hurled towards the ring, splattering the ringsiders, and the new champion had to crouch for cover on the canvas and then be hustled away under police escort without even hearing himself proclaimed champion.

Whatever hopes Minter may have entertained of a second chance vanished when the Syrian Mustafa Hamsho outpointed him in Las Vegas in June 1981 and, after British rival Tony Sibson knocked him out in three rounds in September, smashing his nose so badly that it needed plastic surgery, Minter quit.

There was no comeback, nor even a rumour of one. He owned a restaurant in Crawley for a while, but when his marriage broke up he left the town and is now involved in the building business. He remains a high-profile figure, an inveterate fight-goer who does regular commentary stints for both radio and television.

In another time, against a less formidable contender than Marvin Hagler, he might well have kept the title for a couple of years. But he should not be judged by the brevity of his reign. He earned his title by beating the best men around, and he didn't try to dodge a man who he must have known would beat him. That, as much as anything, is the mark of a real champion.

CAREER RECORD: 49 fights, 39 wins (23 inside schedule), 9 defeats, 1 'no contest'.

Cornelius Boza-Edwards
(born 1956)

CORNELIUS BOZA-EDWARDS had a background as colourful as his name. He was born in Uganda, whence he fled to escape the Idi Amin terror, and mastered his fighting trade in England. But Boza really blossomed in America, where he won the WBC super-featherweight title and, in a series of wildly exciting fights, established himself as the most popular performer of the boom years of American TV boxing.

He has known tragedy and trials on a greater scale than most of us, but through them all has remained the same affable, easy-going, genuine man that he was when he first arrived in Britain to join his amateur boxing mentor from Kampala, the English plantation owner Jack Edwards. Boza – whose surname is properly spelt Bosa – had taken up boxing at eleven in Uganda, in the same club as Ayub Kalule, another brilliant southpaw who went on to win the WBA light-middleweight title. But life in Idi Amin's Uganda offered little hope for an intelligent and ambitious young man, and so when Edwards decided to return home to London in 1974 after his farm and business had been confiscated by the Government, Boza followed him there and even added Jack's surname to his own in token of the debt he owed him.

He picked up the threads of his boxing career, first with the New Enterprise and then the Fitzroy Lodge club in South London, in whose colours he won London titles at bantamweight in 1975 and featherweight the following year. Boza was a hot tip for the 1976 ABA title, but came unstuck in the semi-finals against Pat Cowdell, who had already won titles at bantamweight and lightweight and was seeking a unique treble.

The Midlander produced a masterly display of precision boxing to outpoint the aggressive African southpaw, but Boza learned much in defeat from the Warley craftsman. Cowdell would go on to fight twice for the world featherweight title, and to complete European and British title doubles at both featherweight and super-featherweight, but their paths never crossed professionally.

Boza turned pro in December 1976 with London manager Mickey Duff. It was a wise choice, for Duff had the kind of international contacts that Boza's career development would need. Duff knew that, exciting though Boza undoubtedly was, the London boxing public were unlikely to take a black African to their hearts. Boza had his first 13 fights in Britain, losing only on a cut to Des Gwilliam, and then Duff took him on the road.

Wherever a Duff-connected fighter appeared on a major bill around Europe, Africa or America, Boza would usually be found a spot on the undercard. It was an exacting apprenticeship, but it paid off. The experience of so many fights away from home helped to harden Corny and knock the rough edges off his style, while at the same time keeping him out of the limelight and free from the pressure that a fast-rising young prospect must normally endure.

Between July 1978 and March 1980 Boza boxed ten times, and seven of them were abroad in venues as disparate as Zambia, Italy, America and Monaco. By now Boza had reached the lower fringes of the world rankings, but Duff, knowing that it would be difficult to advance his career without American TV exposure, gambled on accepting a non-title match with the dazzling Nicaraguan holder of the WBC title, Alexis Arguello.

Boza fought well and bravely, and although he retired at the end of the eighth round he had done quite enough to impress both Arguello – who predicted a championship future for him – and the US TV money-men, who wanted to see more of the exciting free-hitting African with what they fondly imagined to be an English accent. Just three fights later, the gamble was rewarded when Boza landed a title fight against the Mexican hard man Rafael 'Bazooka' Limon, who had taken over as champion when weight-making difficulties forced Arguello to move up.

Few thought Boza had much chance, especially as he had to face Limon in Stockton, California, but by now Corny was well used to fighting far from home. Limon, like the critics, expected an easy night's work. Instead, fifteen rounds later, he was an ex-champion after a gruelling, foul-filled and bloody battle.

Boza's first defence, less than three months later, was even tougher. Bobby Chacon was a charismatic Californian who had held the featherweight title before moving up a weight. He was a big favourite with the West Coast fans and, like Boza, was rarely in a dull fight. Again like Boza he, too, knew great tragedy in his personal life, when his wife Valerie shot herself because of his refusal to give up boxing; in 1979 Boza's English wife, Jackie, had died of kidney failure, leaving him to rear their infant daughter Michelle.

Their fight in Las Vegas in May 1981 was a classic, one of the epic encounters of the decade. It finished in Boza's favour when the American, battered and bleeding but still defiant, was retired by his corner.

Two such punishing fights in such a short space of time should have earned Boza a spell of rest and recuperation, but instead he was back in the ring in August in Viareggio, Italy, defending against Rolando Navarette, a crude Filipino southpaw. Boza had nothing left to give, and took a one-sided pounding before Navarette finally knocked him out in the fifth.

With Boza's stock temporarily devalued in America, Duff began the rehabilitation process in London. At that time the qualification period for boxing for a British title was ten years, and so with that avenue closed to him Duff concentrated instead on getting Boza back into world title contention via the European championship, which had a shorter eligibility period. Champion Carlos Hernandez of Spain had made eight successful defences, but Boza ended his reign at the Albert Hall on 17 March 1982, when the Spaniard surrendered in the fourth round.

The low-key ending denied Boza the chance to display his talents properly to what he still regarded as his home crowd, and in fact he boxed only twice more in Britain for the rest of his career. Five weeks later, another of Duff's inspired gambles had short-routed him back up the ratings, as Boza butchered the previously unbeaten John 'The Heat' Verderosa in three rounds at Atlantic City. The win re-established Boza as a TV favourite, and over the next couple of years he figured in some of the great American fights of the early eighties.

He moved back and forth between lightweight and super-featherweight, but despite his unmatched reputation as a crowd-pleaser he found it difficult to land a title fight in either division. He came close when a rematch was arranged with Chacon, who by now had won the WBC title, but championship recognition was withdrawn amid a welter of writs and counter-writs. The fight went ahead anyway, billed as the 'People's Championship', and Chacon won a savagely fought twelve-rounder. A further loss, to the future champion Rocky Lockridge, moved Boza permanently into the lightweight class, where he resumed his patient search for a title chance.

It took him seven fights, six wins and a draw before he got it. The flashy Puerto Rican Hector Camacho defended the WBC title against him in Miami in September 1986, and was too fast and clever for the by now battleworn Boza. He rested for ten months, then came back with a typically thrilling points win in New York over Ali Karim Muhammad which earned him one final crack at the WBC title. This time, though, José Luis Ramirez knocked him out in five rounds in Paris, and Boza never fought again.

He had remarried in 1981, to a beautiful part-Japanese girl named Rumiko Moore. They met in Las Vegas, where they still live. He now has a Mercedes dealership, but also plans to get back into the business as a trainer: like so many great competitors, he has found it impossible to break the links with the game to which he has already given so much.

CAREER RECORD: 53 fights, 45 wins (34 inside schedule), 1 draw, 7 defeats.

Charlie Magri (born 1956)

IT IS easy to see why, with his uniquely appealing combination of power and vulnerability, the London fight crowd loved Charlie Magri. He hit harder than any British flyweight since Peter Kane half a century earlier – but if the opponent connected first, then Charlie could be in trouble. With a stouter chin, Magri could have been one of British boxing's all-time greats in the lighter divisions. He had everything else: power, skill, a knockout punch in either hand, and a charming personality which endeared him even to his critics.

He was born in Tunisia on 20 July 1956, one of seven children, and the family emigrated to England when he was a child, settling in east London. At eleven, Charlie joined the Arbour Youth club and launched a brilliant amateur career. He won four ABA titles, one at light-flyweight and three at flyweight, as well as a host of junior honours. At international level he took a silver medal in the 1974 European Under–21 championships, and a bronze in the senior event in Katowice a year later.

Magri, who was working at the time as a tailor's cutter in Whitechapel, went to the Montreal Olympics in 1976 as one of Britain's hottest tips for a gold medal, but flopped; an unknown Canadian, Ian Clyde, stopped him in his first contest. It was Charlie's fourth defeat in around a hundred bouts, and significantly all the losses had been inside the distance.

The vulnerability was apparent, but once he announced his intention to turn professional with Terry Lawless in 1977 the publicity machine ensured that this flaw was glossed over by the national press, if not by the trade paper. Magri knocked out the former Irish amateur champion Neil McLaughlin on his debut on 25 October 1977, and three weeks later he repeated the result of the 1976 ABA flyweight final when he stopped the Welshman Bryn Griffiths in two rounds. Griffiths never boxed again.

Forty-two days after his debut, Magri won the vacant British flyweight title. It was no great achievement: there were only four flyweights active at the time, and Magri had already beaten two of them. The third, and his title opponent, was Eltham's Dave Smith, whom he met at the Albert Hall on 6 December. Magri was much too good for the twenty-four-year-old Smith, who had been an international-class amateur himself. Smith fought heroically, climbing up from seven knockdowns before referee Roland Dakin rescued him in the seventh round. It was the quickest British title success in the sport's history, and it had an odd footnote ten years later, almost to the day.

On 9 December 1987, the Boxing Board of Control held a ceremony at their London office to present Magri with a Lonsdale Belt to keep, on the grounds that the lack of suitable opposition had denied him the chance to earn one in the ring. The Board had done that only once before, more than twenty years earlier, when the recipient was Walter McGowan, another former world flyweight champion.

Smith was the last British opponent Magri faced until his final fight, nearly nine years later. The remaining 31 contests were against an assortment of Continentals, Orientals and Latin Americans, of varying abilities and accomplishments. Some of the early opponents had spectacularly poor records: Nessim Zebelini had won 10 of 31 fights, Dominique Cesari boasted 13 wins in 31 outings, Filipo Belvedere had won 11 out of 32, and Raul Pacheco had 19 wins in 33 fights.

Mixed in with the dross, however, were some competent performers such as the Spanish southpaw Manuel Carrasco, who took Magri the distance for the first time, and the Italian veteran Francio Udella, from whom Magri won the European title in his twelfth fight at Wembley on 1 May 1979. Udella, who had been the first ever world light-flyweight champion, had held the European title since 1974, but never boxed again after losing to Magri.

The old weakness, though, reasserted itself in Magri's first fight as European champion when Freddie Gonzalez dropped him briefly before going under in the third round. Charlie may have had other matters on his mind that night: three weeks later he married nineteen-year-old Jackie Britton, who presented him with a daughter, Emma, in 1982.

Throughout the rest of 1979 and 1980 the build-up continued. He retained his European championship twice, being taken the distance again by the durable Carrasco and stopping Italy's Giovanni Camputaro in three rounds. There were two notable victories during this period: Alfonso Lopez, a former WBA flyweight champion, was outpointed, and Santos Laciar of Argentina floored Magri in the first round but lost on points in a superb ten-rounder at the Albert Hall.

With hindsight, that was the supreme performance of Magri's career. Laciar, a few fights later, won the WBA flyweight title for the first of several times, and went on to establish himself as one of the division's best champions of the 1980s. When his flyweight days were over, he moved up to super-flyweight and won that title as well, and at the time of writing he is still highly rated by all the various authorities. Yet Magri had beaten him beyond argument, and the merit of that result should never be undervalued.

Enrique Rodriguez Cal, a grossly overmatched Spaniard, was floored four times and stopped in the second round of a European title defence in February 1981, and in August that year Magri relinquished the British title to allow a couple of lesser performers, Kelvin Smart and Dave George, the chance to contest it.

In October the bubble burst. Juan Diaz, a squat, slab-faced little Mexican who had lost 16 of his 39 fights, was not expected to provide Magri with anything other than a brisk work-out at the Albert Hall, but instead he smashed Charlie to sixth-round defeat. When Magri was floored again in his 'comeback' fight by Cipriano Arreola, and finished with his right eye battered shut, all prospects of a world championship seemed to have disappeared.

On 4 May 1982 another Mexican, José Torres, appeared to have administered the *coup de grâce* to Charlie's aspirations when he survived some hard early rounds to wear down and stop the Londoner in nine rounds at Wembley. But it never pays to underestimate the ability of Magri's promoter, Mickey Duff, to retrieve apparently impossible situations.

In just two fights, Magri was rehabilitated. He went to Spain for a ridiculous rematch with Cal, ordered by the European Boxing Union, and knocked him out in two rounds. Then, on 23 November at Wembley, he won a magnificent ten-round return fight with Torres to set up the world title chance at Wembley on 15 March 1983.

The WBC title carried something of a jinx, as its champions seemed unable to retain it for even one defence. The present incumbent was Eloncio Mercedes, a twenty-five-year-old from the Dominican Republic. Magri could not have hand-picked a better opponent: Mercedes was strictly a non-puncher, who won only three fights inside the distance in his entire career. He had taken the title from the former light-flyweight champion Freddie Castillo in November 1982, and had won only 12 of his 20 fights, drawing two. He, too, had been stopped by Juan Diaz in 1979, but had outpointed Diaz in a twelve-rounder immediately before taking the title from Castillo.

Mercedes was fast and stylish, but lacked the power to keep Magri at bay. There were few real highlights until the sixth round, when Mercedes was cut badly over the left eye. Referee Rey Solis of Mexico consulted the ringside doctor, Adrian Whiteson, who ordered that the fight be stopped, and Magri leapt in jubilation as he realized that after all the detours, disappointments and setbacks he had finally become champion of the world.

But the jinx held as Magri, too, lost the title in six rounds on his first defence to a Filipino, Frank Cedeno, at Wembley six months later. (Cedeno was also dethroned by his first challenger. In fact, six champions came and went before one managed a successful defence.)

It was a bad night for Charlie – so bad that it was assumed he had retired – but he reappeared almost a year later to challenge Franco Cherchi for the European title in Cagliari, Sardinia. He had opened a sports-goods shop, and business was not as brisk as he would have wished. The injection of a few healthy fight purses into the project would make a difference, and besides, he felt that at only twenty-eight he had not achieved everything that was within his power.

It was a dream return: Cherchi was cut by a clash of heads in the opening round, forcing the referee to stop the fight as soft-drink cans and fruit rained into the ring in protest.

And then boxing politics, which have so often hampered the careers of British boxers, worked to Magri's benefit. Mickey Duff's new and aggressive young rival Frank Warren was anxious to stage prestige fights in a bid to establish himself as a force in the game, and he paid the formidable Thai Sot Chitalada $100,000 to defend against Magri in London. Under normal circumstances Lawless would not have entertained an offer from Warren, but the shrewd Warren had timed his approach well.

The existence of a cartel involving Lawless, Mickey Duff, Jarvis Astaire and Mike Barrett had recently come to light, and it was politic for Lawless to show that he and his boxers were not tied exclusively to one promotional group. In any case, the offer was too good to decline, and at that stage of Magri's career there would not be many more chances.

Magri made his second challenge at Alexandra Palace on 20 February 1985. For two rounds he boxed brilliantly, blasting home punches from all angles on the impassive Thai. But Chitalada took them all unflinchingly, and from the third round he began to break Magri up. The cut which opened on Charlie's right eyebrow in the fourth saved him the embarrassment of a worse defeat, as Lawless was quick to pull his man out at the end of the round.

Once more it was assumed that Magri had fought his last fight. He had relinquished the European title in January to facilitate the world title challenge, and there seemed little point in continuing. But a £14,000 offer to face Cherchi again, this time on mainland Italy at Alessandria in October 1985, persuaded him to change his mind. The money was a powerful incentive, but there was also the lure of joining Henry Cooper and Joe Bugner as the only British boxers to have won the same European title three times.

Cherchi, a local government officer, was hopelessly outclassed and the towel fluttered in from the Italian corner as he went down for the second time in the second round. Magri had looked so impressive that a third world title chance was suddenly a possibility; but Duff had other ideas.

He managed Duke McKenzie, who had recently won the British title, and he felt that the time was right to move McKenzie up the ladder at Magri's expense. The pair met for both titles at Wembley on 20 May 1986, and Charlie could do nothing with the tall, lightning-fast McKenzie. At the end of the fifth round, after Magri had been floored, Lawless draped a towel round Charlie's head and signalled the end of the fight – and, this time, of his career.

No one who has been in the business for over twenty years, as Magri had, can walk away from it, and Charlie has been busy since his retirement coaching the Lions Boys' Club in east London. He continues to run his sports shop in Bethnal Green Road, and has also flirted with the professional side of the game. He remains a popular and well-respected figure on the London fight scene, and his place in the records of British boxing is secure – and unique.

CAREER RECORD: 35 fights, 30 wins (23 inside schedule), 5 defeats.

Barry McGuigan (born 1961)

THE TRUE yardstick of Barry McGuigan's unique place in the affections of the Irish people is not that 10,000 of them travelled to London to watch him win the WBA featherweight title in 1985, but that when he returned in triumph to Dublin more people thronged the streets of the capital than had come out a few years earlier to welcome John Paul II. The country boy from Clones outdrew the Pope.

The Irish, as a race, have a giant inferiority complex which ignores the contributions they have made to the world in so many different fields of endeavour. Whenever an Irish person does well on the international stage, the rest of the country tends to stand back in amazement, so that the success attracts quite disproportionate national interest. So it was with McGuigan, although in his case the story was complicated by the cleverly orchestrated PR campaign which created for him the image of 'The Peacemaker', the man whose achievements united the divided communities of Northern Ireland.

In reality, this was arrant nonsense. Boxing has always crossed easily over the sectarian divides. The Irish international amateur team is drawn from the 32 counties, and in the professional game – traditionally a Northern preserve – the victories of a Catholic from the Falls like Hugh Russell drew just as much enthusiastic acclaim as those of a Shankhill Road Protestant like Davey Larmour (who, as if to emphasize the point, was trained in the later part of his career by another Catholic ex-champion, Paddy Maguire).

But the peacemaker image was powerfully emotive and effective, and the British media, who for a decade had handled nothing but bad and bloody news from Northern Ireland, suddenly had a pleasingly positive story on their hands.

McGuigan was born south of the border in Clones, Co. Monaghan, and qualifies for inclusion in this volume only because his manager, Barney Eastwood, persuaded him to become a British subject in order that he might win a Britsh title. Becoming champion, of course, would also enhance his marketability in Belfast, Eastwood's operational headquarters and home of the

King's Hall, the marvellously atmospheric arena in which McGuigan's progress to the world championship was shaped on a series of unforgettably exciting nights.

McGuigan was an immensely appealing young man, whose attraction transcended all barriers of age, sex, nationality and politics. Mothers wanted to cuddle him, daughters longed to date him, fathers jostled to shake his hand and boast of his acquaintance, and sons dreamt of emulating him. He was a very marketable commodity, but unlike so many other products of the PR men's imaginations, McGuigan was much more than just a handsome face and a quick wit: he really could fight, at the highest level. In his case, the charisma was just the window-dressing on the real product, rather than being the product itself.

He was swept to the top on a tidal wave of national fervour, but once the bell rang on that warm summer evening at Loftus Road football ground to send him on his way against the magnificent Panamanian Eusebio Pedroza with the world title on the line, McGuigan was on his own, beyond the help of his army of supporters – and he was not found wanting. McGuigan was not just a fighter: he was something much more complex, and the emotions which he generated and which fuelled his drive to the top of his profession were unique to his time and his place.

Like all the great champions, he started young. His father Pat, a showband singer, had been a useful amateur in his youth and his enthusiasm for the game infected his sons. When he was twelve, Barry made the short trip across the Monaghan–Fermanagh border to join the amateur club at Wattlebridge. After a couple of bouts he switched to the Smithboro club, eight miles from the family home above their grocery shop in the Diamond, Clones. The club was run by Frank Mulligan, a dedicated enthusiast who, with club trainer Danny McEntee, soon realized that McGuigan was no ordinary youngster.

McGuigan's first success was in the national U–14 championships, and after that the titles flowed in. By the time he was seventeen he was an established international, and already the framework for his pro style was built.

He was hard, even ruthless, in the ring, and was none too particular where the punches landed: that would be a recurring complaint from beaten and aching opponents throughout his career. Unlike most amateurs he had long since appreciated the value of body punching, and spent hours studying videos of his favourite professionals.

In 1978, having won the Irish senior title, he went to Edmonton and came back with a Commonwealth Games gold medal: although a southerner, he had boxed for Northern Ireland because both his parents had been born there. It was a punishing final, and there were plenty who thought him lucky to get the gold after taking two mandatory eight counts and getting a public warning against the customs officer from Papua New Guinea, Tumat Sogolik, who showed splendid sportsmanship by immediately congratulating the winner.

But it was the image, relayed around the world, of the Irish teenager weeping on the winner's rostrum which launched the McGuigan legend, and which captured the country's heart.

McGuigan's amateur career blossomed. He won gold medals in two multi-nation tournaments, but lost two shocking decisions in the European junior championships and in the ABA Centenary tournament at Wembley to the Scot, Ian McLeod. He went to the 1980 Olympics as Ireland's best medal prospect, but boxed below his best and was outpointed in his second contest by a lanky Zambian, Wilfred Kabunda.

The loss to McLeod a few months later convinced him that he had gone as far as he could in the amateur game, and he set about interviewing the impressive line-up of prospective managers. He could have had his pick of Terry Lawless, Mickey Duff, Eddie Thomas or Peter Keenan, but he opted instead for Belfast bookie and property speculator Barney Eastwood.

Eastwood was one of the wealthiest men in Ireland, but his spectacular successes in the business world had not satisfied him. He had a life-long interest in boxing, and had dabbled in small-scale promotions a decade or so earlier. McGuigan's potential was unlimited, and Eastwood believed that he had the resources and the ability to channel it properly. Pat McGuigan, on whose opinions Barry always relied heavily, favoured the local man. Barry had no desire to move far from home, particularly as he was by this time engaged to his childhood sweetheart, Sandra, and so Eastwood got the job.

His pro career began on a wet, cold night in a Dublin football stadium. The Irish star of the day, Derry's Charlie Nash, lost his European lightweight title to Joey Gibilisco in the main event. Nash was badly knocked out and was detained overnight in hospital, and the uncaring attitude of some of the men who were involved in Nash's career gave the Clones youngster an insight into the callous side of the pro game which he never forgot.

The wins piled up rapidly after that, apart from a hiccough in his third fight when Peter Eubanks got a controversial eight-rounds verdict over him in Brighton, which was comprehensively avenged in the rematch in Belfast. In his fourth fight, McGuigan came off the floor to outpoint Jean-Marc Renard, later to become a two-weights European champion, in the Ulster Hall. The compact little hall is a wonderful venue for boxing, and with Eastwood doing the hard sell to the media the great Belfast fight nights began. By mid-1982 the McGuigan phenomenom was established, and he had created his own unique aura.

When the tragic Nigerian Young Ali lapsed into irreversible coma after McGuigan knocked him out in June 1982, though, McGuigan had to endure an emotional crisis before deciding to box again.

By now McGuigan, acting on Eastwood's advice, had taken out British citizenship in order to become eligible to contest a British title. It was a controversial step, and for a time the unbroken adulation which he had hitherto enjoyed was marred by taunts of 'Barry the Brit'.

But McGuigan was young, naïve, and prepared to do whatever Eastwood told him was required. In any event, it made great copy for the tabloids – the young boxer who crossed the sectarian divides to unite the warring factions, the battler for peace. (The 'flag of peace', later to become part of the McGuigan trappings, was in fact adapted from the symbol of the Holiday Inn in London, where the McGuigan camp stayed prior to a European defence at the Albert Hall.)

The marketing strategy worked brilliantly, and McGuigan rapidly became one of the most identifiable faces in British sport. He stopped Vernon Penprase in two rounds for the vacant British featherweight title in April 1983, flooring the stylish West Country-man in the most impressive performance of his career so far.

After that, it was open throttle and all systems go for the world title. McGuigan roared up the world ratings in 1983–84, and his continued success prompted Eastwood to re-open the King's Hall in Belfast to boxing for the first time in over twenty years.

It was a crucial stage in McGuigan's development. The King's Hall, a 7000 capacity stadium in the Balmoral district of Belfast, provided an unmatched setting for the high drama of McGuigan's victories over the likes of Valerio Nati for the European title, Charm Chiteule, Jose Caba, Paul DeVorce and Felipe Orozco.

Of them all, only Chiteule gave him trouble. McGuigan was lucky to escape disqualification, and struggled through nine unimpressive rounds before catching up with the classy Zambian in the tenth.

But there was one final, formidable hurdle to cross first: the former WBC champion Juan Laporte. The fight was shown live on American TV, and now the rest of the world knew what we were getting so excited about. It was perhaps the most complete performance of McGuigan's career, although others might prefer his climactic win over Eusebio Pedroza three months later. Laporte rocked him twice, in the fifth and the ninth, but the way McGuigan survived full-blooded rights from the division's hardest puncher removed any lingering doubts that he was ready to make his bid for Pedroza's WBA title.

It took long and costly negotiation by Eastwood to lure the veteran Panamanian to London for his 20th and last defence of the championship, but it was worth it. Around 26,000 fans packed the Loftus Road ground, home of Queens Park Rangers football club, on 8 June 1985, on a night of nerve-tingling excitement and emotion. Pedroza was as good as his record indicated, and my ringside report described him, rightly, as 'one of the finest craftsmen ever to grace a British ring'. But this was Barry's night, and after he had floored the champion with a brilliant right in the seventh round there was little doubt that the title would change hands.

Pedroza fought a dogged, dignified rearguard action, and there was little of the foul play which had earned him such a notorious reputation in previous defences. He held his boxing together immaculately in the face of the most ferocious pressure, but at the final bell he immediately acknowledged that he had met his master.

McGuigan was never quite so good again, and the fighter who struggled through difficult defences against Danilo Cabrera and Bernard Taylor was a jaded, fight-weary shadow of the force that had almost swamped Pedroza.

He needed a long break from the rigours of training and fighting, and from the hectic social demands which his position imposed on him. Instead, and against his own better judgement, he signed to fight in Las Vegas on 23 June 1986, and embarked on a gruelling coast-to-coast promotional tour of America. The venture was doomed from the start, with training injuries and squabbles in the camp as his already fraying relationship with Eastwood degenerated into cold war. The last straw was when he had to accept a substitute opponent, Texan Steve Cruz, and agree to fight in the early part of the show when the afternoon sun would be at its fiercest.

Cruz was a competent but unexceptional performer, and under any other conditions McGuigan would have beaten him. But the heat was intolerable, almost literally lethal, and it drained and dehydrated him. By the closing rounds he was fighting on blind instinct, but it still needed two fifteenth-round knockdowns to swing the verdict Cruz's way.

That finished him with Eastwood: there could be no going back, and later that summer he started legal proceedings against him. Eastwood counter-sued, but then settled on the steps of the Belfast High Court on the morning the case was due to open, for an amount generally accepted to be around £600,000.

McGuigan tried to retire from the game, and dabbled in show business and car racing. But the call of the ring was too powerful and in late 1987, some months after the death of his much-loved father, he began preparations for a comeback, this time as a super-featherweight (9 st 4 lb). London promoter Frank Warren bought out the options which Eastwood held on the boxer, and McGuigan moved his fighting base across the Irish Sea.

He looked so good in his first two wins, over Nicky Perez and Francisco Tomas Da Cruz, that there seemed real hope of a world title. IBF champion Tony Lopez was the target, although WBC title-holder Azumah Nelson – who had dogged McGuigan's featherweight reign with endless taunts and challenges – was desperate for a money match with the charismatic Irishman.

But the third comeback test almost went wrong, as the rugged Argentinian Julio Miranda gave McGuigan a tough eight rounds at Edmonton before being ground down. Barry had won that one on guts and heart, and was quick to write it off as just a bad night. Not everyone was convinced, though, and when the former European featherweight champion Jim McDonnell stopped him on a cut in the fourth round in Manchester on 31 May 1989, McGuigan was forced to accept that the old fire had gone out. He announced his retirement within minutes of leaving the ring, and now plans to get involved in the business as a promoter or manager.

That nightmare in Las Vegas robbed McGuigan of his title and its repercussions kept him out of the ring for more than two years. Now we will never know just how great he might have become had his career been allowed to reach its full flower, but at least we can savour the memories of those three fabulous years when the little Irishman was the most thrilling performer in the whole of British sport.

CAREER RECORD: 35 fights, 32 wins (28 inside schedule), 3 defeats.

Terry Marsh (born 1958)

TERRY MARSH always wanted to be the only British world champion to walk away from the game undefeated. He made it, but not quite in the style he had planned. Instead of a euphoric post-victory announcement, Marsh's retirement was bannered across the front pages of the tabloids. The day after signing a contract for a defence which would have earned him more than he had ever made before, Marsh told the world that he was an epileptic who had been risking his life by boxing at all.

The news was greeted with a large amount of scepticism within the trade; Marsh had, after all, passed the usual medical examinations which precede any title fight, and had given no hint of his condition to those people most closely involved with his career. (A magazine which was rash enough to print Marsh's suggestion that his manager Frank Warren knew of the epilepsy had to make Warren a substantial out-of-court settlement.)

But then Marsh himself added to the mystery. In early 1989 he announced his intention to get back in the ring under the auspices of the IBF–UK, which was then attempting to gain a foothold in British boxing. He explained that he had been suffering not from epilepsy, but from a condition which was induced by gorging on chocolate and other sweet foods. But by then the damage had been done, and Marsh's career, instead of ending in a blaze of glory after a winning world title defence, petered out in a series of bitter recriminations between boxer and manager.

His farewell to the sport was the only aspect of his long and distinguished career which did not work out exactly as scheduled. Marsh was always different – more articulate and perceptive than the average fighter, a man who knew what he wanted from boxing and from life and was determined to have his way.

His background contrasted dramatically to that of most of Britain's world champions. He had been a London chess champion as a schoolboy, and tended to approach his boxing in the same cerebral fashion, regarding it as being as much an intellectual as a physical challenge. Such an approach seemed certain to turn off professional promoters and managers. After all, Chris Finnegan, his nearest equivalent in the amateur ring (although, of course, a southpaw), had been obliged to abandon his naturally cautious, slippery style and become a brawler instead in order to be marketable in the professional world.

But Marsh did it his way from start to finish, and when late in his career he opted for two-fisted aggression rather than points-pinching, that too was his own decision. He was never an outstanding crowd-puller, but his articulate delivery and appealing 'cheeky chappie' personality endeared him to the media world of chat shows and quiz-game panels.

He was one of the outstanding British amateurs of the late 1970s and early 1980s, winning three ABA titles in four finals between 1978 and 1981. He was lightweight champion in 1978, light-welterweight runner-up in 1979, and welterweight champion in 1980 and 1981, when his opponent in the final was the future European and British pro champion Chris Pyatt. He had already won a string of schools and junior titles, and boxed regularly for England.

In 1981 he decided to turn pro, and became the first big-name amateur to sign for Frank Warren, who was then battling to establish himself as the second promotional force on the London scene. By now the twenty-three-year-old Marsh had left the Marines, with whom his service had included stints in Northern Ireland, and was working in the Fire Service in his home town of Basildon. The shrewd Warren was quick to exploit the publicity angle of the 'Fighting Fireman'.

Marsh made an unspectacular start to his career. His fast-jabbing, fleet-footed approach was not calculated to have the customers queuing in the street, but it kept him unbeaten and trainer Ernie Fossey was sensible enough not to interfere with the style in which Marsh felt most comfortable.

The only blemish on the record was an eight-round draw with Lloyd Christie in April 1982. Christie then was regarded as a win-a-few, lose-a-few type without the flair and talent of brother Errol, but in fact after drawing with Marsh Lloyd he went on to win a Lonsdale Belt outright at light-welterweight while Errol's career fizzled out disappointingly.

In April 1983 Marsh acquired his first professional championship, outpointing Vernon Vanreil for the Southern Area title. But he boxed only once more that year, returning to action in April 1984 to outpoint Tony Sinnott in a final eliminator for the British title held by the Croydon veteran Clinton McKenzie, who was managed by Warren's arch-rival, Mickey Duff. The managerial rivalry gave the fight extra spice, and Warren won the first round by securing the right to promote it.

Marsh made his title bid on a sweltering September evening at Shoreditch Leisure Centre, and the TV lights made the clammy, suffocating heat of the hall almost intolerable for the spectators, let alone the boxers. The well-matched pair could have been forgiven for turning in an insipid, mauling match, but instead they staged a battle which ranked with the very best in the history of a division which had produced more than its share of thrillers in its relatively short life. Marsh drove himself to exhaustion and beyond, flailing away with uncharacteristic abandon at the veteran southpaw in the last couple of rounds to edge the decision.

The next target was the European championship, held by the Italian Olympic gold medallist Patrizio Oliva. Oliva obliged by winning the WBA title and vacating the European, which Marsh collected by travelling to Monte Carlo to knock out another Italian, Alessandro Scapecchi, in the sixth round of a live TV show. It was the first count-out victory of his career, and suddenly there was a real possibility that the Fighting Fireman might go all the way up the ladder.

He retained the European title twice in early 1986 while Warren manoeuvred him towards a world title bid. Tex N'Kalankete provided stiff opposition throughout their twelve-rounder, and later proved his worth by winning the title when Marsh was stripped of it a year later. The other challenger, Francesco Prezisio of Italy, was more durable than dangerous, and Marsh coasted to a points win in the only European championship ever staged on the Isle of Man.

Warren thought he had pinned down Oliva to a 12 July defence in Monte Carlo, but the Italian opted instead to meet an obscure American, Brian Brunette. Throughout 1986 the backstage haggling went on, while Marsh fretted in idleness. The European Boxing Union stripped him of the title for failing to defend within their deadline, ignoring the fact that he had injured a hand in training and then hurt his nose in an accident with a fire hose at work while practising drills. He had, in any case, packed three title fights into little more than five months and was entitled to expect a little grace from the EBU.

There were rumours of various world title dates and opponents, but then Warren wrong-footed everyone by announcing that he had booked the International Boxing Federation champion Joe Louis Manley to face Marsh in a circus tent pitched on the outskirts of Basildon on 4 March 1987.

It was a typically bold and imaginative stroke, calculated to achieve maximum publicity. The IBF was not recognized in Britain, one of the obstacles being their insistence on retaining the fifteen-round championship limit that the other two bodies, and the British Board, had abandoned. Warren relished the free publicity as the newspapers debated the issue, and the fact that the fight was being held on Marsh's wedding anniversary, which was also his photogenic little daughter's birthday, was a happy bonus for promoter, hacks and photographers alike.

The tent provided an odd setting for a night of high drama and uninhibited emotion, as Marsh hurled himself at the champion in round after round with what I described in *Boxing News* as 'a display of ruthless, brawling aggression that would not have been out of place in the harsher environs of Philadelphia or Mexico City'.

Manley had been briefed to expect a jab-and-move English stylist, but found himself confronted instead by a punching machine. Long before the finish, the outcome was inevitable. Manley looked a beaten man from four rounds on, and he folded at last at the end of the ninth. He was up at five as the bell rang, but the minute's respite was not enough and Marsh needed only 20 seconds of the tenth to bring referee Randy Neumann rushing to his dazed compatriot's rescue.

For months it seemed that the media could not get enough of Terry Marsh. He was strikingly different from the average pro fighter, and the image he conveyed was good for the game. He let it be known that his ambition was to defend his title once and then retire undefeated, and Warren set out to find the easiest acceptable opponent for a showpiece defence. He came up with a Japanese, Akio Kameda, whose early record was impressive enough; but because of a dispute between the IBF and the Japanese Board, he had been very inactive in the preceding three years, with only four insignificant contests between October 1984 and his title bid at the Albert Hall against Marsh on 1 July 1987.

What should have been a safe and easy defence for Marsh became instead a nail-biting struggle to hold on to his championship. Once more, Marsh abandoned his boxing skills and fought like a street brawler. He was flirting with disaster, and he paid a high price: in the second round he was cut over the right eye, and another vertical gash opened up in the next. From then on it was a case of whether the tall Japanese southpaw would crack before Marsh's cuts – which needed 13 stitches – forced him out of the fight.

But it came right in the end, as Kameda wilted dramatically in the sixth. He had been down for six late in the round, and at the bell was so dazed and disorientated that he went to a neutral corner instead of his own, leaning over the ropes in utter bewilderment. Board of Control doctor Adrian Whiteson immediately ran up the ring steps and told referee Randy Neumann and the challenger's cornerman that the fight was over.

Watching at ringside was the exotic Hector 'Macho' Camacho, resplendent in a bullfighter-style suit of lights. Marsh had had second thoughts about retirement, and the colourful Puerto Rican was lined up as the big-money opponent for the next defence.

Warren negotiated the contract, reportedly worth $250,000, which Marsh signed – and then the very next day the *Sun* carried a banner front page announcing Marsh's retirement. The rights and wrongs of the Marsh *v* Warren dispute will probably never be known publicly because of the rigorous libel laws that apply in this country, but Marsh – while disputing many aspects of Warren's statement – agreed that he had grossed around £250,000 in his career. Considering that few in the trade expected him to make the grade at all as a pro, that is a considerable achievement.

Wherever the truth lies, it was a sad, shabby and unseemly finish to what had promised to be one of the brightest success stories of modern British boxing. Marsh tried to have his licence reinstated in 1989, but the Board of Control refused. He then announced that he would return to action anyway under the auspices of the IBF–UK against another ex-Warren fighter, Sylvester Mittee. But wiser counsels prevailed and, at least at the time of writing, Marsh's comeback appears to be a dead issue.

CAREER RECORD: 27 fights, 26 wins (10 inside the distance), 1 draw.

Duke McKenzie (born 1963)

You COULD no more keep a Croydon McKenzie out of the ring than a Barrymore off the stage, or a Churchill or Kennedy out of politics. Winston was a neat-boxing pro lightweight, Dudley a useful middleweight, and Clinton won the British light-welterweight title three times and the European championship once. Cousin Lee was the Southern Area champion at the same weight, but the most successful of the bunch was the baby of the family, flyweight Duke.

The plethora of championships that exists following the formation of the International Boxing Federation and the World Boxing Organization, which themselves jostle for space with the long-established WBC and WBA, has substantially diluted the value of one of their 'world titles'. But McKenzie's capture of the IBF flyweight title in 1988 remains an outstanding achievement by a British fighter in a division which for the last forty years has been the traditional preserve of the Latins and Orientals.

McKenzie has had to accept that being a black British flyweight does not command a high public recognition factor. Ironically, the only time he has ever attracted national attention, as opposed to the odd slot on the sports pages, was when a crashed commuter train ploughed into his back yard in Thornton Heath, south London in March 1989, four days before he was due to defend his world title against Tony De Luca.

McKenzie's professional success has been all the more remarkable in view of the modest results he had as an amateur, first with the Sir Philip Game club in Croydon and, when that folded through lack of funds, subsequently with Battersea ABC. There was no string of ABA championships or international honours to ease his path when he turned professional in 1982, unlike brother Clinton who was ABA light-welterweight champion in 1976 and represented Britain in that year's Olympic Games.

Duke won around 60 of almost 90 contests, taking the London title in 1981 and boxing for Young England, and turned pro after being beaten in the 1982 London final by his south London rival Steve Nolan. He approached Mickey Duff, who was at first reluctant to take him on; after all, the only British flyweight in recent years who had made any significant money was Charlie Magri, whose world title potential was always evident.

He had considered joining the Terry Lawless camp, but knew that if he did so he would be very much in Magri's shadow. Duff warned him that there were no instant fortunes to be made for an unknown black fighter in an unglamorous division. Magri had enjoyed a high amateur profile which included four ABA championships and Olympic competition, but for McKenzie it was an uphill struggle all the way.

At least the advantages of being managed by someone with Duff's extensive international connections were considerable. Unable to guarantee him regular work in Britain, Duff used his transatlantic contacts to get McKenzie experience on the American circuit, and five of Duke's first ten fights took place in America at venues from Las Vegas to Los Angeles, Reno and Atlantic City. It was his East Coast success against David Capo that first suggested McKenzie might go further than his critics believed. Capo had beaten the 1976 Olympic champion, Leo Randolph, who went on to win a version of the world super-bantamweight title, and yet McKenzie handled him easily.

By June 1985, the British flyweight title was vacant. Charlie Magri was not interested, having recently lost to Sot Chitalada for the WBC title, and so Duff matched his man with Danny Flynn of Edinburgh for the title. It proved a painfully one-sided exercise as Flynn bounced around the canvas at the Albert Hall, taking count after count before McKenzie finally stopped him in the fourth.

Wins over a pair of imports, Orlando Maestre and Sonny Long, convinced Duff – ever a gambler – to try a short-cut for McKenzie into the world ratings. Magri had come back strongly to regain the European title, but Duff sensed that the time was right to risk McKenzie against him. It was a bold move, but sensible: there would be no disgrace in defeat by a former world champion, while if McKenzie won he would progress immediately into the world ratings, which might otherwise have taken another year and half a dozen fights.

They met at Wembley on 20 May 1986, with both titles at stake (McKenzie defending the British title, Magri the European). Magri was the crowd's favourite, but even his most committed fan could see from early in the fight that Charlie's career was about to end. He struggled to get the near the tall, long-armed McKenzie, and even when he did break through, the punches which had brought him 23 quick wins in 34 fights had little effect. Magri was floored in the fourth, looking thoroughly dispirited, and his manager, Terry Lawless, pulled him out at the end of the round.

It is never enjoyable to watch a big-hearted, popular battler like Magri having that one fight too many, and sympathy for the loser may have dulled appreciation of just how good a performance the winner had given. Certainly, it did not bring McKenzie any instant rewards – he did not even manage another British appearance that year. Instead, Duff took him back to America to outpoint Lee Cargle in Atlantic City, and to the Italian spa resort of Acqui Terme to return his European title against Giampiero Pinna, although one judge plumbed new depths of incompetence by scoring all twelve rounds even.

McKenzie spent 1987 and most of 1988 marking time in relatively meaningless wins over a succession of South American imports, and an absurdly one-sided European defence against the out-classed Spaniard Agapito Gomez. Duff was in a difficult position: the WBC title was held throughout this period by the formidable Thai Sot Chitalada, who was considered virtually unbeatable, while the WBA champion, Fidel Bassa, was not interested in meeting McKenzie.

The establishment of the IBF was a stroke of luck for Duff and McKenzie. As the newest and least recognized of the (then) three world authorities, it tended to attract fewer of the big-name contenders and so IBF title fights were cheaper to make than those involving WBC or WBA champions. The current holder of the IBF flyweight title was a Filipino, Rolando Bohol, and Duff succeeded in luring him to Wembley to defend against McKenzie on 5 October 1988.

The show – televised live by BBC – was hardly a box-office smash, but at least Duff got the result he wanted as McKenzie outboxed and gradually demoralized the inexperienced and fragile champion before knocking him out in the eleventh. It was a sweet moment for Duke, and for his band of loyal and highly vocal brothers who cheered him on from ringside. Clinton, a sadly undervalued boxer who deserved to fight for a world title himself, carried the winner around the ring as Duke showed off the championship belt, borrowed for the occasion as no new belt was available.

After years of struggling for a living, McKenzie at last had the chance to earn financial security. He made his first defence in March 1989, stopping a hand-picked American, Tony De Luca, in four rounds at the Albert Hall. De Luca, who had won 14 out of 18, was more a light-flyweight than a flyweight, and although the fight was halted because of a cut on the American's eye, there had not been the slightest hint that he was equipped to trouble McKenzie.

His next defence, against the hard-hitting Irishman Dave McAuley at Wembley on 7 June, saw the end of his brief championship reign as McAuley hustled him to a clear points defeat. But at least Duke, unlike the rest of his talented family, had been able to reap some rewards for all those years of quiet professionalism.

CAREER RECORD: 24 fights, 23 wins (12 inside schedule), 1 defeat.

Lloyd Honeyghan (born 1960)

BACKING Britsh world title challengers is not, on the whole, a quick way to get rich. Just occasionally, though, the outsider comes home to defy the odds: Randolph Turpin against Sugar Ray Robinson, John H. Stracey in Mexico City against José Napoles, and the brash, flash and brilliant Lloyd Honeyghan in Atlantic City against the supposedly unbeatable Don Curry.

Those were probably the three most astonishing upsets recorded by British fighters this century, and of them all Honeyghan's is the one most deserving of applause. There were convincing excuses for the other two losers: Turpin fought Robinson when the great man was at the end of a gruelling European tour, while Napoles was a weary thirty-five-year-old at the tail-end of his career when Stracey got to him. Curry, though, was a different proposition: a young champion, supposedly at the peak of his powers, who had annihilated virtually every man he had ever faced, and whose chilling two-round knockout of rival claimant Milton McCrory to unify the title seemed to confirm the Texan as the outstanding performer, pound for pound, of his generation.

And yet Lloyd Honeyghan, a man of whom few outside the trade had ever heard, went to America and thrashed the fighter who seemingly had no flaws. The result amazed everyone, except the winner and his manager, Mickey Duff – but then, total self-belief had always been a central part of Honeyghan's weaponry. The British like their heroes to be unassuming – Frank Bruno is seen as the ideal role model – and they have never really warmed to the extrovert and decidedly unorthodox Honeyghan to the extent that his talent and achievements merit.

Honeyghan has made a career out of flouting convention, in his private life as much as in the flamboyant, swashbuckling style he brings to the ring. He has fathered children by three different women, and (at least at the time of writing) married none of them. He does not slot easily into Britain's image of the sporting hero, which has its roots in the Brylcreem days of the Compton brothers and Stanley Matthews.

Honeyghan has always been an individualist, who does things his way. Maybe that was why his face and style never quite fitted with amateur officialdom in the days when he was boxing for Fisher ABC in Bermondsey, near Walworth, where the family had lived since arriving in Britain when Lloyd was nine. He was a good, though not outstanding amateur, his 1979 London welterweight title being the summit of his achievements, along with a couple of England vests.

He turned professional with Terry Lawless in late 1980, and served the time-honoured apprenticeship that Lawless and his managerial and promotional partner Mickey Duff have perfected. In just over two years Honeyghan fought 15 times and won them all, but they were generally low-key, down-the-bill affairs with minimal television exposure.

In his 16th fight he was matched with Cliff Gilpin in a final eliminator for the British title, then held by Colin Jones, but when Jones relinquished the championship Honeyghan v Gilpin was recognized as being for the vacant title. They met at the Albert Hall on 5 April 1983, 17 days before Honeyghan's twenty-third birthday, and the Jamaican-born Londoner had to come off the floor to outpoint the cagey Midlander in a tough twelve-rounder.

He beat Gilpin again in another hard twelve-rounder in December 1983, but injuries restricted him to only one appearance in 1984. Public recognition was still virtually zero, even after Honeyghan travelled to Perugia in Italy in January 1985 and scored a rare British knockout success there, taking the European title from local favourite Gianfranco Rosi (who went on to win the WBC and IBF light-middleweight titles).

Soon after that, the friction which had been building up in the Canning Town gym between Lawless, Honeyghan and trainer Jimmy Tibbs boiled over, forcing manager and boxer to agree that they had no future together. Lawless released him to be managed by Mickey Duff, whose international contacts and influence immediately paid off. Wins over Roger Stafford and Danny Paul moved Honeyghan up the world ratings, while in the gym his technique was being greatly improved by the expert tuition of the former British featherweight champion Bobby Neill, the man who deserved much of the credit for making Alan Minter a world champion.

A British title victory in November 1985 over another defector from the Lawless stable, Sylvester Mittee, provided him with a well-paid sidestep on the road to the world title, and also gave him outright ownership of the Lonsdale Belt. The WBC's number one contender was an ageing American, Horace Shufford, whose qualifications for the top contender position were unconvincing. Duff brought Shufford to Wembley to risk his rating, and Honeyghan duly battered the American to eighth-round defeat.

That success qualified him for the dubious honour of challenging Don Curry for the undisputed world title, and the fact that Honeyghan had to make his bid in America stacked the odds even higher against him. No one, outside Honeyghan's own entourage, shared the fighter's positive attitude, but Honeyghan himself was so confident that he even backed himself to win $25,000 at odds of 5–1.

The fight was staged in a casino showroom in Atlantic City on 7 September 1986. Few on the American circuit had heard of Honeyghan, and as the fight was viewed there as a routine defence for Curry, there was no interest from any of the major venues in promoting the match. Within a couple of rounds, though, Honeyghan had shown how wrong the critics were.

Curry was never allowed to get into the fight, as Honeyghan, arms pumping maniacally, swarmed all over him. Curry was at a loss to know how to deal with him, and by the fourth round the champion was bleeding and thoroughly disheartened. Honeyghan kept driving forward in the fifth and sixth, smashing the American around the ring, and at the end of the sixth Curry walked wearily to his corner and shook his head in resignation and surrender.

It was a magnificent victory, and while Curry's subsequent claims to have been weight-drained were valid (he had boiled down from 21 lb over the welterweight limit), that should not blur the quality of Honeyghan's achievement. It takes enormous strength of character to win a world championship under any conditions, but a special kind of courage is required when the whole world seems to be predicting your defeat.

As champion, Honeyghan suddenly became a 'personality' in Britain. The details of his extravagant love life fascinated the tabloid press, and he happily went along with the image they created for him as the wild man of the ring, the playboy champion. His first defence enhanced that reputation, when he raced across the ring to attack the former WBA light-welterweight champion Johnny Bumphus as he was still rising from his stool at the start of the second round. Bumphus never recovered, and was stopped later in the round. Honeyghan remained cheerfully unapologetic: 'The bell went ding, and I went dong,' he explained laconically.

That fight had involved only the WBC and IBF titles, as Honeyghan had relinquished the WBA belt on the somewhat shaky grounds that he might be asked to defend against a South African, Harold Volbrecht. That statement lost some credibility when Volbrecht claimed that Honeyghan had made advances to fight him before becoming champion, so that he could take over the South African's number one contender spot. The more likely explanation was simply that, as champion of three bodies each with different official challengers and defence deadlines, life was threatening to become too complicated.

His second defence was considerably more demanding, when the balding American stylist Maurice Blocker forced him to his limits. Not everyone agreed that Honeyghan deserved the twelve-round points verdict, but at least his performance in battling through the closing rounds in an exhausted condition proved that his heart was as big as his ego.

From here on, Honeyghan's championship reign became ever more controversial. He knocked out the hapless American Gene Hatcher in a Marbella bull-ring in either 40 or 45 seconds – the official timing did not seem to correspond with the actual duration – and then, against his own better judgement, went through with a defence at Wembley against Jorge Vaca, a moderate Mexican who was a substitute opponent. Honeyghan had been plagued by hand trouble and wanted to pull out, but claimed that Duff persuaded him to fight.

It was a dreadful night; he boxed as if his mind was elsewhere, and in the eighth round Vaca sustained an ugly S-shaped cut over his right eye in a clash of heads. The clash was accidental, otherwise Honeyghan should have been disqualified, but the crazy WBC rules meant that a point had to be deducted from his score because he was not cut. This made the points total at the end of the seven completed rounds 67–65 Honeyghan, 67–65 Vaca, and 67–66 Vaca. Without that point deduction Honeyghan would have retained his title on a draw, but instead he was judged to have been outpointed on a 'technical decision'.

The IBF had refused to sanction the match on the grounds that Vaca was not a worthy challenger, and they declared the title vacant. Honeyghan at first threatened to retire, then decided to carry on – but sought to dump Duff, with whom he had signed a four-year deal in 1986. Duff commented, memorably, that, 'There's nothing in our contract that says we have to like each other,' and got on with the job of persuading Vaca back to Britain for a rematch.

This time, Honeyghan got it right. He stormed into the Mexican with a kamikaze attack, throwing everything at him from the first bell, and in the third Vaca was counted out from a body shot. The win set up a big-money match with the WBA champion Marlon Starling, whom Honeyghan could not abide. The feeling was heartily reciprocated by the American, and the prospect of a genuine 25-carat grudge match was alluring. To showcase the pair, defences were arranged for each of them on the same show in Atlantic City against their respective number one challengers, neither of whom was too threatening.

But what should have been a straightforward afternoon's work for the rivals degenerated into farce. Honeyghan was first into action, against a limited Korean called Young-Kil Chung. The Londoner was chugging towards a comfortable win, although not looking overly impressive, when a low left sent Chung sprawling theatrically in the fifth round. He rolled around for several minutes, clutching his foul-proof protector in the hope that he might earn a sympathetic disqualification. Instead, when it became clear that the Korean had no intention of resuming, Honeyghan was declared the winner on a 'technical knockout'.

That had been bad enough, but there was worse to come. Starling was taking charge of his defence against the Colombian Tomas Molinares when, at the end of the sixth round, Molinares threw a punch several seconds after the bell and Starling was knocked unconscious, twisting his ankle badly as he fell. It seemed a clear-cut disqualification, but instead Molinares was proclaimed the winner and Honeyghan's dreams of a million-dollar showdown evaporated.

He and Starling finally got together in Las Vegas in February 1989, for much less than a million, and Honeyghan must have wished he hadn't bothered. Starling was a classy thirty-year-old who had mastered his trade in 50 tough fights on the American circuit, and he knew far too much for Honeyghan, who by now had fired the faithful Bobby Neill.

The champion took a fearful pounding: his jaw was horribly swollen, and he had bruises around both eyes and on the forehead. He showed limitless courage but little else to suggest that he could salvage the fight, and referee Mills Lane ended his reign in the ninth as Honeyghan, who had survived a knockdown earlier in the round, took unanswered punishment against the ropes.

He flirted with the idea of retirement, but has decided to box on. It will be a hard road back, maybe too hard for a twenty-nine-year-old who has already endured the emotional and physical strains of eight world title fights. But at least he reached the top twice, and along the way gave us some of the most colourful and controversial moments in the history of the British ring.

CAREER RECORD: 35 fights, 33 wins (22 inside schedule), 1 technical points loss, 1 defeat.

Dennis Andries (born 1953)

As THE final pages of this book were being written, the news came through that the Canadian glamour-boy Donny Lalonde had pulled out at three weeks' notice from his fight with Dennis Andries for the WBC light-heavyweight championship. His decision cost Andries around $400,000 in lost earnings, and was typical of the bad luck which has pursued this likeable and honest professional throughout his eleven hard and ill-rewarded years in the business.

The Lalonde fight should have been the pot of gold at the end of Andries' rainbow, the fight which would at last have set him up for life. But then, very little has ever gone the way that Andries wanted, and even less the way he deserved. It would have been a fairytale ending if the man who got £75 for his first fight could have earned around £300,000 for what may not even have been his farewell appearance. But life is not like that, and Andries has already stretched the fairytale metaphor to breaking point by winning the WBC title twice after having had to absorb more criticism than any British boxer I can recall in nearly twenty years in the business.

Much of the criticism, of course, was well founded. Andries has only a basic grasp of the arts and crafts of boxing, and has never pretended otherwise. But what he does possess, in overflowing abundance, is natural physical strength, iron determination, and unquenchable will. These qualities have carried him far beyond what was even remotely conceivable in his early days in the game.

Andries was born in Guyana (then British Guiana) and the family arrived in Britain in stages during the 1960s. Dennis was nine when his turn came. He got into boxing in his early teens at the suggestion of a friend, after a brief flirtation with wrestling ended when he learned, to his naïve horror, that professional wrestling was not quite the honest endeavour he had assumed it to be. He became an enthusiastic if unpromising member of the Colvestone Club in north-east London, where his clumsiness in the ring became a matter for sniggers and jokes among those who imagined themselves to be the *cognoscenti.*

But Dennis has a thick skin; he ignored the jibes, jeers and giggles, and worked determinedly at his chosen sport, wisely choosing to build on his strengths rather than gloss over his weaknesses. As a crude but powerful amateur, Andries developed slowly under the patient tuition of London cabbie Harry Griver – known inevitably as 'Griver the Driver' – who was the guiding force behind the Colvestone Club.

Andries never made any real impact at championship level, apart from winning the North-East London divisional title in 1978. He reached that year's London final, losing to Devon Bailey, and when it was discovered that he had broken Bailey's jaw Dennis replaced his conqueror in the English semi-finals, where he lost to the eventual champion, Vince Smith.

Over the amateur course of three rounds there were always going to be a great many slicker movers than Dennis. But he learned enough to know that he could make a reasonable living at the game, and so in 1978 he turned professional.

The prospects for a crude, ill-connected black fighter were not good, but then neither were Andries' expectations of success. He knew his limitations, and he set his sights no higher than they permitted in those early days. But his first year was more successful than anticipated: he lost only once, and among the six men he defeated were Tom Collins – later to figure prominently in his story – and Ken Jones, Colin's light-heavyweight brother. He also fought a bruising draw with the former British middleweight champion Les McAteer, which persuaded McAteer to abandon his comeback plans.

In his ninth fight, he got one of the few lucky breaks that have ever come his way. Tony Sibson had been matched for the British light-heavyweight title against champion Bunny Johnson, a good left-hooker from Birmingham who had formerly held the British heavyweight championship. Sibson decided, quite sensibly, that what his manager thought was a good match and what he considered to be one were not always the same thing, and pulled out. Promoter Ron Gray scoured the country for a save-the-show substitute, and Andries was offered the job.

Few outside the London fight trade had heard of him, but he almost pulled off one of the shocks of the season as he harassed and harried Johnson throughout the ten rounds to lose only narrowly on points. His showing was good enough to earn him a rematch for the title, and after Dennis had notched up another three wins, including one over Johnny Waldron for the Southern Area title, his chance came.

Pat Brogan promoted the fight in a dinner show at Stoke on 27 February 1980, and it remains the worst British championship I have ever seen. Dennis was simply awful, even falling through the ropes three times in the same round. He lasted the fifteen rounds to lose on points, but if anyone had told me that night that Andries would twice win the light-heavyweight championship of the world I would have sent the house wine off for chemical analysis.

But he plodded on, winning more than he lost and regaining the Southern Area championship which he had vacated to meet Johnson. He took the jobs where he could find them; promoters were not lining up to offer him work, and in order to keep busy he took on opponents such as David Pearce, a future British heavyweight champion, who stopped him in seven rounds.

He was now under the management of Greg Steene, who from 1982 to 1985 also promoted the majority of his fights. Andries supplemented his meagre ring earnings with a variety of occupations: at different times he worked as a tailor's cutter in Hackney, a plasterer, and a general assistant in the ticket agency run by Steene.

When Johnson relinquished the title, Andries was matched with a man he had already beaten twice, Tom Collins of Leeds, for the vacant title. He was entitled to feel confident about facing Collins, but he was weakened by an attack of flu in the weeks leading up to the fight and, over the fifteen-round course, Collins lasted the pace better to win a deserved decision. So Dennis went back to the Area title circuit, defending it three times to earn a rematch with Collins.

It took place finally at the Lyceum Ballroom in the Strand on 26 January 1984, and this time at last Dennis thumped out a clear points win. Collins, though, had grounds for complaint: the ring in which they boxed was found to be below the minimum permissible dimensions, which favoured a brawler like Andries rather than a smooth boxer like Collins. The Board of Control ordered a rematch three months later, and Andries settled the arguments with a repeat points win. A twelfth-round knockout of old amateur rival Devon Bailey completed a very satisfactory 1984 by giving him outright possession of a Lonsdale Belt.

Steene sent him to America to work under the guidance of Beau

Williford, the engaging southerner who later made a world cruiserweight champion out of Glenn McCrory. Under Williford's guidance Andries won three out of three in the States, and gained invaluable experience. When he came back to Britain to challenge world number one Alex Blanchard for the European title, he was a vastly improved fighter – but not yet quite good enough to dislodge the Dutchman, who survived a couple of knockdowns to cling on to his title with a twelve-round draw.

Andries' performance lifted him high in the WBC world ratings, and when he scored an impressive sixth-round knockout of Keith Bristol in defence of his British title, promoter Frank Warren decided to gamble on the year's most unlikely world title bid. The title, previously held with such distinction by Mike Spinks, had split three ways when Spinks moved up to take the heavyweight championship from Larry Holmes. The WBC portion was won by an undistinguished ex-Marine, J.B. Williamson. In boxing circles J.B. stood for 'Just Bad', which was exactly what the American was when Warren brought him to Pickett's Lock in north London to risk his title against Andries on 30 April 1986.

It was an abysmal world title fight. Williamson showed virtually nothing to indicate how he had become champion in the first place, while Dennis fought as ineptly as he had ever done in his novice days. When the twelve dreary rounds were over, two of the three judges ruled that Andries' crudities had been more effective than Williamson's inadequate efforts, and, unbelievably, the brawler from Hackney via Guyana was the new light-heavyweight champion of the world.

His first challenge came from the rejuvenated Tony Sibson, who had put together a few good wins since returning to the ring under Warren's direction. It was a bold move, to step up from middleweight straight into a world title challenge, but Andries firmly repelled him with a conclusive ninth-round defeat at Alexandra Pavilion.

There was big money to be made, for once in Andries' long, hard career, in a defence against the Detroit hitman Tommy Hearns, who was chasing his third world championship. The negotiations, offers and counter-offers were the subject of legal action as this book went to press, so let it suffice to say that Andries was unhappy with the deal which sent him to Detroit for a defence he felt should have taken place in London, and for a better purse.

He fought with unforgettable bravery against Hearns. He was outclassed in every aspect of the business except the most fundamental – the heart, the will to continue, the desire to win. Andries hauled himself off the floor time after time, until Hearns was moved to question the referee's judgement in letting him continue. But Andries even dropped Hearns with the penultimate punch of the fight in the tenth round, although it was not ruled a knockdown. Hearns got up and floored Andries yet again with his next punch, and this time the referee finally waved a halt.

Andries' reign was over, and so, most assumed, was his career. Dennis had other ideas. He had not made anything like the money he had hoped to earn from the business, and certainly not enough to provide the kind of future he wished for his wife, Odette, and two daughters. Instead of going home to lick his wounds, Andries turned up at the Kronk gym in Detroit, the training headquarters of the man who had just taken his title, and asked Hearns' mentor Emanuel Steward to take him over.

Steward had been hugely impressed by Andries' raw courage and natural strength, and he believed that given the professional polish that the Kronk environment could provide, Andries could still regain the title. So began the third and most extraordinary phase of Andries' career. At thirty-three – or possibly thirty-five, or even thirty-seven, for his age has always been a matter of conjecture, most of it fuelled by himself – Andries set out to prove himself all over again. He did it with a string of five wins over opponents of mixed abilities, and each time he looked better and better.

When he trounced the former IBF champion Bobby Czyz, Steward knew that Andries' rehabilitation was complete. Sugar Ray Leonard had relinquished the WBC title without defending it, and Andries was paired with the unbeaten North American champion Tony Willis, who had stopped 12 of his 16 opponents. They fought in Tucson, Arizona, for a cut-price purse of less than $50,000 apiece, four days before Andries' infinitely more publicized compatriot Frank Bruno challenged Mike Tyson.

Andries' fifth-round knockout victory got minimal coverage in the British press. He returned home in muted triumph, passing completely unnoticed through Heathrow – and yet when Bruno, a fifth-round loser, walked through the same arrival hall a few hours later he stopped the traffic.

But Andries was used to such slights from the British public, and consoled himself with the thought that the bumper payoff he expected to earn against Donny Lalonde would compensate for everything that had gone before. But that fell through, and instead Andries took a pay-cut of around 50 per cent to face an unbeaten but untested Australian substitute, Jeff Harding. Andries dominated the fight for three-quarters of the way. Harding absorbed a fearful beating; he was cut around both eyes, floored in the fifth round, and had his nose smashed in the tenth. His courage and endurance defied belief, as he walked through endless punishment to pound away at Andries' body.

Gradually the body punches began to take their toll of the veteran, until by the end of the eleventh Andries had slowed to a standstill. He was an open target for the young Australian in the twelfth and final round, and Andries was put down twice before the referee rescued him. There were just 97 seconds left in the fight, and Andries would have saved his title with a draw had he been able to survive the round.

It was a cruel end to his championship reign, and typical of the bad luck which continues to dog this quiet and undervalued man.

CAREER RECORD: 44 fights, 34 wins (21 inside schedule), 2 draws, 8 defeats.

Glenn McCrory (born 1964)

GLENN MCCRORY went past the local dole office on his way to the Louisa Leisure Centre in Stanley where he was to fight Patrick Lumumba for the vacant IBF cruiserweight title. He could not have had a more powerful reminder of the cost of failure, because for so long McCrory himself had been just another dismal statistic, another name on the over-long register of unemployed in that most depressed corner of the country.

Most world title challengers are acutely aware of their fans' expectations, but for McCrory the pressure that night must have been near intolerable. His world title bid was a community effort, sponsored by the local council and backed by local businessmen, financed by what money there was in an area where youngsters often reach their twenty-first birthday without ever having had a job.

The early summer of 1989 was a bad time on the sporting front for the region, whose chief passion is football. The two local sides, Newcastle and Sunderland, had both been relegated in the League and a McCrory victory would be a real morale-boost. It says much for the twenty-four-year-old's strength of character that he shrugged off all these additional pressures and concentrated instead on boxing his way to a decisive points win, which gave the North East its first world champion in the first world title fight the region had ever hosted.

His success was a sweet last word to the critics who, just three years earlier, had written him off as a fat, failed heavyweight. McCrory, from a big Irish family of five boys and two girls, began his pro career full of promise after a decent amateur run with the Consett Club had brought him a junior ABA title and a Young England vest.

All went well for his first 13 fights, and the readers of the trade paper *Boxing News* voted him their 'Prospect of the Year' for 1984. Even if he was not knocking his opponents over – ten of those wins were on points – he had the advantage of being white and handsome in a sport increasingly populated by blacks. (Such considerations matter in boxing, more than in any other sport; the good white heavyweight can write his own pay cheques.) He had the right connections, too. His manager was Doug Bidwell, who had taken his son-in-law, Alan Minter, to the world middleweight title, and the major promoters were only too keen to feature the promising young Geordie.

But all the time, McCrory was only kidding his body that he was a heavyweight. He had the height for it, at 6 feet 4 inches, but it was not his natural weight, and when John Westgarth knocked him out in four rounds in September 1985, the rot set in. In the course of one fight, McCrory plummeted from championship hopeful to trial-horse. He lost four in a row in 1986. The ill-fated Rudi Pika, an unbeaten Welsh–Estonian who later took his own life, outpointed him at the Albert Hall, and the former European champion Anders Eklund made full use of a huge weight advantage to outpoint him in Denmark.

North-Eastern rival Dave Garside stopped him in seven rounds in June 1986, but it took a clubbing right hand from the former British champion Hughroy Currie four months later to convince McCrory that enough was enough. Currie knocked him cold in two rounds at Oldham, and McCrory's career seemed to be in tatters.

But then Beau Williford, the amiable American who had transformed Dennis Andries' career, took a hand. He had watched McCrory spar with Andries at the Thomas à Becket gym in south-east London, and seen what should have been obvious to everyone – that McCrory's frame was carrying two stone of surplus weight, and that his natural division was the recently created cruiserweight class whose limit was 13 st 8 lb.

Williford took him in hand and brought him to America, where he began patiently to rebuild Glenn's career with a couple of wins. The opposition did not amount to much, but the renewal of confidence that the wins gave him was priceless. All the time, McCrory's weight was coming down to what Williford felt was his most efficient poundage. He had scaled a heaviest-ever 15 st 8 lb against Currie, and only seven weeks later Williford had trimmed him down a full stone for his first American appearance. Four wins in Britain in 1987 completed the rehabilitation, for in the last of them he took the Commonwealth cruiserweight crown from the veteran African holder Chisanda Mutti in front of his home fans at Gateshead.

In January 1988, hardened by heavy duty as chief sparring

partner for Mike Tyson, McCrory became a double champion by outscoring British title-holder Tee Jay. The Tyson experience – more than 90 rounds as the heavyweight champion prepared for defences against Larry Holmes and Tyrell Biggs – was both lucrative and satisfying. The man who had once been flattened by Hughroy Currie survived against the world's most lethal heavyweight without once going down – and even got a joke certificate to prove it.

McCrory's only defence of the British title, an eighth-round retirement win over Londoner Lou Gent, recalled their last meeting as sixteen-year-old amateurs, when McCrory outpointed him in the 1981 junior ABA final.

With two titles behind him, and Williford becoming increasingly influential, McCrory moved up the world ratings. He had by now broken acrimoniously with Bidwell, McCrory able to secure his release only by agreeing to continue to pay Bidwell his managerial percentage throughout the remaining duration of their contract.

McCrory went back to America with Williford, and won a further three routine engagements against 'knockover' opposition. The matching was abysmal, but the wins kept him high in the world rankings and stretched his unbeaten run as a cruiserweight to 11.

Evander Holyfield was world cruiserweight king, and had unified all three versions of the championship. He was unbeatable at the weight, but in early 1989 – to the great relief of the rest of the world's cruiserweights – he relinquished the title to chase Mike Tyson's heavyweight crown. All three bodies nominated their own challengers. McCrory was highly ranked by the WBC and the IBF, but wisely opted to contest the IBF vacancy with Patrick Lumumba, a Kenyan who had become a Swedish citizen and was now fight-based in America.

McCrory's world title chance captured the imagination of the North-East. Middlesbrough promoter John Spensely put the sponsorship package together with the involvement of several leading businessmen, and he arranged the backing of the local council. Nothing was too much trouble: a road was even specially laid to facilitate access to Glenn's training quarters which had been set up in the grounds of the Royal Derwent hotel, where his heavyweight brothers Gary and Shaun provided him with sparring. A Newcastle brewery gave him a car to use, while a Darlington firm laid on a mini-bus to shuttle the McCrory entourage between the training camp and the gym – which, naturally, had been provided free of charge at the Consett Sports Centre.

On fight night, the Louisa Centre was sold out. The fans did not, in all honesty, see a great world title fight, but they almost had a spectacular first-round victory to cheer when McCrory sent Lumumba reeling with a perfect left hook. But the African was cagey and clever enough to survive that crisis and several subsequent ones, although at the end of the twelve rounds he was in an overwhelming points deficit.

McCrory's success earned him around £20,000, a pittance by modern championship standards. Now, though, he has the prospect of earning some real money to provide lifetime security for his wife, Amanda, and daughter, Victoria. The dole queue, finally, is just a bad memory.

CAREER RECORD: 31 fights, 26 wins (9 inside schedule), 5 defeats.

Dave McAuley (born 1961)

Nothing ever came easy to Dave McAuley. He spent much of his career in the considerable shadow of his stablemate Barry McGuigan, and failed twice in attempts on the WBA flyweight title before his persistence finally paid off when he took the IBF version from Duke McKenzie in June 1989. Such perseverance deserves reward, and the man who almost quit the ring only a year ago because, he claimed, he could earn more on the dole than from boxing now finds himself in a position to demand some worthwhile purses.

His success is all the more extraordinary considering that only twenty years ago the flyweight division was on the verge of extinction in Britain. Between Walter McGowan's world title win in 1966 and Charlie Magri's in 1983, there was no British flyweight good enough even to contest a world title. Yet McAuley did so three times in only 17 fights.

His career may have been overshadowed by McGuigan's, but indirectly he owes his present eminence to the former featherweight champion, who is also his close friend and confidant. McGuigan's manager, Barney Eastwood, who was also handling McAuley's career, formed very close business relationships with powerful and influential figures in Panamanian boxing. Their association proved mutually rewarding during the years of McGuigan's triumphs, and has continued. It was because of those links that Eastwood was able, in 1987, to arrange for McAuley – then a virtual unknown in world terms – to challenge Panamanian Fidel Bassa for the WBA title at the King's Hall.

No one gave the inexperienced Irishman even an outside chance of victory, and the pessimism looked well founded when McAuley was floored in the opening round. Yet he fought back so effectively that he came agonisingly close to the championship, in a thriller which was rightly named as the 1987 Fight of the Year. Bassa was on the floor five times in all, although only three of them were classed as official knockdowns. He was down twice in an electrifying ninth round, and under WBA rules one more knockdown would have meant the automatic finish. But Bassa survived, and McAuley had spent himself in his efforts to end it.

By the twelfth he had nothing left, and a couple of punches were sufficient to end his challenge in the thirteenth round. Ironically, had the fight taken place a few months later, when the WBA's championship distance had been reduced to twelve rounds, McAuley would have won since he was ahead on all three judges' cards at the end of the twelfth. It was a superlative effort by the Irishman, and was viewed live on BBC TV. The man who had conducted his career hitherto in near-anonymity found himself suddenly a star, and his days of playing the supporting role on Barry McGuigan's fight nights were over.

He had turned professional in October 1983, by which time McGuigan was already on the road to greatness. Like McGuigan, he had been an accomplished amateur who had won the Irish senior title and boxed many times on the international scene, but the star treatment which Barry enjoyed was denied him. He was relegated to down-the-bill appearances on the shows which McGuigan headlined, although he was an exciting performer in his own right.

Maybe there was only room for one star in the Castle Street gym where Eastwood's fighters trained, and McAuley had arrived a couple of years too late for the part. While much was made of McGuigan's role as a bridge-builder between the divided communities, no one even bothered to ask which 'side' McAuley belonged to – or to consider why a matter which in his case was rightly regarded as a total irrelevance should be seen as of paramount importance in McGuigan's.

The Larne man, who supplemented his ring earnings by working as a chef in his father-in-law's restaurant, was one of the hardest-hitting flyweights in Europe, but for the first two years of his career he was obliged to box bantamweights and featherweights in order to keep active. In fact, the first time he actually fought at the flyweight limit was on the McGuigan v Pedroza world title bill, when he beat the Glaswegian Bobby McDermott in an eliminator for the British title in which both men were on the floor twice. It was a bitter war of attrition which, on any other night, would have been acclaimed as an epic, but here it was dismissed with a one-sentence report in all but the trade paper, *Boxing News*.

McAuley plodded on with a 'bit part' appearance on McGuigan's world title bill in Dublin before, on 22 April 1986, he at last topped a show in his own right and celebrated by stopping Charlie Brown of Glasgow in the first round of their British title final eliminator. In October, he took the vacant British title by knocking out yet another Glaswegian, Joe Kelly, in the ninth round in front of a members-only sporting club audience.

By now McGuigan had split acrimoniously with Eastwood, and his defection left the promoter needing to find another bill-topper in a hurry. Thus McAuley was suddenly pushed to centre stage against Bassa, and so nearly justified Eastwood's gamble. The fight was so gruelling that McAuley rested for eight months before getting back in the ring again, and Eastwood could not have found a less demanding exercise for his return: he was matched with his own sparring partner, Roy Thompson, and to nobody's surprise he won on points over ten untesting rounds.

A rematch with Bassa was a big attraction, and Eastwood made it for the King's Hall on 26 March 1988, eleven months after their first meeting. It proved a damp squib. The fight never caught fire: it was as if both men, having pushed each other to breaking point last time, had no desire to go that far again and were content merely to go through the motions. McAuley later claimed he was drained and over-trained, and certainly that was consistent with the way he boxed. Bassa did just enough to stay out of trouble and keep in front to take a comfortable points decision in a dull, disappointing twelve-rounder.

McGuigan's dispute with Eastwood had induced McAuley to consider his own position carefully, and when he totalled his ring earnings from a four-year career and found them considerably short of what he regarded as adequate, he aired his grievances publicly in a series of sensational newspaper articles, in the course of which he vowed never to box again if he had to do so under Eastwood's management. But peace was eventually made between them, and the price of the truce was the world title opportunity against McKenzie which Eastwood was able to deliver.

Now the fighting outside the ring has all been done, and McAuley, Ireland's first world flyweight champion since Rinty Monaghan nearly forty years earlier, has at last got the chance to step clear of McGuigan's shadow.

CAREER RECORD: 17 fights, 13 wins (7 inside schedule), 2 draws, 2 defeats.